THE CASE FOR

Spiritual Healing

THE CASE FOR
Spiritual Healing

by
DON H. GROSS

THOMAS NELSON & SONS

Edinburgh   NEW YORK   *Toronto*

All Biblical quotations in the text are from the Revised Standard Version of the Bible by permission of Thomas Nelson and Sons.

ⓒ, 1958, by Don H. Gross

All rights reserved under International and Pan-American Conventions. Published in New York by Thomas Nelson & Sons and simultaneously in Toronto, Canada, by Thomas Nelson & Sons (Canada), Limited.

Library of Congress Catalog Card No.: 58-9037

MANUFACTURED IN THE UNITED STATES OF AMERICA

TO

My Mother

Author's Preface

This book is written with a sense of a ground-swell of popular interest in healing through spiritual means. Fifty years back, the Emmanuel Movement was almost alone in representing spiritual healing in the major Protestant churches. Ten years ago we heard almost nothing about it in our seminaries; the books on the subject were few; and not many of the people in our congregations knew anything about religious healing except to connect it with Christian Science or Unity.

Now magazine articles and books are beginning to flow forth in profusion. Healers of the evangelistic type have long been with us, but spiritual healing on nation-wide television is a novelty introduced by Oral Roberts. Its impact on people at the "grass-roots" is far-reaching indeed. This sort of resurgence of faith healing, mostly outside our larger denominations, has called forth the first major book of our generation aimed *against* such healing, *Faith Healing and the Christian Faith,* by Wade H. Boggs, Jr.

At the same time, new advances are being made in relating the Church's work to medical and psychological care. Our seminaries are increasingly offering clinical training and preparation for pastoral counseling. In several leading theological schools we see new programs to relate religion with psychotherapy. And in several of the prominent churches of the United States and Great Britain we observe clinical teams of clergy, psychologists, psychiatrists, and other doctors.

All this is an increasing challenge to the leaders of our churches. Whether they are ministers or laymen, the times demand that they come to grips with the ministry of healing.

It is our hope that this book will help them to do so. The book is intended as more than a review of what is happening in spiritual healing. Its purpose is to put those events in a fuller theological background, so that both the principles and the meaning of that healing will be more clearly seen. Its purpose, even more, is to help our churches to *practice* Christian healing.

What is said here is necessarily imperfect and incomplete. It is only a stepping stone on the way. Jesus said, "Heal the sick"; and after almost two thousand years we are only scratching the surface in fulfilling that command. If as much devotion were to be given to healing through spiritual means as is now dedicated to scientific healing, Christianity would be bound to the heart and pulse-beat of the people of the twentieth century. Whether loved or hated, Christ could not be ignored. Divine healing is judgment on spiritual Laodiceans. The message of the Son of Man to the church in Laodicea is, "I know your works; you are neither cold nor hot. Would that you were cold or hot! So, because you are lukewarm, and neither cold nor hot, I will spew you out of my mouth. . . . Those whom I love, I reprove and chasten; so be zealous and repent."

I wish especially to express my thanks to my wife, Anne, for her invaluable help both in the composition and preparation of the manuscript; to Bishop Pardue, for his constant help and encouragement, not to mention his over-generous Introduction; to Emily Gardiner Neal for her good advice; to Jane Ramsay Tyrie for her conscientious help in getting the manuscript in final order for publication; and to the people of St. Peter's Episcopal Church, Brentwood, whose faith and responsiveness made my healing ministry and this book possible.

D. H. G.

Introduction

The author walked into my office at the end of World War II and stated that he wanted to study for the Episcopal Priesthood. I had never met him before. He was tall, good-looking, and wore the uniform of a junior officer in the United States Navy.

Upon routine questioning, I discovered that he was a physicist doing research work for the Navy and a recent graduate from Carnegie Institute of Technology. He said that he had long been torn between science and theology and finally had decided to switch professions. However, he assured me that he would never lose his interest and devotion for the field of physics and hoped to continue it as a hobby in some form throughout his life. This was top news for us and we immediately made him a Postulant for Holy Orders, waiting for his term of service to end and theological training to begin.

In the year 1946 he entered the Episcopal Theological School at Cambridge, Massachusetts, where again he proved to be an honor student. However, he was more than a topflight scholar. He was an aggressive contender on behalf of the supernatural aspects of the Gospels. At theological seminary, he did not hesitate to openly disagree with faculty members who leaned toward the side of what he thought was too drastic an emphasis in New Testament higher criticism. He told me that his scientific training left him unconvinced as to their de-emphasis of some of the "mighty acts" of Christ. He was anything but a fundamentalist, but believed and accepted much of the life of Christ on faith and therefore felt that there was insufficient evidence on the part of the scholars to make him believe less in the miracles of Our Lord.

The seminary faculty members were understanding, tolerant, and interested in this excellent and challenging mind. A calm but vigorous debate continued in a friendly manner throughout his seminary course. To this day he is a welcome guest at the Episcopal Theological School at Cambridge and has been invited back to lecture on the theme of healing.

For the past six years, he has been a successful pastor, rector, preacher, and teacher at St. Peter's in Brentwood, a suburb of Pittsburgh. Recently he resigned his post as rector in order to attend the University of Pittsburgh and obtain a graduate degree in psychology. His main motive is to approach the healing ministry from the viewpoint of science and theology, thus joining together his talents in both fields and dedicating them to the ministry of health of mind, body, and soul. He is married and has two children and is part-time assistant at Calvary Church, Pittsburgh, as Minister of Religious Education.

I have been interested in the healing field for many years and it is my belief that Don Gross is on his way toward making a real contribution to this cause. His investigations for a number of years have been broad and objective as he has observed the movement and its manifestations from the evangelistic tent meetings to the dignified sacramental approaches of the Anglican and Roman Catholic Churches. I know of no person in America who is more familiar with the movement or more qualified to write this book. Don Gross is dedicated to the cause and hopes to return to his own beloved seminary as well as to others and offer his findings to faculty and students. He is aware of the grave dangers that accompany an overemphasis on the healing side of Christianity, but he is likewise aware of the equal dangers that have resulted from the neglect of this all-important ministry. He feels that because the Church has neglected its duty in this direction, it is responsible for many of the bizarre cults that have developed as a result of the starvation of communicants for the healing that can be wrought through the ministry of the Church. He is equally interested in working with the medical profession since he knows how all-important a part of God's revelation is being manifested through the scientific discoveries being made in our laboratories and hospitals.

I am not sure where this young man will be led in his ministry, but his consecration to the cause of Christ and His healing message is most impressive. He is singularly equipped in mind and temperament for the task and I venture to say that the contribution he has already made in this field will be greatly enhanced and increased throughout the coming years.

AUSTIN PARDUE
Bishop of Pittsburgh

September 23, 1957

Contents

THE CASE FOR

Spiritual Healing

CHAPTER I

Where Is the Healing?

"Not every one who says to me, 'Lord, Lord,' shall enter the kingdom of heaven, but he who does the will of my Father who is in heaven."
Matthew 7.21

John Ellis Large, rector of New York's Church of the Heavenly Rest, was travelling through Europe when a conference was being held on Christian Healing. His interest was known, so he was invited to speak. When he arrived, a physician raised an earnest question. The good doctor had been studying the Gospels, filled as they are with the healing work of Jesus. He compared it with the Church life of his own experience. His heavily accented words still ring in Dr. Large's ears: *"Where is the healing?"*

It would be easy to say, "What do you mean, doctor? Surely you know about Church hospitals, about Christian doctors and nurses, about Sisters and Deaconesses who spend their lives helping the suffering. You must have heard about hospital chaplains and pastoral visits to the sick. What do you mean, 'Where is the healing?' "

And he might answer that of course he knows about these things and about many more. We may be sure that he would thank God for them all. But he knew that Jesus did something more—something so obvious with Him, and so rare in His Church today. Jesus healed directly through spiritual means—through prayer, through faith, through love, through hope,

3

through the touch of His hand and the power of the Holy Spirit. The Christian Church now counts its members in the hundreds of millions. But the healing love that flows through the typical Christian today is a mere trickle compared with the torrential waterfall that poured from Christ. When the disciples of John the Baptist asked Jesus, "Are you he who is to come, or shall we look for another?" (Luke 7.19,20) Jesus could not say, "See my millions of followers. See their love for the sick, their hospitals, their physicians, their nurses, their research and their scientific victories." None of these things had come to pass. What He did say was, "Go and tell John what you have seen and heard: the blind receive their sight, the lame walk, lepers are cleansed, and the deaf hear, the dead are raised up, the poor have good news preached to them. And blessed is he who takes no offense at me." (Matthew 11.4–6; Luke 7. 22–23)

Even a superficial reading of the Gospels shows how deeply imbedded healing was in the ministry of Jesus. The book of Acts shows its continuing place in the work of the Apostles. Did not Jesus commission them to heal, right along with His command to preach the Gospel? "And he called the twelve together and gave them power and authority over all demons and to cure diseases, and he sent them out to preach the kingdom of God and to heal." (Matthew 10.1; Mark 6.7; Luke 9.1–2) "So they cast out many demons, and anointed with oil many that were sick and healed them." (Mark 6.12–13; Luke 9.6) The story is similar when He sent out seventy others: "Whenever you enter a town and they receive you, eat what is set before you; heal the sick in it and say to them, 'The kingdom of God has come near to you.' " (Luke 10.9) "The seventy returned with joy, saying, 'Lord, even the demons are subject to us in your name!' And he said to them, 'I saw Satan fall like lightning from heaven. Behold, I have given you authority to tread upon serpents and scorpions, and over all the power of the enemy; and nothing shall hurt you. Nevertheless, do not rejoice in this, that the spirits are subject to you; but rejoice that your names are written in heaven." (Luke 10.17–20) Jesus healed and His disciples healed as a part of their proclamation of the kingdom of heaven. It is the kind of healing that they did which is so rare in His Church today. "Where *is* the healing?"

Edward Weiss, M.D. and O. Spurgeon English, M.D. have written an 803-page medical text-book called *Psychosomatic Medicine*.[1] It spends less than one page on the contribution of religion to healing. It reads as follows:

Undoubtedly many cures, *more temporary than permanent*, have taken place through religious assurances. These may take the form of affirmation, blessing, anointing, ingestion of consecrated bread, utilization of the sign of the cross, visit to a shrine, or reassurance by a religious personage. When we attempt to explain this phenomenon scientifically we should bear in mind that love has a beneficial effect upon disturbances of emotional origin. The suffering child is helped by the security which he feels in the presence of his mother and father. Religion has much to do with mother and father figures. It is the childish parts of the personality which are in great need of love and reassurance in illness of emotional origin. Hence, when conflicts produced by guilt, hostility, and sexuality produce pain and suffering, contact with a religious force may do much to bring relief. Physicians recognize the spiritual values of religion for themselves and their patients but *they possess neither the religious training nor the desire to utilize religious assurances psychotherapeutically. A rare exception may be made; occasionally a patient is so inaccessible to psychotherapy that religion must be called upon to perform a function for which it is not intended.* In the great majority of patients, however, as we have repeatedly emphasized, it is the direct working with the patient's emotional conflicts by the physician himself, based on his knowledge of the personality structure, which will have more controlled and more lasting results.

[1] W. B. Saunders Co., Philadelphia and London, 2nd ed., 1949.

There is only one large religious order which specializes in healing the sick and its method of doing so does not deviate from the principles mentioned above. Christian Science has undoubtedly made many people feel better and function better, but it has also delayed scientific help to thousands of people until it was too late to be of any value. *We feel that there is no power in Christian Science which is not possessed by clergyman, priest, or rabbi, none of whom attempts to heal the sick. They comfort and help the sick but the cure of disease is left in the hands of the medical profession.* (Italics mine.)

There is no reason to doubt that this was written with all the good will in the world. But it is hard to imagine a more damning indictment of the Christian clergy for their failure to follow their Lord's command to heal the sick. Its complete innocence of any attempt to condemn makes it just that much more effective. It is based upon simple observation of typical Church practice.

"Where is the healing?"

Some such puzzle raced through the mind of a mother whose daughter was born deaf, blind, and without normal muscle coordination. There was no known medical solution—only the advice to commit the child to a state hospital for hopeless cases. In desperation the mother turned to her Bishop, Austin Pardue of Pittsburgh. The Christian Scientists had offered help and she was about to turn to them. What could the Bishop say?

He might have reviewed all the shortcomings of Christian Science. He might have told her that she should resign herself, that it was God's will, hopeless to battle. He might have said, "Religion can help functional disorders, illnesses caused by emotional disturbances by restoring proper emotional balance through the Christian virtues of faith and hope and love. It can overcome guilt feelings and relieve pent-up hatreds. But your child has an organic affliction. There is a physical impairment of her nervous system. We could not deal with such a thing, nor could we provide even the beginnings of religious instruction. How could we now teach even a normal baby—so young? But this handicap will make it impossible to reach her even when she is older. How do we know that even if her blindness and deafness could be overcome, she would have the mental capacity to understand religious faith? How could she ever express herself to tell us? It is a tragedy indeed, but neither the doctors nor the Christian Scientists nor anyone else can heal your child. Under the emotional strain that is natural in these circumstances, you are grasping at every straw. But common sense will tell you that you must seek to accept this affliction, and we can pray that God will give you the strength to accept it."

The Bishop *might* have said something like that—perhaps more tactfully. And the chances are that the mother would then have become a Christian Scientist. She was not the type of person to accept defeat.

As a matter of fact, he listened patiently to all she had to say. He said that he understood how she felt. But before she left, he gave her a copy of Agnes Sanford's book, *The Healing Light*.

She read the book; and she found hope and strength within her Church. These are now her words: "God's word shall not return to Him void, and even the most afflicted 'word' shall have its purpose when it is given to God in faith and prayer." God had a purpose and plan for this child. Through her, the mother has been instrumental in forming prayer groups and has been led to other people who had the same desire to help the child serve God. This has resulted in initiating and supporting programs for other severely handicapped children.

But the chain of events in God's plan reached out yet further. Although Bishop Pardue had been active in the healing ministry long before, his experience with this desperate mother alerted him to the challenge to the Church: how shall we remedy our failure to keep Christ's command to "heal the sick . . . and say to them, 'The kingdom of God has come near to you' '"?

Dr. Alfred Price, who has carried on a notable ministry of healing at St. Stephen's Episcopal Church, Philadelphia, was invited to preach and to conduct healing services for a week each Lent at Pittsburgh's Trinity Cathedral. The response of the people was immediate and enthusiastic. In 1949 Bishop Pardue invited Dr. Price to address the fall conference of the clergy of the Diocese of Pittsburgh, and other priests also reported on various phases of spiritual healing. Not long afterwards he appointed a Healing Commission to further the work in the diocese. Other leaders in the field, such as Agnes Sanford, Gladys Falshaw, and Fr. John Maillard, have likewise contributed to the movement among both clergy and laity in the Pittsburgh area. Interest has grown to the point where a large proportion (though still a minority) of the Episcopal churches of the diocese hold regular services of spiritual healing, and where a much larger percentage of the clergy consider spiritual healing a normal part of their ministry, with their congregations increasingly expecting this to be so. Lay participation and even leadership in prayer and the laying on of hands is also growing.

This development within the Episcopal Diocese of Pittsburgh is only one instance of a widespread revival of interest in spiritual healing, a resurgence touching many places and many denominations. It takes infinitely varied forms: from the practice of verbal affirmations of health and the cultivation of "positive thinking," to visits to shrines of the saints; from simple prayers during private visits to the sick, to emotionally charged "miracle services" with hundreds of people joining their voices in song and their hearts in supplication; from the healing centered in a gifted personality, to the objective power of the Sacraments.

Whatever may have brought forth the current upsurge of Christian healing, the history of the Church shows it to be a return, an approach to an earlier, more "normal" Christian life. This is true despite the fact that any full development of spiritual healing strikes most people as quite a novelty. But the true novelty, the real peculiarity, in the Christian Church is that its ministry of healing should have fallen for so long into neglect. It belongs in the life of every Christian congregation today.

An interesting report that gives some idea of the percentage of ministers of the larger Protestant denominations actually engaging in healing is the "Study of Spiritual Healing in the Churches" by Charles S. Braden, which was published in *Pastoral Psychology*. A total of 982 questionnaires was sent out, and 460 replies were received. The question, "Have you ever as a minister attempted to perform a spiritual healing?" was answered affirmatively by 34.5% of those who responded.

Of the 460, only 248 gave an unqualified "no" answer to the question. This is just under 54%. Forty-eight, or 10.4% of our respondents qualified their negative answers . . . Percentagewise the Episcopalians rated highest in the number of healings in proportion to the number reporting; 65% had engaged in healing by spiritual means. Other percentages were: Presbyterians, 39%; Lutherans, 33%; United Brethren, 30%; Methodists and Disciples, 29%; and Baptists, 25%. Actually a much larger number of Methodists responded to the questionnaire than from any other denomination. I incline to think that the number involved is too small to serve as a basis for a denomination-wide generalization. There is too much possibility for chance selection to account for the higher or lower percentages.[2]

These figures show that a substantial minority of Protestant ministers have practiced spiritual healing at one time or an-

[2] *Pastoral Psychology*, May, 1954, p. 10. This survey was sponsored in 1950 by the Commission on Religion and Health of the then Federal Council of Churches. A further discussion of it is to be found in Chapter 9 and Appendix C of *The Healing Power of Faith*, by Will Oursler (Hawthorn Books, N.Y., 1957.)

other—a greater percentage than one might expect. The fraction is high enough to make us wonder about the statement of Weiss and English that clergymen do not attempt to heal. But Weiss and English were speaking from an observation plain enough to all: that on the whole, insignificant time and effort have been spent on healing as compared with other sides of the ministry. A minister could answer "yes" to Dr. Braden's questionnaire even if he had attempted a spiritual healing only once in his entire ministry. The majority of those polled apparently could not think of even a single instance when they had so much as tried to heal through spiritual means.

It is also true that many who have practiced spiritual healing have done so shyly, hesitantly, fearfully, often limiting their attempts to rare occasions. At a recent conference on the subject, a clergyman told of some of his experiences in healing through faith and prayer, and immediately explained that he had told no one in his church about it—as a matter of fact, he had not even told his wife! It is no wonder that only a crack of the light of spiritual healing shows from under the covering bushel basket.

Where is the healing?

⋅§ CHAPTER II §⋅

A Physician Is Healed

"The wind blows where it will, and you hear the sound of it, but you do not know whence it comes or whither it goes; so it is with every one who is born of the Spirit."

John 3.8

On Saturday evening, November 18th, 1950, a physician, his wife, and their grown son began a strange journey. The doctor's father had been a doctor (and an agnostic). His brother is a doctor. His education was, of course, in medical science. In his general practice he had gained that mature wisdom that only a lifetime of experience in restoring the suffering could develop. Yet he had somehow been persuaded to travel hours from his home, expecting to spend the night in a hotel in order to be in good time for a seat Sunday morning—a seat in a tabernacle where a young woman, Kathryn Kuhlman, conducted services for healing through faith!

The initiative that led to this odd state of affairs had come from his wife. She had heard Miss Kuhlman on the radio and some months before she had written to ask for prayers for her husband. The reply and the improvement in his health at that time had encouraged her. At the time of this trip, the doctor had the following afflictions:

(1) A painful sinus condition. This was in his right antrum

11

and frontal sinuses and had been treated medically ever since his college years.

(2) The loss of most of the hearing in his right ear.

(3) A broken collarbone. Earlier that year he had fallen down a flight of steps and injured both his right knee and his right collarbone or clavicle.

The right clavicle had been fractured, but the bone kept in alignment well enough that no break was apparent at first. It pained, but this was considered the result of one of the many bruises caused by the fall. However, before long he used his right arm and shoulder even more than usual, because his knee condition required crutches, then a cane. The knee healed, but the clavicle did not.

I remember visiting him early that November of 1950. The pain radiated into his right arm and up his neck into his head, keeping him in misery. Without thinking, he lifted his coffee cup at dinner; when it was raised about half-way to his mouth, his hand shook violently, and coffee spilled every which way. He simply could not use his right arm normally, especially when he would begin to raise it.

An X-ray of the right clavicle had been taken on March 28, 1950. It indicated a rather clean fracture on a plane approximately perpendicular to the bone, not too far from the point midway between the ends. A reddish, angry-looking lump could be seen on the skin at this spot. Movement of the right arm often gave a painful grating sensation, apparently caused by movement of the ends of the bone at the break. The doctor diagnosed his own affliction as a "false joint."

The symptoms continued unabated, but he continually put off the day when he would have to return to the hospital and have the ends of the bone scraped and set so that normal knitting would occur. He has always been thoughtful of others, but at times he has not done so well in taking care of himself. He dreaded having his work interrupted again for a hospital visit. Whatever other reasons he had for procrastinating, the fact remains that on Sunday, November 19th, 1950, he came to the service of healing with all the symptoms of his injured clavicle, his partial deafness, and his old sinus trouble.

He wrote a letter five days later—a letter to the young woman who led the service he had attended. This is what it said:

November 24, 1950

Dear Miss Kuhlman,

This letter is both an expression of gratitude and an apology: gratitude to God and to you (may He bless you always), and an apology to you for not recognizing a healing when it was taking place. I shall try to make this letter as short as possible, so here goes the "blow by blow" account.

I had been suffering from an enlarged and tender thyroid, rapid pulse, and high blood pressure. I had been taking medicine for this condition, but after a while the medicine began to cause me to have a sore throat. If I stopped the medicine (propylthiouracil), my pulse and blood pressure became worse, and if I took it, my throat became sore and fear was expressed that I might be getting agranulocytosis and a blood count was ordered. I have not had to have that blood count, for my wife wrote to you asking for your prayers for me. I began to notice a steady improvement after her last letter until I was symptomless. No more rapid pulse, tenderness of the thyroid, hypertension, or extreme fatigue. My wife wrote to you expressing her thanks. THEN: Old man Devil began to whisper, "How do you know that this is not just a natural remission?" Then the article in *Redbook* [1] was brought to my attention, and this increased my confidence. When my wife suggested driving up to hear you at Faith Temple, I agreed, though, to my shame, with a certain slight degree of unbelief.

Saturday, Nov. 18th, was a hard day for me. Up at 6:00 A.M., going hard all day until 5:30 P.M., when I arrived home for dinner. Rushed to get ready and drove to Franklin. There, in the

[1] "Can Faith in God Heal the Sick?" by Emily Gardiner Neal, *Redbook Magazine*, November, 1950, pp. 28ff.

hotel, I had very little sleep, due to an infected right antrum which caused me no little pain, and an old fracture of the right clavicle which had not healed together but had formed a false joint with a callus around it about the size of a walnut. It has been very painful so that I could put my coat on only with difficulty, and my hand would shake when I endeavored to raise my right arm. I assure you that the pain from my neck down to my wrist was really severe.

Sabbath Morning: Up again at 6:00 A.M. in order to get break- fast and get out to Faith Temple before 9:00 A.M. I want you to know that I truly had no thought as to any healing for myself. I have always been able to stand pain, so my chief concern was for my wife, who had her left breast removed in April for signet-cell carcinoma, (a very malignant type), and my fear that she might have metastases. Also I was concerned and praying for our son, who has had a very nervous condition due to multiple petechial hemorrhages in the brain, which resulted from whooping-cough when he was just one year old.

During your healing period you began to state that there was "a sinus opening up. Some one is regaining hearing in an ear." (I have been deaf in my right ear for at least fifteen years.) You went on to say, "I see a lump the size of a walnut beginning to dissolve." My dear wife nudged me and whispered, "She means you," but I, just thinking of her and our son, felt nothing but a burning in my right ear which I thought was the result of mental suggestion. Then you said, "This is a man. I do not want this man to lose this healing. Please speak up." I can see you now as you looked earnestly in our direction waving your left hand almost directly at our group and at the same time pounding the pulpit with your right fist. My wife kept nudging me but even when you said that the man had a burning in his ear, I couldn't believe that I was being healed. After all, I had asked nothing for myself. I was accustomed to the deafness in my right ear and gave it no thought.

I drove the eighty-five miles home through the rain, a condition not conducive to helping sinusitis. On the way home my wife kept speaking to me in an ordinary tone of voice. She was sitting beside me, *on my right.* Then she called my attention to my ability to hear her and we both realized that I was not asking her to repeat. Just after we arrived home, all of a sudden I had to blow my nose. My sinus had opened and the pain had gone. The antrum kept draining freely all evening. I slept well all night and in the morning I was entirely free from drainage and pain. To add to my amazement, I found that I was able to use my right arm in normal motion without pain. I cannot state that the hearing in my right ear is perfect but I need not turn my left ear to my wife and ask her to repeat. Perhaps the rest of the hearing will return gradually.

I have tried to make this letter short. I could write a lot more, but you are too busy to be bothered with lengthy letters. I must, however, express my gratitude to God, to you Kathryn Kuhlman, to my dear wife, my daughter and her husband . . . who have all been praying for me. The best part is that I have had a real spiritual uplift and I hope that God will continue to bless you all and be merciful to me, a sinner.

Gratefully yours,

———— ——————, M.D.

P.S. Please do not mention my name or location in the city, because some people might consider that I am seeking notoriety.

I also wrote a letter to Miss Kuhlman on the same date, confirming the change that occurred so rapidly. It said, in part:

We knew that (Dr. B. and his wife) were going to your meeting in Franklin last Sunday, and we remembered them in our prayers. We were very anxious to know what happened, and when they told Anne (my wife) over the phone, we were overjoyed . . . They have told me in detail what happened during and after last Sunday's meeting at Faith Temple, but I will not repeat that story here. I will say, though, that I know them very well and I don't question for a minute the accuracy of what they have told me.

Now as to what I see as the result of the healing that took place during and following your meeting: (Dr. B's) arm gives him no pain in normal use. He can lift it as high as he wishes, even straight over his head, with no pain or trouble at all. Last night, without thinking what he was doing, he threw his right arm straight up, to show us how you raise your hand and ask the people to raise their hands in your meetings. His arm acted perfectly normally, and he forgot how he had raised it until I reminded him of what he had just done.

He still has a lump on his right shoulder, but they tell me it is growing smaller. (I didn't see the lump until yesterday.)

His sinuses have cleared up. He has no headache.

He can hear from his right ear. It is not quite as good as his left ear yet, but he can understand what you say perfectly well, with his finger in his left ear.

For the first time in years, when you meet him and ask him how he is, he says enthusiastically, "Just fine!"

He is happy. He can do his work without any handicap. He has a vigor and endurance that I have not seen in him for a long, long time.

His faith in God has been strengthened and deepened, and he is eager to make a new start in serving our Lord.

Dr. B. never received any medical or surgical treatment for his broken collarbone. It might not be impossible for a false joint to heal naturally, but any normal healing would take a number of weeks. Usually an operation would be prescribed, to scrape and set the bone ends, and even then several weeks would be needed for complete healing. The doctor's symptoms of pain and limitation of motion disappeared during one day. The callus dissolved completely within a few weeks. An X-ray taken for another purpose on June 20, 1952, shows a perfectly knit bone, and an outward examination shows no difference between the right and the left clavicle at the present time. The healing of this fracture has been permanent and complete.

Since about 1954, Dr. B. has had some trouble in a quite

different sinus region, but he has never had a recurrence in the areas originally infected. There has been no noticeable change in his hearing since November, 1950.

When this account was published in *Tomorrow* magazine,[2] inquiry was made by a California surgeon. I sent him a copy of an earlier article [3] in which photographs of the X-rays mentioned above were included. (This is, unfortunately, a poor way to examine X-rays, since details showed up under strong light that did not appear in the photographed and printed reproduction.) Since the ensuing correspondence sheds further light, I quote the pertinent passages:

———————————, California
July 17, 1955

Dear Reverend Gross,
I want to thank you very much indeed for your detailed and honest answers which you gave me on my questions, as well as your article, "A Physician Is Healed."

It is unfortunate that the X-rays which are reproduced in your article are not good enough to allow a definite diagnosis. Maybe that is the fault of the reproductions and not of the originals.

On X-ray One you can see distinctly the proximal part of the clavicula and the line of fracture. The distal end of the bone is not visible probably due to a strong atrophy of the peripheral bone distal from the fracture.[4] On the basis of this X-ray, however, one is not entitled to make the diagnosis of a "false joint." I also feel that your definition of a "false joint" (page 69 of *Tomorrow*) [5] is misleading. You write "such a condition means that the fracture does not knit." (That is correct.) But it is incorrect to continue

———

[2] Spring, 1955 issue: "Prayer That Heals," by Don H. Gross, pp. 56–62.
[3] In *The Pittsburgher* magazine, November, 1954: "A Physician Is Healed," by Don H. Gross, pp. 6ff.
[4] The outer end of the bone did not appear in the published picture, but it does appear in the X-ray under strong illumination. It was very faint, not because of atrophy but because the intensity of the X-rays fell off toward the edges of the film.
[5] He means *The Pittsburgher*, not *Tomorrow*.

"The outer covering of the bone grows over each broken end, and a callus grows around the fractured area." Now that is the description of a normal bone healing but surely not of a "false joint." A "false joint" is always characterized by the lack of new bone formation, and you will never find in those cases a "painful lump" as was the case with Dr. B.

On the X-ray and clinical basis I actually have the impression that the fracture healed without any "false joint" in a completely normal way, and that the remnant was a periostal thickening as shown in the second X-ray more than 2 years after the fracture occurred.

I do not deny psychic influences in the suddenly improved pains, and movements in this case, but I am not able to declare it as a healing of a collar bone "false joint" due to prayer.[6]

Dr. B. wrote me a comment on the surgeon's letter.

I have read with interest the letter you received from Dr. L. I feel that he is rather too cynical in regard to the healings which took place in regard to the fracture of my right clavicle. Let us review the case. On January 7, 1950, due to a fall, the right patella was struck in such a downward force that all the tendonous and ligamental attachments to the upper and lateral aspects of the patella were completely torn loose and the patella was located down over the head of the tibia. In addition to that, the anterior half of the knee capsule was split wide open exposing the cartilages of the knee. It was necessary to put a hollow silver pin laterally through the patella and wire the ligaments and tendons back in position. Of course it was necessary to close the knee capsule. I was informed by the orthopoedic surgeon that "a man your age, 63 years, cannot expect to get off without some stiffness of your knee."

[6] The rest of the letter concerns a reported healing of cancer which was included in the *Tomorrow* article, and which subsequent inquiry showed as probably involving a mistaken diagnosis. This sort of problem is not uncommon in accounts of spiritual healing. It has led to the policy which I now follow, which is normally to cite only those cases which I know or have carefully investigated first-hand. For that I am grateful to the doctor from California. (I have made an exception in quoting and commenting on Rebecca Beard's story of the healing of Alice Newton, Chapter X, and Appendix C. The indications are that it was carefully observed.)

I was up and around on crutches in less than a week and by the middle of Feb. the cast was removed and I was given an elastic bandage. I then started using a cane and in another week the surgeon said to take the elastic bandage off and "use that knee." I did just that, in spite of the pain and to this day I have absolutely NO limitation of motion. By the end of June I was walking without a cane. Now, does it sound reasonable to you that my knee should heal so well and a simple fracture of the clavicle should take ten months? I am sorry Dr. L. cannot see the original pictures but I must take issue with him when he states that "a false joint is always characterized by lack of bone formation and NEVER by a painful lump." He should know that circumstances alter cases. I kept using crutches and cane and thus prevented union of the bone. That nature tried to heal is evidenced by the fibrous callus formation. The fact that the proximal end of the bone was seen is evidence that the fractured ends had been misplaced by use of cane and crutches. Then also false motion could be felt. The callus was much larger than would have been the case in a completely normal healing and it was an angry red and extremely tender and painful, after ten months.

As to psychic influence, that is completely out. My entire religious and scientific training had taught me that the age of miracles was past and I walked out of that meeting with no thought that any "healing" had taken place.

Afterward, when I realized that I was able to hear with my right ear and when my sinuses suddenly drained freely that night and I was able to use my right arm without pain, then I remembered how Miss Kuhlman had said, "This man is receiving a healing of sinus trouble, his right ear is regaining its hearing, and there is a lump, the size of a walnut, beginning to dissolve." That was in Nov. 1950 and, though I had suffered from frontal sinusitis and antrum trouble every year since I was a freshman in medical school, 1908, I have had none since. Personally I am convinced that "Nothing is impossible with God" and that was His way of teaching me that I was having too little faith. If I see a cancer patient, I immediately refer it to the best surgeon I can get and I have not as yet seen a cancer patient healed by prayer; however, I pray for them and encourage them to have faith that God will be merciful. In the case of my own wife, who had a mastectomy in April, 1950, I was told that her case was so malignant that she could not live more than six months. Now, five years and nine months later she shows no evidence of metastases, and we feel that we have God to thank for that, and, of course, a very capable and conscientious surgeon.

All this is told in detail so that it can be examined in detail. Case histories of spiritual healing have been published in considerable numbers, but usually with brief descriptions and with little analysis by anyone with medical training. The approach here is different: to see what is revealed by more careful scrutiny.

The scientific-minded might wish that they could have been watching through a fluoroscope, seeing the rapid knitting of the collarbone and taking a movie of it all the while. But life-situations are seldom so neat as this. That the healing described should have happened at all is rare enough; that it occurred in the context of as much medical knowledge as we have in the case is rarer still. It is not the sort of thing that could be reproduced on command, and no doubt it will fail to convince anyone who is resolute in his determination not to be convinced of the reality of spiritual healing. However, it is not presented to "prove" something to the unwilling, but to be instructive to those who would prefer to learn from it.

First, may we note that at least two of the three afflictions were organic and physical. The partial deafness may have been, but we cannot be sure. Every physical illness probably can be affected by psychological factors. But basically we consider a sinus infection as caused by microbes and a broken bone as caused by a physical impact. These would not normally be called psychosomatic illnesses; that is, brought on or to be removed by emotional readjustment.[7]

[7] It is true that some psychology looks for a psychological cause for *all* illness. But this point of view would not set apart an area considered organic or physical, to be isolated from the effects of spiritual healing. It is this isolation which we are here concerned to overcome.

As a matter of fact, the evidence indicates that Dr. B. did not undergo any strong emotional reaction, except when he discovered later in the day that he had been healed. He did not seem particularly responsive to suggestion. Evidence for this is his initial refusal to believe that he was healed, and his failure to come forward when Miss Kuhlman asked, "Please speak up." He acknowledged the healing only after seeing the results. May I say, too, that his personality is not an especially suggestible type. I recently sat beside him at an evening gathering led by a hypnotist. He gave no appreciable reaction to the hypnotist's suggestions and certainly did not qualify as one of the subjects for the evening's demonstration.

The California surgeon, diagnosing at a distance, did not think that the collarbone developed a false joint. But he gave no explanation for the continuing symptoms, all of which were originally caused by the fracture. The natural inference from the persisting symptoms is a persisting cause: the unhealed fracture. And in any case the healing involved physical disorders.

The evidence in this case, as in so many others, is that healing through spiritual means is not confined to functional, emotionally-caused, or psychological illnesses. The theory that would eliminate physically caused disease from the realm of spiritual healing is not based upon an examination of actual case histories.

Secondly, the healing of Dr. B. is unusually clear-cut in its relation of cause and effect. In many examples of spiritual therapy it is easy to say that the cure "would have happened anyway." It may be possible someday to develop statistical evidence of the effectiveness of spiritual healing. But until enough documented cases, compared under carefully controlled conditions, are available for such a study, the evidence for effectiveness will lie in individual cases such as the one at hand.

Here we have Dr. B.'s presence at a service where healing

is claimed. The three afflictions are accurately described by Miss Kuhlman, who has no previous knowledge of these conditions or that the doctor and his family are present. She looks in his direction, but cannot distinguish him indivdually in the crowd of several hundred people. She says that the healing is being received. Within the day it comes to pass, as it would not have in the normal course of events. It is impossible to give a mathematical estimate of this happening by chance, but intuitively we feel that the odds against it are enormous. Unless we cherish some philosophy that inflexibly eliminates inconvenient evidence, we will conclude that the healing was caused by some power working in conjunction with Miss Kuhlman's ministry.

✦ CHAPTER III ✦

The Challenge of the Fringe

"John said to him, 'Teacher, we saw a man casting out demons in your name, and we forbade him, because he was not following us.' But Jesus said, 'Do not forbid him; for no one who does a mighty work in my name will be able soon after to speak evil of me. For he that is not against us is for us.' "

Mark 9.38–40

      It seems more than a bit embarrassing to the Church to ask where spiritual healing is today, and then to answer with an example in which the spiritual ministration was so far removed from conventional Church life. Yet some of the most publicized claims of healing through spiritual means come from those who would be considered on the "fringe" of the Church by members of the traditional, conservative Christian denominations. On the one hand we see well-known and successful Oral Roberts; on the other hand, some (who shall remain nameless) who have run into trouble with the law. The fringe ranges from orthodox fundamentalists to the self-centered Father Divine in America or to the spiritualist Harry Edwards in England. It has included individualists such as the late Aimee Semple McPherson and tightly knit organizations such as the Christian Scientists. What is the meaning of this fringe healing?

      It would be simple to dismiss the whole thing by denying that anything occurs beyond psychological and ordinary psychosomatic effects. Unfortunately the brute facts do not allow this easy solution. The case of Dr. B. does not allow it, and this case happens to be only one of a multitude.[1] And if some genuine spiritual healing is happening in the fringe, the acute questions are, "Why do we not see more of it in the typical Church? If it belongs in the normal life of the Church, how can we introduce it?"

There are two possible answers that lead to opposite results:

1. Spiritual healing simply does not belong in the life of the Church. This approves the general *status quo* and discourages any further introduction of spiritual healing; or

2. The Church needs repentance, and will find anew the power to heal when it returns once more to Christ's command to heal the sick.

It is easy to argue for the first answer by pointing out the faults of the various fringe types of healing. Basic errors of Christian Science, for instance, can be demonstrated by the scientific study of medicine. Or its fundamental premise, that nothing but God has real existence, can be shown to contradict Biblical Christianity. Its underlying thought-pattern can be seen as similar to Oriental dualistic religions, only dressed up in selected Bible quotes. Psychologically speaking, its approach to life is bound up with an attempt to escape harsh realities, following the pattern of Mary Baker Eddy's neuroses. And the experience of medical doctors abounds with patients whose health has suffered or whose life has been lost because of the influence of Christian Science.

The trouble is that a review of faults only gives reason why something should *not* exist. The question that remains unanswered is, "Why, if all this is true, *does* Christian Science exist?" Perhaps many reasons could be given, but the usual

---

[1] For example, many of the case histories collected by Emily Gardiner Neal for *A Reporter Finds God through Spiritual Healing* are instances that took place through Miss Kuhlman's ministry.

experience of a convert to Christian Science is that he had an affliction which no one helped until a Christian Scientist came along and offered to meet the need. But what if someone from the Church had offered the help? What reason would there have been then to become a Christian Scientist? The story of the woman who came to Bishop Pardue makes the point.

Would we have to mimic Christian Science to offer healing? The Rev. Dr. Elwood Worcester and his associate, the Rev. Samuel McComb, did not think so when they launched a healing program (eventually called the Emmanuel Movement) at Emmanuel Episcopal Church, Boston, shortly before Mary Baker Eddy's death. Their critics were often so unobserving as to confuse their project with Christian Science. But in reality they carefully cooperated with medical men.[2] "They studied Christian Science also, and tried to analyze the reasons for its spread. Although they say modestly that their movement had no relation to Christian Science, by way of either protest or imitation, yet they profited by what was commonly regarded by the old, established Churches as its errors."[3] The Emmanuel Movement was the pioneer work in the restoration of healing to the life of the larger Protestant Churches in modern times, and much of what it stood for has been expressed in the later ministries of such men as Dr. Leslie Weatherhead, Dr. Norman Vincent Peale and Dr. John Sutherland Bonnell. With a somewhat different emphasis, the ministry of spiritual healing has been continued in the Episcopal Church, and in complete harmony with medical care, under the leadership of such men as the late Dr. John Gaynor Banks and Dr. Alfred Price. It would appear that spiritual healing need not be con-

[2] Including Dr. Joseph H. Pratt, Dr. James J. Putnam, Dr. Richard C. Cabot, Dr. Isador Coriat, and other leading physicians, neurologists, and psychiatrists. A valuable treatment of the Emmanuel Movement is to be found in Chapter XII of *The Church and Healing*, by Carl J. Scherzer, (Westminster, 1950), pp. 169–183.

[3] Scherzer, op. cit., p. 170.

fined to the fringe groups, nor need their limitations be reproduced in the Church.

While Christian Science, as a new movement, was particularly in the minds of Church people a half-century ago, it would seem that the fringe individuals popularly known as "Faith Healers" often draw more attention now. What pastor has not been asked, "What do you think of Oral Roberts?" Dr. Wade H. Boggs, Jr. has recently written on the subject in his *Faith Healing and the Christian Faith*.[4] While there is much in this volume to commend it, there is also much that betrays a lack of first-hand acquaintance with the subject. Dr. Boggs' lumping together of Elsie Salmon, Agnes Sanford, Oral Roberts, Henry Branham, Aimee Semple McPherson, "Little David," Lourdes, Fatima, St. Anne de Beaupré, Christian Science, New Thought, Unity, Father Divine, the "snake handlers" and others is not exactly a model of discrimination. His unfortunate habit of making one stew out of selected tidbits of teaching from sundry scattered sources puts everyone who believes in healing through spiritual means, through brute faith, through right thinking or through almost anything not encompassed by orthodox medicine, in the same unsavory pot. His discussion seems to boil down to a plea for the *status quo* in Church life, justifying the present example of typical Protestant practice. His explanation of the fringe type of healing is to couch it in "psychosomatic" terms, as follows:

["psychosomatic"] is a term which is enjoying immense and growing prestige in medical circles. It is taken from two Greek words meaning "spirit" and "body" and it conveys the idea that many diseases, previously thought to be purely physical and chemical, are closely connected with, if not caused by, mental conditions . . .

Perhaps the most reasonable explanation of the successes of the faith healers, therefore, is to suppose that they have stumbled upon this psychosomatic principle, and that while they operate in

[4] John Knox Press, Richmond, 1956.

accordance with it, they more or less imperfectly understand it, and use it in hit-or-miss fashion. This view of the matter contradicts the contention that God's power is being released in a miraculous way through them. Rather, it would seem that in using their accidental discovery of the psychosomatic principle, they are no more and no less effective than non-religious practitioners or even charlatans.

By Dr. Boggs' definition of "Faith Healers," Miss Kuhlman, whose work was considered above in Chapter II, would surely be included. Yet the healing of Dr. B. does not fit Dr. Boggs' hypothetical explanation. Anyone who has been directly associated with the healing work of Agnes Sanford [5] will realize how far it transcends this hypothesis of the "psychosomatic principle." Many of the healings at Lourdes certainly do not support the hypothesis; in fact, they alone would rule it out as a complete explanation. If the "psychosomatic principle" were extended to include all cases where the state of someone's mind has an influence on the condition of someone's body, then it would be a principle that would describe (but not explain) all cases of spiritual healing. But when Dr. Boggs' limitation of "curing diseases that have been caused by mental or spiritual condition," is applied, the evidence uproots the theory. It is always unsafe to propose an explanation before becoming familiar with the events that need explaining.

This is not to say that many of Dr. Boggs' criticisms do not deserve careful consideration. He brings out genuine problems which we will consider in later chapters. But even if we were to accept all his negative criticisms, the failure of his thory of the "psychosomatic principle" makes necessary a serious revision of his positive philosophy of health. Because if spiritual healing has an effectiveness in its own right, a factor not included in orthodox medical and psychological healing, this factor cannot be omitted in the Church's approach to healing.

[5] Which is reported in her books, such as *The Healing Light*.

It would seem obvious from the New Testament alone that Christian healing through spiritual means does have a distinctive contribution to make. But Dr. Boggs says:

If the purpose of Jesus' healing ministry was, as we discovered in the last section, to reveal the compassionate love of God for mankind, then there is every reason to believe that the followers of Christ have a perennial obligation to reflect the compassion of God as best we are able to those who are sick. So we believe that signs of the divine compassion should continue during the entire era when the Gospel is being preached and the Kingdom established; that is, to the very end of history. But these signs will, I believe, have only a slight, if any, connection with the freak phenomena of the faith healers. We should look today for signs which effectively express the divine spirit of compassion in the the area of healing primarily from Christian doctors, surgeons, dentists, medical scientists, psychiatrists, nurses, and technicians who have put forth sacrificial efforts to learn the principles, the techniques, the means by which God heals, in order that they may co-coperate with Him.

In other words, the Church should now expect its ministrations of healing to be carried on primarily through scientific knowledge. Indeed the Church should bless and use every available bit of scientific knowledge. But is its healing work to be primarily scientific and only secondarily spiritual? Jesus healed and He commissioned His apostles to heal, but it would take more than a little anachronism to suggest that their approach was scientific. Where has Dr. Boggs left room for their New Testament type of healing? Is their compassion all that is to be left, while their power to heal through strictly spiritual means lies forgotten in the shadow of modern science? Would it not be fitting for Christ's Church to give some attention to the kind of healing that Christ did?

Dr. Boggs comes right up to the main point in this paragraph:

Recall in the next place that Christ demonstrated the spirit of divine compassion by doing all that was in His power to fight against disease. The very least that may be deduced for our guidance from the healing ministry of Jesus is that we should have in us His spirit of compassion, and do whatever lies within our power to fight against disease. Just as Jesus did the will of God in His ministry of healing, so we may be sure the human family also does the will of God when it strives to wipe out the scourges which afflict us. This point is so plain that there can be no debate about it. The only question here is how the human family can best express the divine compassion in its fight against sickness. It is my conviction that the spirit of compassion for the sick is most effectively expressed, not by the bizarre practices of the faith healers, but by more generous support of scientific medical research, and by the use of the skills of men who have put forth sincere and arduous efforts to learn how to co-operate with God in the healing of the sick.

Here he grants a major premise of those who stand for spiritual healing. That premise is that it is always God's will to strive against disease. Then he comes to the one essential decision to be made: "The only question here is how the human family can best express the divine compassion in its fight against sickness." Indeed that is the question. Dr. Boggs then makes an "either-or" out of what (if it were stated a little differently) should be a "both-and."

As for the "bizarre practices of the faith healers"—they all depend on one's point of view. Let us, for example, see whether Jesus might not qualify as a "faith healer" (in Dr. Boggs' sense), and whether his practices might not have met some people's definitions of "bizarre." The fact that most of the religious leaders of His day considered Him "a glutton and a drunkard, a friend of tax collectors and sinners." (Luke 7.34), a blasphemer (Mark 14.64), a traitor to the emperor (John 19.12), demon-possessed (John 8.48), in league with the devil (Mark 3.22) makes Him a member of the fringe. Let us not forget the condition of our spiritual ancestors.

Jesus had healing hands (Luke 4.40); felt God's healing power go forth from Him (Mark 5.30); drew great crowds because of His healing (Mark 1.45); healed physical (Luke 22.51), mental (Mark 1.23–27), and spiritual (Mark 2.5) afflictions; performed miracles (John 6.2); healed those who had not benefited from medical care (Mark 5.25–26); and claimed that healing came through faith (Mark 5.34; 10.52). He seems to meet every requirement for inclusion among Dr. Boggs' "faith healers"!

Let the reader judge for himself regarding the bizarre practices of Jesus. He healed incurable cases instantly (Mark 1.42), rebuked the wind (Mark 4.39), multiplied a few loaves and fishes to feed five thousand people (Mark 6.30–44), cast a multitude of demons out of a man and into a multitude of pigs who then rushed into the sea and were drowned (Mark 5.1–4), raised Lazarus from the dead after four days, coming to his tomb and calling with a loud voice, "Lazarus, come out," whereupon "the dead man came out, his hands and feet bound with bandages, and his face wrapped with a cloth" (John 11). Perhaps long acquaintance with the Bible has made such things seem commonplace. But what if Oral Roberts were to do them? Would they be bizarre?

At this point someone may be ready to say, "Now you have done it! What are you trying to do? Equate Oral Roberts with Jesus?"

Of course not! What has been done is to carry out an argument to its logical conclusion. For a blanket condemnation of all "faith healers" unfortunately includes the condemnation of Jesus. This is a plea for a measure of tolerance and understanding love, and even for people who seem at first sight completely outlandish. The "fringe" no doubt is piled high with chaff, laden with nonsense that has no meaning beyond being bizarre. But in among its freak phenomena there just *might* lie nuggets of gold. You never can tell until you look. Is it inevitable that the majority will never look for the gold until a generation has blessed part of the fringe and thus removed it from *their* fringe?

If instead of being merely defensive against the fringe, we decide to be patient and constructive and (shocking thought!) even *learn* something from it—what is the meaning of the lesson that it teaches?

First of all, the fringe contains a real element of the Judgment of God upon the Church. When the Lord says, "I was sick and you visited me" (Matthew 25.36), many a Christian Scientist will pass where many an orthodox churchman will fail. When He reminds us of His command, "Heal the sick" (Luke 10.9), many a "faith healer" will find approval while many a "respectable" minister will be found wanting.

If the members of the Church had remained true to Christ's commission to heal, there would be no reason or excuse for healing sects or for individual healers working in pathetic isolation from the main stream of Church life. They need the balancing influence of the whole Church desperately. The Church needs them, too.

In the New Testament Church it was common for Christians to exercise all sorts of unusual gifts of the spirit—gifts that were gladly accepted. As St. Paul wrote to the Church at Corinth:

Now there are varieties of gifts, but the same Spirit; and there are varieties of service, but the same Lord; and there are varieties of working, but it is the same God who inspires them all in every one. To each is given the manifestation of the Spirit for the common good. To one is given through the Spirit the utterance of wisdom, and to another the utterance of knowledge according to the same Spirit, to another faith by the same Spirit, to another gifts of healing by the one Spirit, to another the working of miracles, to another prophecy, to another the ability to distinguish between spirits, to another various kinds of tongues, to another the interpretation of tongues. All these are inspired by one and the same Spirit, who apportions to each one individually as he wills. (I Corthians 12.4–11)

Now everything is done so "decently and in order" that many spiritually gifted individuals have no decent place to go and no orderly way to fit into the life of the Church. Even Agnes Sanford has had many doors closed to her although she is the wife of an Episcopal clergyman. Now Dr. Boggs has ranked her with Father Divine. Should we be surprised when less patient souls cut loose from the Church to follow an independent path? Is the fault all theirs, or does some of the blame rest on us in the orthodox Church?

The fringe contains elements of judgment, too, on the secular thought of our day. For the present secular frame of mind is intolerant toward whatever human reason cannot dominate and manipulate. It is uncongenial to psychic phenomena, not just because spiritualists have so often been frauds, but because the subject matter of parapsychology does not fit neat, comfortable, predictable materialism. It rejects the supernatural because it is a threat to the lordship of man over the universe. As a result, both the psychic and the supernatural aspects of healing tend to be suppressed into the dark corners of the fringe. The wife of a certain leader in the academic world, for instance, claims to have an astonishing clairvoyant gift by which she describes diseased states. A medical doctor has worked together with her for a number of years. Although her husband fully accepts her claims, when they come into contact with his academic friends, no hint is ever given that she has such a gift. It would identify her with the fringe, not quite proper for polite society. Is this not really a judgment on society for its narrow-mindedness?

The Christian answer to the fringe cannot stop with easy condemnation of obvious faults. The Church must boldly embrace whatever is true in the fringe, open the door for those with true spiritual gifts (however unusual), and in humble penitence respond once more to Christ's command to heal the sick. When the Lord is followed, His works within the Church will surpass those outside. Their quality will partake of the wholeness of the truth that the fringe does not have, a wholeness that includes the best in scientific medicine and, in addition, that which science cannot provide—the crowning glory of the power of the Holy Spirit.

CHAPTER IV

The Well-Springs of Reason

"There are more things in heaven and earth, Horatio, Than are dreamt of in your philosophy."

Hamlet, Act I: Scene 5

The philosopher Descartes once spent a day inside a dark stove meditating on his own mind. His conclusion was: "I think, therefore I am." He made this the foundation stone of his philosophy. But his own existence had started with one single cell with no consciousness at all. It multiplied and grew into the amazing form of a human baby, and he was born. Still he had no conscious thought. He slowly became more aware of the world around him and of his own existence. At last he began to think. His thinking was not yet governed by logic, but by his inner feelings. His knowledge was mostly what he absorbed from others who were more mature. As he grew toward manhood, he established the attitudes and habits that made up his own individual personality. His feelings, his training and experience, and his reason all grew and wove themselves into his own individual pattern of thought. If Descartes had said, "I am, therefore I think," he would have spoken the truth. Instead he concentrated on only one special part of his life, his conscious thought, and in this way he afflicted himself with a peculiar sort of blindness that has misled many another brilliant man. For the mind of man is not and never was the beginning or the measure of all things.

To pretend that it is, is to make an idol of the mind just as surely as if it were an idol hewn of wood or cut of stone.

The worship of thought is avoided by respect for simple experience, for actual life-situations, for events as they occur. The understanding of reality progresses through stubborn refusal to let our dear little theories and the workings of our ever so limited minds interfere with first-hand experience. Nothing blocks either science or religion more than the attempt to deny the existence of the obvious just because it would upset neat notions of how God, man, or the world ought to behave. One of the reasons many people rejected Jesus during His lifetime was that He did not fit their preconceived picture of the Messiah. Today He is more likely to be rejected because the things He did do not fit our preconceived notion of the laws of nature. Of course, we do not now say that we reject Him— we merely "reconstruct" His life in our own image—a sort of historical brainwashing of the records.

It is disconcerting to pick up a book hoping to study the life of Jesus and discover instead an expression of the pet theories of the "historical critic" who wrote it.[1] (The first-century Gospel writers, we are given to understand, recorded a mass of illusions, and the true history of nineteen centuries ago has only recently been discovered.) It is similarly disconcerting to find that cases of spiritual healing one has seen with his own eyes are likewise discredited as illusion—and simply because they do not come within the thought-patterns of the hearer. These things are especially puzzling to a student of modern physics. The greatest advances in that science have come through experimental results which could not possibly have been fitted into any known theories. Nature is no respecter of human mental pictures. The advances of physics have been made when

---

[1] This is not a refusal to allow historical criticism of the Bible. It is a criticism of those critics who are so subjective in their approach that their work is of value mainly in the study of the psychology of the critics themselves.

the mind arrived at a new level of understanding which included the new phenomena along with the old, and which
at the same time opened new corridors of exploration which
had previously been barred. Thus, through happenings which
at first seem absurd and illogical, the broadening imagination
opens the gates to more things in heaven and earth than were
ever before dreamt of in our philosophy.

After all, what is logical, and what is not? Logic is an
excellent means of careful and precise thinking. Yet even the
most carefully reasoned logic is anchored to beginning points
which are beyond the reach of logic. These are the "postulates,"
certain truths that are assumed to be correct before logic gets
under way. Geometry, for instance, begins with "axioms,"
starting points for which no justification is offered. The axioms
of ordinary geometry, such as the assumption that a straight
line is the shortest path between two points, are usually easy
to accept. They fit everyday experience and appeal to "common
sense." However, other axioms of geometry could be assumed,
and in some scientific studies they are assumed. For instance,
it may be helpful in the study of the vastness of outer space
to imagine that space is curved and that a certain type of
curved line is the shortest distance between two points! When
different axioms are chosen, a different type of geometry results. Each type of geometry is equally logical. Yet the calculations made using one type of geometry may lead to answers
different from those given by another type of geometry. The
difference has nothing to do with logic, but is determined purely
by the axioms.

There is nothing in this that is peculiar to geometry. All
human reasoning works this way. It depends on postulates that
cannot be proved by reason. And most of our postulates are
assumed unconsciously, without examination. They are simply
taken for granted. Each civilization and each age in human
history shows much of its character in those postulates its
people take for granted. It is the common assumptions shared

by a people that make up the background pattern of their thinking.

We are likely to get a perspective on ourselves when our postulates are challenged. Thus the members of Western civilization have been driven to a new self-examination by the challenge of the enemy ideologies of Naziism and Communism. The well-known psychiatrist C. G. Jung gives an illuminating contrast between the thinking of primitive men and that of modern civilized men. He tells of the case of two primitive women who were eaten by a crocodile. Fellow-tribesmen "said that an unknown sorcerer had summoned the crocodile and had bidden it to bring him the two women." Dr. Jung's comment is as follows:

This story is a perfect example of that capricious way of accounting for things which is a feature of the "pre-logical" state of mind. We call it pre-logical, because to us such an explanation seems absolutely illogical. But it only strikes us in this way because we start from assumptions wholly different from those of primitive man. If we were as convinced as he is of the existence of sorcerers and of mysterious powers, instead of believing in so-called natural causes, his inferences would seem to us perfectly reasonable. As a matter of fact, primitive man is no more logical or illogical than we are. His presuppositions are not the same as ours, and that is what distinguishes him from us. His thinking and his conduct are based on assumptions other than our own. To all that is in any way out of the ordinary and that therefore disturbs, frightens or astonishes him, he ascribes what we should call a supernatural origin. For him, of course, these things are not supernatural; on the contrary, they belong to his world of experience. We feel we are stating a natural sequence of events when we say: this house was burned down because the lightning struck it. Primitive man senses an equally natural sequence when he says: a sorcerer has used the lightning to set fire to this particular house. There is nothing whatever within the experience of primitive man—provided that is at all unusual or impressive—that will not be accounted for on similar grounds. In explaining things in this way he is just like ourselves: he does not examine his assumptions. To him it is an unquestionable truth that disease and other ills are caused by spirits or witchcraft, just as for us it is a foregone conclusion that an illness has a natural cause. We would no more lay it down to sorcery than he to natural causes. His mental activity does not differ in any fundamental way from ours. It is, as I have said, his assumptions alone that set him apart from ourselves.[2]

The common tendency either to isolate Christian thought or to subordinate it to secular thought hides the very real conflict between what is likely to be taken for granted in our secular culture and what is assumed in Biblical Christianity. In truth the chasm between the secular and the Christian assumptions is every bit as deep as the gulf between the thinking of primitive tribesmen and that of civilized citizens.

How can we describe the first principles of Christianity in the most simple and crystal-clear way? The answer lies in two affirmations of loyalty, from which all else follows. The first is from the Old Testament, from Judaism, from the deep root of the Christian faith: "Hear, O Israel: The Lord our God is one LORD; and you shall love the LORD your God with all your heart, and with all your soul, and with all your might." (Deuteronomy 6.4–5; Mark 12.28–31). This is monotheism. It is expressed at the beginning of the Ten Commandments—at the beginning, as having first priority: "You shall have no other gods before me. You shall not make yourself a graven image, or any likeness of anything that is in the heaven above, or that is in the earth beneath, or that is in the water under the earth; you shall not bow down to them or serve them; for I the LORD your God am a jealous God . . ." (Exodus 20.3–5). In the worship of one God lies the power of Judaism, of Islam, and of Christianity. In it, too, lies both narrowness and breadth. The worship of one God is utterly narrow because it rejects all man-made substitutes for the living God. It distinguishes

[2] *Modern Man in Search of a Soul*, by C. G. Jung, Harcourt, Brace & Co., N. Y., 1939, pp. 145–146.

sharply between true worship and false worship. It is not inclusive of all religions. It can see in all religions a response to God, but this is usually a confused response.

Sun worship, for instance, can be seen as a reaching toward the Source of light and power, God Himself; yet this is a confused worship, mistaking the visible sun for the invisible Creator. The truth of sun worship is hopelessly tangled with its falseness. Human religion looks at God through frosted glass, so to speak, and sees a blurred image. The God of the Bible insists that no human image, whether of wood or stone or of pure thoughts, is an acceptable object of divine worship. He also insists that nothing in creation, whether it be a hewn idol, or nature, or the human mind, or ideals, or science, or the nation, or a political party, or a church, or a family, or a lover, or one's own self, or the whole human race—nothing in creation is worthy of that absolute devotion which belongs to Him alone. He, the God of Abraham, of Isaac, and of Jacob, the God of Jesus Christ, stands majestically alone as God, Lord of all creation, the Father Almighty, Maker of heaven and earth, and of all things visible and invisible!

If this monotheism is utterly narrow, it is, in another sense, boundlessly wide. This is because it is God's will that His whole creation serve Him. Monotheism is insatiably missionary in nature. This is not to say that God desires forced or merely outward conformity: the commandment is "you shall love." Christians can never improve upon their Master, Who did not lift a finger to stop Judas; Who refused the protection of the sword when He was made a prisoner; Who said to Pilate, "My Kingship is not of this world"; Who endured the cross, despising the shame; Who prayed for His crucifiers, "Father, forgive them . . ." But if Christ refused to conquer by force, He set out to conquer by love. "Thy kingdom come. Thy will be done, On earth as it is in heaven" means that everything and everyone on earth is to be brought into subjection, in love, to God. "You shall love the Lord your God with all your heart, and with all your soul, and with all your might" means that every thought, every word, every action, twenty-four hours a day, every day of a lifetime, is to be offered, in love, to God. Even the commandment to love our neighbors derives its force from God as its author. So as we serve others, we serve God. God is Monarch of all; His Kingdom reaches toward the ends of the earth. He seeks an empire of love, a dominion that is to be all-inclusive. Yet this is not by way of democratic federation of gods many and religions many, but by the voluntary, loving subjection of all mankind to the rule of the one true Lord. This is the wideness, the catholicity, of monotheism.

This all-embracing nature of Christianity reaches out to include everything but sin and evil. (We speak now of God's intention, not the actual practice of Christians, who most certainly are sinners.) Non-Christian practices are to be "baptized," if possible, preserving and elevating the good in them, rather than abolishing them entirely. For instance, the ancient sun-worshippers celebrated the birthday of the sun-god at the beginning of winter (when the daylight began once more to lengthen). Rather than abolish the happy feast, the Church transformed it into the birthday celebration of the Son of God, Jesus Christ—and so it is that we celebrate Christmas on December 25th. The sun-god is forgotten, but the joy, now "baptized," remains, and is centered on its proper object. Thus the good of pagan worship is preserved, while its idolatry undergoes a purge. Of course, in practice, things are not nearly so neat and perfect as in this idealized example. But the worship of the one God does reach out in such ways to draw to Him all of His creation.

If the first root of Christianity is seen in the Old Testament's proclamation, "Hear, O Israel: The Lord our God is one Lord," the second root is in the New Testament's shout of faith: "Jesus is Lord" [3] "Christian" means faith in Jesus as the "Christ."

---

[3] Acts 2.36, 10.36; Romans 14.9; I Corinthians 12.3–6; Ephesians 4.4–6; Philippians 2.9–11; I Timothy 6.14–16; Revelation 17.13–14, 19.11–16 (cf. John 1.1–14), etc.

"Christ" is from the Greek word "Christos," and this is a direct translation of the Hebrew "Messiah," which means "the Anointed One." In ancient Israel, kings were consecrated to God and His service by anointing with oil. The High Priest, too, was anointed. But Israel especially looked forward to a great Deliverer of the nation, a worthy successor to David. David had given Israel victory and security against all enemies. This new King, this "son of David," was "the Anointed One" expected by their prophets.

Jesus of Nazareth disappointed those who expected an earthly ruler with arms and armies, in David's style. His own successful struggle against the temptation to be that kind of a Messiah is seen in His encounter with the devil in the wilderness at the beginning of His public ministry (Matthew 4.1–11; Luke 4.1–13):

And the devil took him up, and showed him all the Kingdoms of the world in a moment of time, and said to him, "To you I will give all this authority and their glory; for it has been delivered to me, and I give it to whom I will. If you, then, will worship me, it shall all be yours." And Jesus answered him, "It is written, 'You shall worship the Lord your God, and him only shall you serve.' "

Instead, He took upon Himself the role of the suffering Servant of God pictured in Isaiah, beginning with chapter 42. (See especially Isaiah 53.) When Simon Peter recognized him as the Messiah,[4] Jesus "strictly charged the disciples to tell no one," probably for fear of being misunderstood as intending the role of a Jewish rebel king against the Roman occupying armies. And from that time on He began to speak of His crucifixion and resurrection. But this did not fit Peter's idea of the Messiah. So "Peter took him and began to rebuke him, saying, 'God forbid, Lord! This shall never happen to you.' But he turned and said to Peter, 'Get behind me, Satan! You

---

[4] Matthew 16.16, Mark 8.29, Luke 9.20. The most complete account is in Matthew 16.13–23.

are a hindrance to me; for you are not on the side of God, but of men.' " As confessor of the faith that Jesus is the Messiah, Peter is in the eyes of Jesus the rock on which He will build His Church; as expressing the temptation to be a political and military Messiah, Peter is the devil's ambassador! The way of Jesus is the road to a cross.

And as He entered Jerusalem at the beginning of the week of His crucifixion, Jesus deliberately rode a donkey's colt in the middle of a celebration to welcome the coming Messiah to the nation's capital.[5] This curious event, which the Church commemorates on Palm Sunday, is to be understood as an acted reference by Jesus to Himself as the humble and peaceful Messiah pictured by the prophet Zechariah (Zechariah 9.9–10):

> Rejoice greatly, O daughter of Zion!
> Shout aloud, O daughter of Jerusalem!
> Lo, your king comes to you;
>   triumphant and victorious is he,
> humble and riding on an ass,
>   on a colt the foal of an ass.
> I will cut off the chariot from Ephraim
>   and the war horse from Jerusalem;
> and the battle bow shall be cut off,
>   and he shall command peace to the nations;
> his dominion shall be from sea to sea,
>   and from the River to the ends of the earth.

At His trial before the high priest,[6] Jesus is asked, "Are you the Messiah, the Son of the Blessed?" According to Mark, Jesus said, "I am." [7] But in His trial before Pontius Pilate, Jesus

[5] Matthew 21.1–11, Mark 11.1–10, Luke 19.28–40, John 12.12–19.

[6] Mark 14.53–65, Matthew 26.57–68, Luke 22.54–55, 63–71, John 18.12–24. In the translation of words spoken by Jews, I prefer here to go behind the Greek text and render "Christ" as "Messiah." In other respects, I quote from the Revised Standard Version.

[7] The exact accounts of His words vary in the different Gospels.

again made clear His own understanding of what it means to be the Messiah (John 18.33–38):

Jesus answered, "My kingship is not of this world; if my kingship were of this world, my servants would fight, that I might not be handed over to the Jews; [8] but my kingship is not from the world." Pilate said to him, "So you are a king?" Jesus answered, "You say that I am a king. For this I was born, and for this I have come into the world, to bear witness to the truth. Every one who is of the truth hears my voice." Pilate said to him, "What is truth?"

Although Pilate was cynical about truth, he wrote on the cross, "Jesus of Nazareth, the King of the Jews." (John 19.17–22) When the chief priests objected, wanting instead, *"This man said*, I am the King of the Jews," Pilate refused to change the title.

But what good is a dead Messiah? No King, no Kingdom! The touchstone to faith in Jesus as the Messiah is to be found in the climax of the Gospel accounts.[9] The earth-rending event that makes all the difference is the raising of Jesus from the dead on the third day. If He had not been raised, Christians would have had neither reason, courage nor power to continue in their faith that Jesus is the Messiah. They would have disbanded in discouragement and perplexity, never to be heard from again. Instead, on the day of Pentecost (fifty days after the Passover), they experienced an unprecedented inflow of dynamic energy from the Holy Spirit of God (Acts 2) and Peter boldly and publicly proclaimed Good News:

Men of Israel, hear these words: Jesus of Nazareth, a man attested to you by God with mighty works and wonders and signs which God did through him in your midst, as you yourselves know—this Jesus, delivered up according to the definite plan and fore-

[8] That is, to the Jewish leaders who were His enemies. Jesus and almost all of His followers were also Jews.

[9] Matthew 28, Mark 16, Luke 24, John 20–21. See also, especially, I Corinthians 15.

knowledge of God, you crucified and killed by the hands of lawless men. But God raised him up, having loosed the pangs of death, because it was not possible for him to be held by it . . .

This Jesus God raised up, and of that we are all witnesses. Being therefore exalted at the right hand of God, and having received from the Father the promise of the Holy Spirit, he has poured out this which you see and hear . . .

Let all the house of Israel therefore know assuredly that God has made him both Lord and Messiah, this Jesus whom you crucified.

Christians are, by definition, those who share this faith in Jesus of Nazareth, as Lord and Messiah, King of kings, Lord of lords, the very King of the Kingdom of God, the Kingdom that He lived, died, and rose again to bring! When John the Baptist had asked Jesus (Matthew 11.2–6; Luke 7.18–23), "Are you he who is to come, or shall we look for another?" the Messiah replied, "Go and tell John what you have seen and heard: the blind receive their sight, the lame walk, lepers are cleansed, and deaf hear, the dead are raised up, the poor have good news preached to them. And blessed is he who takes no offense at me." The power of Jesus is the power of God. The authority of Jesus is the authority of God. The Kingdom of Jesus is the Kingdom of God. This is the Christian faith.

How does this tie in with monotheism? As devout Jews, the first Christians (or should we translate it "Messianists"?) agreed thoroughly with the prophet Isaiah that

"You are my witnesses," says Yahweh,[10]
   and my servant whom I have chosen,
that you may know and believe me

[10] The personal Name of God as revealed to Israel. This is usually translated either "the Lord," following Jewish piety in not pronouncing the sacred Name, or else as "Jehovah," an artificial word derived from the consonants of "Yahweh" (or "Jahveh") interspersed with the vowels of the Herbrew word for LORD. I prefer to keep the Name as in the Hebrew and will differ from the R.S.V. in this detail.

and understand that I am He.
Before me no god was formed,
      nor shall there be after me.
I, I am Yahweh,
      and besides me there is no saviour . . . (Isaiah 43.10–11
Thus says Yahweh, the King of Israel
and his Redeemer, Yahweh of hosts:
"I am the first and I am the last;
      besides me there is no god . . ." (Isaiah 44.6)

Believing this, and believing that Jesus is King of Israel and of the world, that He is Saviour and Redeemer, the conclusion is inevitable that Jesus is actually Yahweh! [11] In Jesus, God Himself has taken on the nature of Man. We have been visited by the Lord of all creation! This is the faith of Christians, and from it the rest of Christian understanding and teaching is derived.

The implications of the Christian experience with the living Lord Jesus have filled libraries of theology, and we can only deal here with what concerns the subject at hand. Christians believe that their spiritual lives are nourished by the Messiah as branches are nourished from a vine (John 15.1–11; also I Corinthians 12) and that Jesus is the perfect revelation of God in human life. "For in him the whole fulness of diety dwells bodily, and you have come to fulness of life in him, who is the head of all rule and authority" (Colossians 2.9–10).

Faith in Jesus Christ is, of course, not yet universal among mankind. Worse yet, the fruits of the spirit are too often lacking in those who profess Christ. But where genuine Christian faith is to be found, how and why does it appear? In one sense, there are as many answers as there are Christians. In another

[11] John 8.58 tells us, "Jesus said to them, 'Truly, truly I say to you, before Abraham was, I am.' " "I AM" is emphatic in the Greek, and is a Divine name. The same implication appears in the Hebrew tradition. In Exodus 3.13–15, Moses is called by God and asks His Name. "God said to Moses, 'I AM WHO I AM.' And he said, 'Say this to the people of Israel, "I AM has sent me to you." ' "

sense, there is one experience common to all believers. That experience cannot be demonstrated to those who do not wish it. It cannot be transmuted from faith into a sort of scientific knowledge. But it can be shared and demonstrated in the individual lives of those who desire it. Christianity does not come by a mathematical proof, but by accepting an invitation: "Follow me." [12] "Come and see." (John 1.39, 46) It is not a philosophy or an ideal, but a Way of Life. On the other hand, life includes thought, and the presuppositions of Christian thought are part of the Christian's life with his Lord.

It is inevitable that some of the readers of a book such as this will not share the life or the axioms that are basic to Christianity. But such readers need not be discouraged from examining spiritual healing or, for that matter, any part of Christian life. They need not even be discouraged from practicing our suggestions for developing faith and prayer. They should accept whatever they can accept, try whatever they can try, understand with the best of their own understanding, and God, Who alone knows the secrets of all hearts, will manifest His love to each. Jesus said, "Ask, and it will be given you; seek, and you will find; knock, and it will be opened to you." (Matthew 7.7–8; Luke 11.9–10)

By bringing to consciousness something of the Christian presuppositions involved in this book, both Christians and non-Christians should be helped in clarifying their own thinking. Both can take our Christian assumptions into account as they read, and can thus be helped to see the strands of our logic and to relate it to their own thought-patterns.

Perhaps someone will feel that a Christian point of view is merely the expression of prejudice and bias, and that a completely detached scientific approach is the only one worth considering. But once we understand that unprovable presuppositions underlie *all* reasoning, we realize that the "completely unprejudiced" way of doing things is a figment of the

[12] Matthew 4.19, 8.22, 9.9, Mark 2.14, Luke 5.27, John 1.43, etc.

imagination. It can only occur to someone whose own assumptions are so unconscious and so untouched by his own critical faculties that he is completely unaware of his own inevitable prejudices. Some of the most monstrous absurdities have come from those who, like Karl Marx, were quite sure that their theories were strictly scientific. All of us depend on some sort of religious faith—including the atheistic Marxists whose own unconscious religion has done more to deprive oppressed masses of basic human rights and dignity than any other religion in modern times. How much better to try to be candid about religious faith rather than to repress it beyond sight of consciousness or criticism.

May we go on, now, to make some brief contrasts between Christian presuppositions and those postulates that are more likely to be found in the developed intellectual atmosphere of the twentieth century. Perhaps the thought characteristics of many of the so-called "intelligentsia" are likely to be found in less subtle forms in the general population. But the better educated usually are given the responsibility of education; so, theoretically, at least, they tend to condition the rational thinking of all of us. For this reason, and because they are more likely to make clear statements of non-Christian points of view than do most people, we will concentrate on a few of the assumptions of many of the more highly trained.

What kind of water comes from the wells that usually supply our educated minds? First, the water flows from man instead of God. Here the Christian's God-centeredness appears oddly out of place. The relation of man to God is seldom a proper topic of discussion in most institutions of learning (aside from some of the strictly Church-operated). Instead, we hear about "religion" (a human activity) or "ideals" (produced by man's mind) or "goals" (humanly chosen). Tolerance is rightly stressed, but it is likely to intrude itself in ways that cannot be squared with a God-centered view. For instance, most people would think that tolerance of ideas (as distinguished from the understanding of people) is absurd when it comes to arithmetic. That is, we can't be tolerant of 2 plus 2 equals 3 in the usual type of arithmetic! But tolerance of all sorts of religious ideas seems to be reasonably popular. The implication is that religion is a development of man's wishes, desires, emotions (or something else purely subjective), and is therefore a matter of taste, not truth. It is man's striving toward what he considers higher spiritually, not a matter of the true God revealing Himself. The Christian faith, on the other hand, implies positive love (not just tolerance) toward all people, and a complete dedication to the one true God to the exclusion (not tolerance) of the worship of man-made objects or desires.

So far as healing is concerned, the prevalent man-centered view tends to direct itself to immediate personal comfort. It may be expressed in terms of restoring biological equilibrium —or removing psychological conflicts. Religion may be considered a useful means of relieving emotional stress. But some psychiatrists feel that in certain cases adultery might be another proper way of eliminating tensions. Objections to the latter procedure may well be passed off by being labelled "taboos," suggesting that to take God's moral law seriously is just primitive superstition.

The powers of healing are likely to be limited to those known to characterize man. Even when a serious illness is "left in God's hands," the actual meaning may be that it is up to fate. "Nature" (impersonal) is considered as an important element in healing. The implication of the term "nature" is that there are unchanging physical, biological, and psychological laws in operation. They are assumed to be intelligible to the human mind (though much remains to be discovered), and the diagnosis and treatment of disease is likely to be confined within the limits of those natural laws that are already known. If the development of an individual case does not fit the natural laws known to man, the chances are that the original diagnosis will be considered as erroneous. This avoids admitting that a new element (prayer, for instance) could have changed the course of events. "Science," man's knowledge of natural laws, giving man powerful techniques of controlling his world—"science" is practically a magic word, too often invested with some of the awe that belongs to divinity.

Scientific materialism has a strong appeal to many. The physical world is the easiest to study and to control, and from the point of view of a man-made world, materialism has its merits. We do occasionally read some nonsense about the medieval world view (which is supposed to have been man-centered) being overthrown by the modern scientific outlook, which makes man a tiny speck on a wee world in an overwhelmingly vast universe. This is a materialistic evaluation of things, judging importance by physical dimensions. (It should make whales more significant than men, I suppose.) But, more to the point, it is a view of things that seems to leave man free in conscience to navigate his own life to his self-chosen destiny (at least within limits). It is thus completely man-centered in those moral decisions that really count. Its motto could come from "Invictus"—"I am the master of my fate; I am the captain of my soul."

Materialism is most naturally allied with nineteenth-century physics, and prefers to explain everything in terms of mechanical pictures. Any other explanation is considered magical or superstitious and beneath consideration. Parapsychology may be ringing the death knell of this sort of materialism (which is why we see such irrational opposition by materialists to the most careful studies of such things as extra-sensory perception). But it is very influential in today's thinking, probably due to the power it seems to put into human hands to remake the world without interference from God. It not only lacks a real challenge to human pride (though it devastates any thought of personal survival after death), but is the philosophy most suited to express the egotism of the power-hungry, as the Communist movement so vividly demonstrates.

An inevitable result of a radically man-centered view of things is an automatic ruling out of anything supernatural. Prayer is interpreted in simple psychological terms: it can make a person feel better or condition his mind. If a physical ailment is responsive to psychological effects, it could be of help even in physical cases. Intercessory prayer can have value in improving someone else's attitude (with whatever additional effects that change of attitude would produce), *provided* that the other person knows about it. But any power from God above and beyond the natural order is ruled out. The grace of God, in the traditional sense, is meaningless, since this implies the powerlessness of men to construct their own lives without the immediate and personal help of God. To admit such a thing would make us dependent on God, and that would undo the 'man-centered viewpoint! The existence of other spiritual beings—angels or demons—is automatically ruled out. They don't fit a mechanistic universe and they seem to threaten man's assurance of self-sufficiency. The supernatural is not reasoned away, it is merely "pooh-poohed" into the unconscious. It is too discomfiting to face.

Such man-centered assumptions have had a strong influence within the Christian Church, and may be traced in the work of theological leaders. As a young man, Albert Schweitzer wrote most significantly about those who set out to reconstruct the life of Jesus: [13]

But it was not only each epoch that found its reflection in Jesus; each individual created Him in accordance with his own character. There is no historical task which so reveals a man's true self as the writing of a Life of Jesus. No vital force comes into the figure unless a man breathes into it all the hate or all the love of which he is capable. The stronger the love, or the stronger the hate, the more life-like is the figure which is produced. For hate as well as love can write a Life of Jesus, and the greatest of them are written

[13] *Von Reimarus zu Wrede.* English translation: *The Quest of the Historical Jesus,* Macmillan, N. Y., 1950, p. 4.

with hate: that of Reimarus, the Wolfenbüttel Fragmentist, and that of David Friedrich Strauss. It was not so much hate of the Person of Jesus as of the supernatural nimbus with which it was so easy to surround Him, and with which He had in fact been surrounded. They were eager to picture Him as truly and purely human, to strip from Him the robes of splendour with which He had been apparelled, and clothe Him once more with the coarse garments in which He had walked in Galilee.

Despite the changes of the half-century since these words were written, recognition of any "supernatural nimbus" would still be a disreputable blotch on the academic gown.

Liberal Protestant theologians, eager for unsoiled skirts and spotless hoods, are still inclined to give the world its way. If the supernatural offends secular humanists and materialists, theological professors are similarly offended. If the world wants no miracles, liberal Bible scholars can oblige.

As I studied the New Testament ten years ago, the favorite reference of one of my teachers was "The Resurrection—and Ascension-Narratives" by Paul W. Schmiedel, in the 1903 *Encyclopedia Biblica*.[14] It was unusually plain about miracles:

The present examination of the subject will not start from the proposition that "miracles are impossible."

Such a proposition rests upon a theory of the universe (Weltanschauung), not upon exhaustive examination of all the events which may be spoken of as miracles. Even should we by any chance find ourselves in a position to say that every alleged miraculous occurrence from the beginning of time down to the present hour had been duly examined and found non-miraculous, we should not thereby be secured against the possibility of something occurring tomorrow which we should be compelled to recognize as a miracle. Empirically, only so much as this stands fast—and no more—that as regards present-day occurrences the persons who reckon with the possibility of a miracle (by miracle we here

[14] Edited by T. K. Cheyne and J. S. Black, The Macmillan Co., Vol. 4.

throughout understand an occurrence that unquestionably is against natural law) are very few, and that present-day occurrences which are represented as miraculous are on closer examination invariably found to possess no such character.

In other words, it's not that "miracles are impossible"; they just never happen!

Note how Schmiedel has implied that a *Weltanschauung* or "World-View" is beneath him. He then goes on:

The normal procedure of the historian accordingly in dealing with the events of the past will be in the first instance to try whether a non-miraculous explanation will serve, and to come to the other conclusion only on the strength of quite unexceptionable testimony. Needless to say, in doing so, he must be free from all prepossession. He must, accordingly, where biblical authors are concerned, in the first instance, look at their statements in the light of their own presuppositions, even though in the end he may find himself shut up to the conclusion that not only the statements but also the presuppositions are erroneous.

By repressing his own presuppositions and centering his attention instead on the presuppositions and *Weltanschauung* of others, Schmiedel naively believed he had become unbiased. He was instead the child of his academic age, fully sharing its typical unexamined thought-patterns. In the Middle Ages theologians had ignorantly meddled in scientific affairs. The shoe is on the other foot when in the supposed name of science miracles are faithlessly denied in theological schools. But surely God does not intend us to choose either ignorance or faithlessness.

CHAPTER V

Nature and Supernature

" 'What no eye has seen, nor ear heard, nor the heart of man conceived, what God has prepared for those who love him,' God has revealed to us through the Spirit."

I Corinthians 2.9–10

If Christians were to abolish the idea of the supernatural, they would immediately have to replace it with the same idea under a different name. It seems wiser to be straightforward about it and keep the old name. The reason the idea cannot be discarded is that Christians believe in a God Who has revealed Himself and Who can only be known through faith. The supernatural realm is that order of things which faith discerns. It is made known when God is known. It is the spiritual order of things, and can be seen only by faith, through inner enlightenment from God the Holy Spirit, Who dwells within us. The Holy Spirit reveals the inward meaning of God's acts in the external world. These acts are His expression of Himself to us. They are His Word. In Jesus Christ the Word of God became man, so that God came to us as one of us. Some have rejected Him. Some have been indifferent. Some have received Him. He is the same Jesus, whether accepted or refused. Acceptance or refusal lies within each man's heart. The Christian is convinced that his devotion to Christ is prompted by the Holy Spirit. Those who do not believe in Christ have not received the Christian revelation, and do not, therefore, see the realm discerned through the Christian faith. They are not aware of, or are not adequately aware of, the order that we mean by the "supernatural." [1]

This definition of "supernatural" should be carefully distinguished from other meanings. It has nothing to do with ghosts or magic.

Since "supernatural" is derived from words which mean "above the natural," we must now define the "natural" order. It is that order of things which all men perceive, whether or not they share the Christian faith. "Natural science," for example, easily fits into this view of the natural order, since it can be universally understood and accepted.[2] The crucial point, though, is not whether all mankind can perceive this order the same general way, but whether what is seen is independent of the Christian faith. For instance, some people have considered the earth to be flat and some have been sure that it is round. Either way we are dealing with the natural order, because the matter is not decided by accepting or not accepting Christ, but by observing the physical world. In a society of headhunters, a Christian would dissent from hunting heads because he responds to the supernatural. In European society both Christian and non-Christian would disapprove of headhunting, so the prohibition of headhunting there would be according to a natural law. There are some difficulties: unless convinced otherwise, the headhunters would contend that hunting heads is the most natural thing in the world, while to

---

[1] The distinction drawn here is oversimplified and no doubt too sharp. On the one hand, no Christian has a perfect awareness of the supernatural order. On the other hand, non-Christians are not without the witness of God in their hearts: Jesus Christ is the Word of God without Whom "was not anything made that was made." He is "the true light that enlightens every man." Faith in Him may be implicit where it is not explicit. The Holy Spirit works even where He is not consciously recognized. Those who "believe in Christ," then, are not to be simply equated with members of the Christian Church. "Abraham believed God, and it was reckoned to him as righteousness" (Genesis 15.6, Romans 4.3) centuries before Jesus was born.

[2] Our derivation here of the meaning of the "natural order," however, depends in no way upon natural science.

the Christian it would seem not only against the supernatural order but against the natural. One justification for this attitude on the part of the Christian is that it would be possible (though not easy) to show the headhunters the reasonableness of abandoning headhunting even if they did not become Christians.

Of course, this distinction between the natural and the supernatural makes sense only when our reasoning begins with Christian assumptions, in line with what has been said in the preceding chapter. There may be instances when it is difficult to say which order we are dealing with, and cases where it doesn't much matter. But the distinction is still a valuable one.

The natural world is not confined to those things which are perceived by the senses. It can include poetry, humor, the subtleties of thought, ethical standards, and a vast area of experience that is quite beyond the sensual level. It is neither self-enclosed nor self-explanatory. We might describe it as "open-ended" in at least two ways: toward the unknown which is as yet unexplored, and toward the supernatural which is perceived only through faith in God. The radical inadequacy of the natural order alone in providing a satisfactory explanation either of life or of itself is a compelling reason for going beyond it to the supernatural.

Our definition of the natural order should not be confused with any materialistic or mechanistic philosophy. It has no implications of any rigid or absolute rule of a natural law which is independent of God. God is the ruler of His whole universe.

This last statement illustrates the illumination, the transfiguration, the "baptism" of the natural order by the supernatural. It is a statement of faith in God, a vision not shared by everyone. It is a supernatural perception that includes nature and puts it in a different light. It sees the law of gravity, for instance, not merely as the law of gravity but as a pattern in God's creation.

How does this apply to healing through scientific medicine? First, by our distinction of the natural order we have agreed that there is an area of scientific research, understanding, and technique which Christians can share equally with non-Christians. Secondly, no matter who develops an understanding of the scientific laws of healing, the Christian perceives these laws as ways of behavior which God has implanted in His creation. This is supernatural illumination. It follows, too, that Christians may find themselves called to a vocation of medical science, not only out of compassion for the sick but in order to reveal more fully God's acts and their significance, as these acts are seen in the laws of healing in His creation. A Christian doctor might not put it this way as he writes for a medical journal, but in his heart he can know his work as a divine calling. The work of physicians, surgeons, nurses, technicians, orderlies—yes, hospital clerks and bookkeepers, cooks and workmen too—can be undertaken as full-time Christian service in the ministry of healing. Not only Sisters and Deaconesses, but hospital cleaning maids too, can know a religious vocation in healing. Whether registered nurses or practical nurses, God can find a place for each according to her talents. Christ's command, "Heal the sick," knows no limits.

"And God saw everything that he had made, and behold, it was very good." These are the words near the end of the first creation story in Genesis. They express so well the Jewish and Christian attitude toward the world. Because God's creation is very good, we cannot as Christians refuse the gifts He offers through medicine. Shall we pray for healing, then dictate to God how He shall provide it? This is the implication of saying, as some do, "If you don't have enough faith, call the doctor." Who are we to decide that God is not answering the prayer of faith by sending us to the doctor?

An example of this dreadful kind of teaching is seen in a woman who came to a physician friend of mine. She had cancer of the breast, dangerously advanced. She knew of the doctor's sympathy with healing through spiritual means, and she hoped he would agree that she should not undergo surgery.

She had been advised that if she had enough faith, the operation would not be necessary. As a result she felt that any arrangement for medical care would be an act of unbelief, an act which would undermine her cure through faith. For this reason she was afraid to make any plans for treatment. The doctor strongly disagreed with her and recommended immediate surgery. He also wrote to ask the patient's spiritual advisor to urge her to undertake treatment at once. He received no answer to his letter. By all odds the unattended cancer was fatal, but could have been checked if removed in time. What right did either the advisor or the patient have to set God's gifts through medicine in opposition to God's gifts through spiritual healing? "If you don't have enough faith, see the doctor" can be a pious-sounding death warrant.

The way to avoid interference with medical healing is to encourage all who come for spiritual healing to continue medical care strictly in accordance with the doctor's orders. Leave all diagnosis and recommendations for medical treatment in his hands alone. If spiritual therapy seems to produce improvement or a cure, let the doctor make an examination and decide what should be done. If a cure is genuine, he will recognize it. Any decision to modify or to discontinue treatment should be left in his hands. If for any reason the patient questions the doctor's competence, he should consult another doctor, and not limit himself to a spiritual therapist with no medical qualifications. If spiritual healing is to gain the respect it deserves, those who engage in it must accord to medical doctors and their treatment the respect they deserve. Where possible, medical and spiritual care should be coordinated. But at the very least they should not interfere with one another. God is a God of order and harmony. His gifts always supplement one another.

The Christian Science denial of medical care is of an altogether different character from that which we have just discussed. It derives from the basic premise (foreign to the

Scriptures) that only God, the Divine Mind, has any real existence. All else is simply error of "mortal mind." Sin, sickness, pain, the body, the physical world, et cetera, are only illusions. To call a doctor for disease, then, is to affirm its existence. This only makes the error worse. Physicians are sometimes consulted for certain types of anatomical advice and certain limited treatment is allowed. But, fundamentally, Christian Science remains in opposition to scientific medicine. As the oldest of the major healing cults that have arisen in modern times, it has, more than any other group, alienated both the medical profession and the Church from spiritual healing.

Returning to our theme of the natural order, we have seen how the Christian faith affirms and encourages the healing power of scientific medicine. This is true despite the fact that in times past Church leaders have blocked medical progress. Under their influence the Emperor Justinian closed the medical schools of Athens and Alexandria in 529 A.D. and refused any longer to pay money to state physicians and endowed scholars. Pope Innocent III condemned surgery in 1215. The dissection of the body was pronounced sacrilegious and the study of anatomy was condemned in 1248. In some periods physicians were not permitted to relieve sufferers until, if ever, the priest was satisfied and the patient had made his confession. On the other hand, medical manuscripts were copied, as at the monastery of St. Gall in the ninth century and later, and many of the clergy have been interested in and have practiced scientific medicine (despite opposition from twelfth-century councils and popes). The first charity hospital at Rome was founded about 300 by a deaconess, Fabiola. Church-sponsored hospitals have been found for many centuries and in many lands. Orders of Deaconesses, Widows, and Virgins have done nursing, and male nursing orders, such as the Knights Hospitalers and the Teutonic Knights, characterized the period of the crusades. However poor their scientific knowledge, such people contributed to the physical as well as the spiritual care of the sick. St.

Philip Neri and St. Francis Xavier were leaders in healing work through religious orders in the Counter-Reformation movement. Many others also engaged in faith healing in this period, but almost all of them used medicines or surgery in their healing practices. The hospitals served by St. Vincent de Paul and the Order of Lazarists in Paris were used by great physicians and surgeons of the seventeenth century. Deaconesses and Nursing Orders have played their part; only within the last century has lay nursing been a skilled and respected profession.[3] And so things have developed through modern times. In 1950 there were 516 Protestant Church-related hospitals in the United States, while in 1947 there were 1,038 Roman Catholic hospitals in the United States and Canada. In many missionary areas, Church hospitals are the only source of scientific medical care. The name of Albert Schweitzer towers above all others in the medical missionary field today. The contemporary support of scientific medical care by the Christian Church is obvious for all to see.

The relation of Christian faith to the principles of psychiatric treatment is too complex for detailed treatment here, but a few basic principles can be outlined. First, to the degree that psychological theory and psychotherapy are scientifically based upon observed experiences, they deserve the same enthusiastic acceptance by Christians, and the same active participation in their development, as we have indicated is appropriate for the rest of scientific medicine. Unfortunately, however, psychology and psychiatry encompass many fields of thought, much of which is unscientific and part of which is based on theological principles (usually unexpressed) that contradict the Christian faith. As long as this situation remains, it is impossible to give unreserved Christian assent to present-day psychotherapy. It seems urgent, in fact, that distinctively

[3] It became so through Florence Nightingale in 1860. It should be noted that she received some of her training, and found an expression of her ideals, at Kaiserswerth, where Pastor Theodor Fliedner had developed a notable training center for deaconesses.

Christian psychotherapy be developed to an extent which has not yet been attempted.

Psychotherapy and spiritual principles overlap each other. The psychiatrist, for instance, must have a standard of mental health. This in turn depends on his view of normal humanity. And this is associated with his outlook on human nature, which in its turn has inevitable theological implications. Some psychotherapists have considered religious experience a neurosis—an obvious journey into the land of theology. (Weatherhead has a charming commentary on this, saying, "If this really is a 'disease,' it is much more attractive than most people's health.") On the other hand, the Christian virtues of faith, hope, and love all involve psychological states. Religious experience is a psychological experience. Theology and psychology are so often two different ways of describing the same thing.

One practical consequence of this is the problem a pastor faces in referral of cases needing psychiatric treatment. If the psychiatrist does not share the Christian faith, the consequences are quite unpredictable. If the patient's religion is treated as though all religious experience is a neurosis, the psychological "cure" will be his spiritual death. The clergy can scarcely be blamed for being perplexed.

The opposite side of the coin, of course, is that too much religious experience actually is neurotic. Preaching that does nothing beyond reinforcing guilt, for instance, is creating emotional disturbances, not healing. The psychiatrist who must try to untangle the damage done by perverse religion is not to be condemned for dismay concerning some kinds of religious practices.

Beyond psychology is the new science of parapsychology. This deals with such things as telepathy, clairvoyance, psychokinesis, etc. Some might consider it to be dabbling in the supernatural. By our definition, it, too, is a science of the natural order. The work done by such men as Rhine, Soal and Bateman, McConnell, and others is on the highest scientific level, and should be gratefully welcomed by the Christian Church. It will have the effect of weakening the materialistic and deterministic philosophies—a consummation devoutly to be wished. It will also shed light on many spiritual practices: prayer, guidance, prophecy, and so on.

This is certainly no proposal to prove scientifically the power of Christ to heal. That can never be done, because it involves recognition of the working of the Holy Spirit, and this is supernatural—perceived by faith. Without that faith, looking from the natural level only, spiritual healing will always present a sort of uncanny mystery, an unexplained something, above and beyond, as we peer out the "open-end" of the natural order into the supernatural. All sorts of rationalizations will be brought to bear to try to plug the hole, but they will never quite fit. There will be a strong inclination, therefore, to deny that the events really happened the way they did happen. At this point scientific studies can be a great help. They can keep the "open-end" in view, the open door to the world of faith.

Seen in the light of faith, of course nothing of this is uncanny, but instead very warm in our Father's love.

We have said a great deal about "spiritual healing." Before going further, we must ask, "Exactly what do we mean by 'spiritual healing'? How does it fit in with the other kinds of healing?"

No words are entirely adequate. "Christian healing" might have been used instead, but a surgeon with Christian motives could justly be described as providing "Christian healing," though his special skill would be on the physical level. An obvious example of this is seen in medical missionaries. "Divine healing" is preferred by some; yet *all* healing, medical or not, is from God and is, therefore, a form of "Divine healing." "Faith healing" fits the words of Jesus when He said, "Your faith has made you whole," but the term has no reference within itself to the object of faith. Any result of suggestion or hypnotism, whether permanent or not, fundamental or superficial, with or without moral or spiritual content, could be called "faith healing." A person paralyzed due to a subconscious desire for attention could walk through "faith healing" at a mass meeting where he is the center of all eyes, yet revert to his former state when he is at last forgotten. But this is not the type of healing that Jesus did. "Spiritual healing" is perhaps the most acceptable term, though it has the disadvantage that "spirit" means so many different things to different people. For instance, spiritualistic mediums believe that they heal through the disembodied spirits of the dead, and they call this "spiritual healing." This is not what we mean. Thus we are left with no description that cannot be misunderstood.

All we can do, then, is choose a phrase and define it to suit the purpose at hand. Suppose we say "spiritual healing," by which we mean healing through spiritual means and for spiritual purposes. By "spiritual" we refer to a close relationship to God, Who is the Holy Spirit and the source of all spirituality. J. V. L. Casserly clearly stated the matter when he said, "Only God is spirit, in the absolute sense of the word, and our spirituality is our orientation *on and into God*." [4] By "God" we mean God as orthodox Christian faith knows Him.

This is not to restrict the operation of spiritual healing to those who share the orthodox Christian faith, but it is to give an interpretation of spiritual healing in unmistakably orthodox Christian terms.

Oh yes—by "orthodox" we do not mean "what is usually done," since much of spiritual healing is quite unorthodox by such standards! By "orthodox Christian" we refer to Biblical, Catholic, and Nicene Christianity. This is intended to include Roman Catholic, Eastern Orthodox, Anglican, and

[4] Seminar on *The Decline of Materialism,* sponsored by the Laymen's Movement for a Christian World, Wainright House, Rye, New York, 1957, p. 84

traditional Protestant views of God,[5] without consideration of the differences between such Christian groups.

If by now, we are reasonably clear about the meaning of "spiritual," we should say a few more words about what sort of "healing" we have in mind. It obviously has to do with the spiritual side of man's nature; that is, his relation to God. But God has created the whole man and is interested in the health of the whole man. So mental and physical healing are also involved. Medical science is increasingly recognizing the closeness of the body and the mind. But we go one step further, and see man as a unity of bodily, mental, and spiritual aspects. Spiritual healing is for the whole person: body, mind, and spirit. To the degree that the spiritual side of man's nature is involved in healing, we may truly call it "spiritual healing."

Though healing does not fall into neatly isolated categories, we can still distinguish different types, and this distinction can be helpful. The four major kinds of healing seem to be as follows: physical, psychological, psychic, and spiritual. The addition of the "psychic" element is to take into account possible healing effects from the sort of phenomena included in the study of parapsychology.

A doctor may prescribe an antibiotic, perhaps a so-called "miracle drug" for a case of pneumonia. This is basically for physical healing. The drug may be marvelous, but in the Biblical sense of the word it is not at all miraculous, since its potency is chemical and biological; it is not peculiarly spiritual. The patient may be cured of pneumonia, but there is nothing inherent in the pills to cure him of sin. The physician has provided a physical means of healing.

Another person may be in intense mental distress due to emotional conflict. A psychiatrist may help him discover the sources of this conflict, and to find a perspective from which he can deal with his problems and overcome the particular inner clash that pains him. This is psychological healing. But as

[5] It would also represent the faith of other smaller Catholic communions.

long as it leaves God out of the picture it is not spiritual healing. As long as it treats guilt but ignores sin, for instance, it is
confined to psychological treatment. A clergyman once fell
in love with another man's wife. It produced a severe emotional
conflict within him. Yet when he consulted a psychiatrist, he
was advised to encourage the woman to divorce her husband,
and to marry her. By thus abandoning his moral standards, he
might, after a fashion, eliminate feelings of guilt and end the
inner conflict within him. I do not believe this would have
been possible even psychologically, but the intention of the
psychiatrist was the healing of a psychological conflict—yet
he was so blind spiritually that he did not realize that his
psychological "cure" would produce a new spiritual sickness.
Psychological healing does not necessarily involve spiritual
healing.

Some people do seem to possess psychic gifts. Healing of
bodily or mental illness may take place through processes still
obscure to present-day science. Some healers sense a flow of
power, usually through the hands, sometimes from another
part of the body, such as the solar plexus, and this power can
heal sickness.[6] On the other hand, some mediums do seem
to be able to get paranormal help (which they feel is coming
from the spirits of the dead) which can combat sickness.[7] Or,
thirdly, some psychically sensitive people appear to be able to
detect the presence of illness, through perceiving auras or some
other means.[8] These are psychic ways of healing. But unless

[6] Ambrose Worrall, for instance; cf. the reports of the spiritual healing
seminars held at Wainwright House, Rye, N. Y., by the Laymen's Movement:
   Third Spiritual Healing Seminar, October 3–5, 1954, pp. 12–26; *Fourth
Spiritual Healing Seminar*, June 24–26, 1955, pp. 17–41, 79–84; *Fifth
Spiritual Healing Seminar*, October 8–10, 1956, pp. 87–89. These are all
Wainwright House Publications.
   [7] Harry Edwards has probably done a greater volume of spiritualistic
healing than anyone else in our time; cf. his books, such as *A Guide to
Spirit Healing* (Spiritualist Press, London, 1950).
   [8] Dora Van Gelder, for example:
   cf. *Spiritual Healing Seminar*, March 25–26, 1954, pp. 39–42; *Third
Spiritual Healing Seminar*, pp. 34–40; *Fourth Spiritual Healing Seminar*,
pp. 68–79, 91–93.

they bring the patient closer to God they are not, by our definition, spiritual healing; they can become, as is typically the case with spiritualism, a barrier to Christian faith, and thus they can become anti-spiritual or dominated by an evil spirit.

True spiritual healing can involve any or all of the other levels, but it cannot be confined to them. A man could be physically healed through the spiritual gifts of one who prays for him, yet if a closer relationship to God does not reflect itself in the spiritual life of the one who is healed, for him it is no spiritual healing. Jesus healed ten lepers, but only one returned to give thanks. It would seem that only one received a true spiritual healing, though Jesus healed all through spiritual means. We might say that as far as Christ's own life was concerned there were ten spiritual healings, but so far as the lepers were concerned, there was only one. The other nine were to Christ's glory, but to their own shame.

Every gift of medical knowledge and skill, of psychological understanding and treatment, of psychic insight and power, can be used for spiritual healing to the degree that it is a means for bringing men into a closer spiritual relationship with God. Thus, though the surgical skill of a medical missionary is not inherently spiritual, it becomes so when he dedicates it to God and through it helps others to draw closer to God. When God is regarded as of first importance, His whole creation can serve in His Kingdom.

When we consider spiritual healing in relation to the overcoming of strictly spiritual sickness, or sin, it becomes indistinguishable from the general application of the Christian Gospel to men's spiritual needs. But it is really just as indistinguishable from the application of the Gospel to other forms of sickness. The only reason for using the term "spiritual healing" at all, is that the Gospel has been so poorly applied for so long in dealing with illness. Jesus did not separate healing the sick from proclaiming the Kingdom of God.

Now that we are clearer as to the meaning of spiritual healing, may we go on to consider the miraculous aspect which often attends it. The miraculous is apparent in the healing works of Jesus and in modern instances such as that of Dr. B. in Chapter II.

What is a miracle? Something that breaks the laws of nature? Or just something unusual? Dr. Boggs says, " 'Miracles' may therefore be defined as unusual acts of God called forth by extraordinary circumstances, according to means unfamiliar to us, but which we may believe to be perfectly normal expressions of God's character." I believe that none of these definitions does justice to miracles as we see them in the New Testament.

The early disciples did not think in terms of "laws of nature" as we do today, though they were as much aware of many of the events that repeat themselves as we are. They show that a belief in miracles (or "signs," as they were more likely to say) is independent of our concept of "laws of nature." Besides, if God sustains His creation, as the Biblical view teaches, then the "laws of nature" are merely the general and regular way that He causes His world to behave. If He makes an exception to that regular behavior, He is not "breaking" a law as though it were made somehow independently of Himself, but making an exception to His own rule in order to attain a special and higher purpose.

A miracle is indeed unusual, but not everything unusual is a miracle. We speak of "miracle drugs" because they are so unusually effective in killing germs. But the New Testament miracles are "signs" pointing to the Kingdom of God. Perhaps the miracle drugs bring us a bit closer to a blissful condition, but they have no *inherent* capacity to bring us into a closer spiritual relationship with God. They are not signs of the Messiah or of His reign. Being unusual is not enough to make a miracle.

Suppose we consider Dr. Boggs' definition. To test it, we might take an unusual astronomical phenomenon, a nova, for instance. This is a sudden temporary flare-up of a star to many times its original brightness. Suppose, to make the case clearer, we are the first to observe a nova. It is surely an unusual act of God. It must be called forth by unusual circumstances. It happens by means entirely unfamiliar to us. But we can be sure it is a perfectly normal expression of God's character as Lord of the heavens. Suppose now that time goes on and other astronomers see other novae. It is still unusual, but we are now becoming familiar with that kind of activity. Now we come to the question: Have we observed a miracle? Did it become somewhat less miraculous as we saw more of them? I have never yet heard anyone propose a nova as a miracle. The definition, "unusual acts of God called forth by extraordinary circumstances, according to means unfamiliar to us, but which we may believe to be perfectly normal expressions of God's character," may express various truths about miracles, but it does not define them.

Jesus was accused of casting out demons by the power of the demons. (Luke 11.14–23) He replied, "Every kingdom divided against itself is laid waste, and house falls upon house. But if Satan also is divided against himself, how will his kingdom stand? For you say that I cast out demons by Beelzebul. And if I cast out demons by Beezebul, by whom do your sons cast them out? Therefore they shall be your judges." Then He said, "But if it is by the finger of God that I cast out demons, then the Kingdom of God has come upon you." His healing work was a sign of God's Kingdom. A nova is not a sign of God's Kingdom, and that is why it is not a miracle. It has no inherent power to bring anyone to repentance or faith in Christ or willingness to let God rule in their lives. It is strictly impersonal.[9]

Note that the effect of Christ's healing depended on the

[9] In conjunction with other circumstances, however, it might on rare occasions bear special spiritual content: for instance, consider the star of Bethlehem (Matthew 2.1–12). It can also be the channel of awe that glorifies God just as any of His creation may be (cf. Psalm 19.1). This is a supernatural perception but it is not anything miraculous.

spiritual state of the observer. His casting out of demons was a sign of the Kingdom, yet Luke says that some of those present, "to test him, sought from him a sign from heaven"! Their eyes were blind. And His enemies, far from seeing the meaning of the sign they had witnessed, said, "He casts out demons by the power of Beelzebul, the prince of demons." It is characteristic of the signs that their true significance is revealed only to eyes of faith. As for the others, they "hear and hear, but do not understand; see and see, but do not perceive." (Isaiah 6.9)

The key to the miracles is in recognizing that in them Person speaks to person, God speaks to this man or to that man, calling him to Himself. Their meaning is supernaturally conveyed. On the natural level they remain incidents incompletely understood. They may be interpreted without reference to God and His Kingdom, but that interpretation is never correct. It leaves out the most important point, the Word God speaks.

I would propose the following definition: A miracle is an extraordinary act of God through which He reveals Himself in a personal way to those who respond in faith; its meaning is perceived through the inner illumination that comes from the Holy Spirit; it is a sign of the Kingdom of God, but it cannot be understood without the guidance of the Spirit. It will be misinterpreted by those who lack that guidance. If it is "explained" in terms that leave out God's personal act of revelation it is completely misunderstood. Without the eyes of faith it may even stand as an inexplicable wonder, but it cannot be discerned as the true miracle that it is.

How may we relate this to our conception of the natural and the supernatural orders? A miracle now appears as something strictly supernatural; that is, seen only by faith. It includes an event in the natural order, but one which cannot be properly understood in terms of the natural order. In Christ's casting out of demons, for instance, His accusers agreed that the demon-possessed were being healed. But they misread God's meaning, the supernatural aspect.

They were likewise mistaken about the ultimate cause of the healings. They knew that Jesus was responsible, but they ascribed His power to heal to an evil spirit rather than to the Holy Spirit. Their rejection of the guidance of the Holy Spirit was so complete and so perverse that they had come to consider the Spirit of God to be the Devil. They had become hopeless cases, unable any longer to repent because they had completely darkened the light within them, losing the means to distinguish good from evil, calling good evil and evil good. That is why Jesus said, "Whoever blasphemes against the Holy Spirit never has forgiveness, but is guilty of an eternal sin." [10]

How does this fit into the concept of "natural law"? At this point it is well to consider the human side of "laws." God does not need a set of "laws" to guide *Him*, as though He lacked the intelligence to take the next step. It is *we* who need laws, patterns standing out of our confusing experience, road maps to guide us out of the jumbled morass of events. A scientific "law" is a human statement that describes the way something has been observed to behave—a "general mode of behavior." It is not absolutely rigid, though for practical purposes it may usually be assumed to be so, providing that the random variations in behavior are within small enough limits of probability. A law is always subject to revision. A child may say, "All sheep are white." After a while he may see his first black sheep. Then he will say, "Most sheep are white." When he grows up and becomes more sophisticated, he may even produce mathematical tables giving the probable ratio of black sheep to white sheep under various circumstances! This is how fluid the reign of "natural law" is.

One of the fundamental and unprovable postulates of nat-

---

[10] Mark 3.29, where this saying appears most clearly in its total context. It is a part of the whole incident told in Mark 3.20–35.

ural science is that of the "uniformity of nature." It is the assumption that nature behaves in the same way everywhere and at every time. It is the basis of scientific prediction and the prerequisite of engineering practice. Suppose a bridge-builder were to say, "I have calculated all the loads and stresses according to mechanical laws. They have proved to be accurate in the past, but who knows what tomorrow will bring?" Can we imagine him paralyzed with his fear of the unknown, demoralized and utterly incapable of building the bridge? What an absurd picture. Yet it is an accurate vision of someone who has lost all faith in the uniformity of nature.

If we were to make the suggestion that perhaps nature really isn't uniform, it might now be greeted with an appropriate shudder of horror. But from a Christian viewpoint, nature is not quite uniform! That is because we believe in the ultimate reign of a Person, which is not the same thing as the ultimate reign of Law. God is not completely predictable, and God is in charge of events. Dr. James Muilenburg has significantly translated "Yahweh" as "I bring to pass what comes to pass." He reveals Himself in specific events of history. He keeps telling a story that cannot be completely predicted. The end of the story is not contained in the process, but remains in Yahweh's hands.

The reason the "uniformity of nature" is such a good working rule for the natural sciences is that science is impersonal. On the impersonal level nature is uniform. This is part of God's wisdom, for without dependable regularity life would be impossible. As a matter of fact, without the contrasting background of ordinary regularity, not even miracles could exist. They would have nothing to distinguish them as miracles. This fact is overlooked when it is assumed that primitive people believe in miracles because they do not know the orderly working of nature. The truth is that they recognize miracles only because they *do* perceive nature's normal regularity. But where God reveals His own personality, He cannot be limited to that rigid uniformity which would confine His acts to the impersonal level.

The greatest psychological difficulty that I had to overcome in changing my life's work from physics to the ministry was in shifting my thinking from the impersonal level to that involving personal relations. Our society is so thoroughly conditioned to think in terms of impersonal laws that perhaps this difficulty in "shifting gears" to personal relationships is a greater obstacle to Christian living than is generally recognized.

Even in relation to God we are accustomed to speak of "laws of the spirit." This has a real value as long as it does not obscure a direct intercourse with God Himself. Some of the spiritual laws may be discovered on the natural level, though full recognition of their meaning depends on supernatural enlightenment. Many of the laws of the spirit can only be discerned through faith.

One way of looking at miracles is to say that the normal course of events, in accordance with the laws of physics, biology or psychology, is changed because of the operation of laws of the spirit. A parallel could be drawn with objects heavier than air. Normally they fall because of the law of gravity. But an airplane flies because other laws are also brought into play—the laws of aerodynamics. An old example along these lines was the mathematically calculated proof that a bee could not fly. The trouble with this proof, I understand, was that it ignored one set of laws, those concerning friction with the air. The bees kept on flying, quite unperturbed, through all these calculations. Similarly, the miracles themselves are completely unaffected by whether or not we understand the higher laws of the spirit that are working to produce them. The concept of these additional spiritual laws rules out the notion that miracles are just capricious nonsense. Christianity differs from pagan magic right here. Its miracles are not meaningless wonders, but have moral and spiritual significance. They are part of the action and purpose of the all-wise God.

It should be emphasized, however, that interpretation in terms of law, even spiritual law, is not sufficient. Such interpretation is helpful, but is not the highest form of understanding. This is because all law is impersonal. It centers our attention on some "thing" rather than on God or on people. By referring to God as being "personal" we do not, of course, think of Him as a sort of glorified human being. But the human person is the highest order of creation. God is *more* than the highest we know, not less. His nature is *beyond* personality, not beneath it.[11] The inanimate, impersonal world of nature is unaware of even its own existence. It *is*, but does not think. To describe God in impersonal terms is to suggest that He is an "It" on a degraded level below our own. It is insulting enough to call a fellow human an "it" without turning on God with the same indignity. That is why we describe God in the highest terms we know, the terms of personality. He gave Israel a personal name to call Him—*Yahweh*. We can know *about* the created world, but we do not have to stop with knowing *about* God. True religious experience begins when we know *Him*.

The Christian response even to the moral laws is not by considering them as abstract principles or as ideals. They are Commandments. Commandments imply One Who commands. And His great Commandments are, "Thou shalt love the Lord thy God with all thy heart, with all thy soul, and with all thy mind . . . Thou shalt love thy neighbor as Thyself." You cannot love an "it" that way. Everything is rooted in personal terms, between an "I" and a "Thou."

Would this leave us at the capricious whim of some unknown spiritual giant? It may seem that way to those who

[11] cf. "Beyond Personality," Book V, pp. 119–175 of *Mere Christianity*, by C. S. Lewis (Macmillan, 1943).

have repressed their awareness of God deeply into their unconscious minds. Yet God is not capricious, He has no whims, and He is not unknown. He reveals Himself to those who respond in faith, and He has shown Himself to be a God of love. "God is love." It is not the regular working of a uniform "nature" that never varies. It is God's love that never varies. God Himself, not some unbending repetition of part of His creation, is the ground of ultimate dependability and security. "Nature" is only approximately uniform, not absolutely so. God never changes.[12]

One other feature of God's revelation of Himself is that some of His acts are intended to be shared by all, while others are of a more private nature. The first type are seen in the Sacred History of Israel preserved for us in the Bible and culminating in the coming of God Himself in the flesh for the salvation of mankind; that is, in the life, death, and resurrection of Jesus Christ. Christ's work was established permanently and effectively in the world through the gift of the Holy Spirit to His Church, and the beginnings of this, too, are to be found in the Scriptures. In these acts God has made Himself known to all Christians.

In an almost infinite variety of ways He has spoken to the multitudes who have come to Him in faith. But not all of God's revealing acts are directed to all the faithful. They may be very private, intended only for one individual or for a small group. By and large, modern miracles rather obviously fit this category. It would seem that in principle all present-day miracles are of this special sort, not necessary for all Christians to receive. However, some may be very widely known.

What might be the result of a present-day investigation of a

[12] That is, God's own being never changes. His actions and attitudes respecting particular circumstances do change. An enlightening discussion of this is to be found in "The Influence of Prayer on God and Man," by L. Harold De Wolf, in *Healing: Human and Divine*, edited by Simon Doniger (Association Press, N. Y., 1957), pp. 144–161.

miracle from the point of view of the natural order? What would a scientific study reveal? Suppose, for instance, that through faith and prayer God were suddenly to restore an optic nerve that had been destroyed by an infection, and that He restored it as a pure act of creation out of nothing. Our argument does not require that we believe that such a thing is actually possible or that it ever has happened. All we are interested in is to see what sort of result might ensue if an investigation were made concerning this hypothetical miracle. We are assuming that somehow we have infallible knowledge of the restoration of the optical nerve and the manner of its creation.

The investigator would begin by collecting evidence as to just what happened. He would discover that several people claim that the sight of one eye had been lost following an infection, that prayer and spiritual therapy were tried, and that the eyesight was immediately restored. Examination would show that the eye appears perfectly normal and that sight is normal. Keeping strictly to the natural order, four approaches are possible:

1. No known explanation can be made. Some mysterious healing power restored the eyesight at the time of the prayers.

2. The healing process can be identified as a known course of natural events. The optic nerve may have been damaged during the infection, but as it healed the vision was inhibited by intense repressed emotional conflict. The spiritual therapy caused a psychological release which allowed the vision to return.

3. The healing was natural, but was only accidentally associated with spiritual therapy. The optic nerve recuperated through physical regeneration. Its recovery just happened to coincide with the prayers.

4. The case history was incorrectly reported. This could

take various lines, depending on the weakest point in
the evidence. It could be said that there had never been
any real blindness or that the recovery had been previous
to the prayers, etc.

The likelihood of one of these approaches being selected
would depend upon the exact nature of the case, the nature
of the evidence, and the personality of the investigator. The
strictly scientific evidence available is always limited. Since
each miracle is unique and cannot be repeated upon request,
a great deal of reconstruction of the case history must be undertaken on the basis of evidence left over from a past event. This
is an art, not a science, and the outlook of the person reviewing the case is inevitably involved.

It is to be noted that in this case only the first of the four
approaches was accurate. Unfortunately it is the least likely
to be encountered in the usual analyses of miraculous events.
Apparently the human mind abhors reserving judgment.

If a really careful scientific study were made of the psychological factors involved in our imaginary case, it would develop that no evidence other than the fact of the sudden cure
could be brought to support the repressed emotional conflict
theory. On the positive side, a great deal might be learned
about the psychology of those involved in the spiritual therapy,
and this could be useful in understanding and applying psychological and spiritual therapy elsewhere.

In some cases of present-day miraculous healing, it may be
possible to obtain clear enough evidence to make the first
approach the only one tenable. Such instances will be especially
revealing. They may lead to the discovery of new natural
phenomena and should point the way more clearly to the
supernatural order beyond.[13]

[13] Such discovery will not reward the half-hearted. Edison is reported to
have said that his inventions were one percent inspiration and ninety-nine
percent perspiration. In 1954 the Archbishops' Commission on Divine Healing asked the help of the British Medical Association in submitting evidence

A possibility suggests itself which has not yet received the attention it deserves. This is to apply the scientific method to case histories, but to analyze the results in the light of the supernatural. It is commonly assumed that the scientific method is applicable only to "public" experience, while religious experience is a private matter. But the Christian faith is not merely a private affair. It is a shared, corporate faith. Therefore the scientific method can be adapted to unfold new understanding on the supernatural level as well as the natural level. Laws of the spirit could be discriminated for the eyes of faith by the scientific examination of present-day acts of God. The best of modern theology has already adapted the inductive approach to the study of the Bible. It should be just as possible to adapt it to the study of healing, conversion, evangelism, and so on. In this way the Church could have the benefit of an

---

of spontaneous cures of apparently incurable disorders and of rapid or accelerated recovery from serious illnesses due to spiritual ministrations. The B.M.A. committee appointed for the task reported: "As far . . . as our observation and investigation have gone, *we have seen no evidence that there is any special type of illness cured solely by spiritual healing which cannot be cured by medical methods which do not involve such claims.* The cases claimed as cures of a miraculous nature present no features of a unique and unexpected character outside the knowledge of any experienced physician or psychiatrist." (Italics theirs. *Divine Healing and Co-operation Between Doctors and Clergy,* British Medical Association, London, 1956, p. 13.) Those of us who have investigated case histories of spiritual healing are well aware that the public questionnaire method used by the B.M.A. committee usually yields such poor results that the truly remarkable thing is that they got as much evidence as they did! They felt that the reports given them often lacked the detailed information that would have been necessary to draw conclusions—but we have seen no evidence that they were willing to perspire a bit themselves in any serious search for the missing details. Had they done so, they would most likely have discovered features similar to the Lourdes miracles which they mentioned and then immediately and blithely ignored. It should be understood, however, that the limitations of the B.M.A. committee report are not only due to the mediocrity of their investigative techniques. No matter how excellent their reports might have become, they would still be couched within the framework of natural science. Inside that framework, even the greatest of supernatural healing miracles can only be seen as a "spontaneous cure"—a medical euphemism signifying, "We don't know why." (A further discussion of the B.M.A. committee report is found in Chapter 18 of *The Healing Power of Faith,* by Will Oursler.)

empirical theology, a branch of theology based on the scientific analysis of what actually happens when Christianity is applied, but analyzed from the distinctive vantage point of the Christian faith.[14]

The power of a definitely Christian psychology would be indeed attractive. It can be developed if some of our most gifted Christians are willing and able to receive training in both theology and psychology, and can relate that background to the needs of both clergy and laymen. It could be a challenging Christian vocation for laymen as well as clergy. Its fruits are desperately needed.

[14] If I may coin a term, it would seem that the most appropriate title for this type of empirical theology would be *"pneumatonomy,"* (pronounced nû'má·tŏn'ŏ·mǐ) which means "the system of laws of the spirit." The derivation is from the Greek πνεῦμα, πνεύματος (*pneuma, pneumatos*) = *spirit* + νόμος (*nomos*) = *law*. The word *"pneumatology"* might have been suitable if it were not already used with other meanings. The word *"pneumatonomy"* has a significant backround in Romans 8.2, "For the law of the Spirit of life in Christ Jesus has set me free from the law of sin and death": "the law of the Spirit" is "ὁ νόμος τοῦ πνεύματος" (*"ho nomos tou pneumatos"*). Psychology deals with the laws of the "psyche," the *"soul."* In Greek thought the *"soul"* signified the vital force that animates the body. *Theology* is from *"Theos,"* which means *"God,"* and means the study of religion. *Parapsychology* studies that which is *beyond* psychology, and tends to approach theology from the side of natural science. *Pneumatonomy* would approach psychology from the side of theology. It is a sort of supernaturally interpreted psychology of man's spiritual life.

CHAPTER VI

The Biblical Basis of Spiritual Healing

"And they went forth and preached everywhere, while the Lord worked with them and confirmed the message by the signs that attended it."
Mark 16.20

Thus concludes the longer of the two additions that were attached to the Gospel according to St. Mark. It expresses the attitude of the early Church but not that of modern liberal Protestantism. It has frequently been observed that in earlier centuries people accepted Christ because of His miracles while now people accept His miracles because they believe in Him. This could only happen in a decaying Christian culture. It does not happen in the youthful vigor of faith. Now we go forth and preach everywhere without signs to attend our message, hoping that our listeners will not be offended by the signs that confirmed the preaching of our forebears.

Of course Jesus did not come as a magician or as a worker of wonders to overawe His enemies into belief. His acts were laden with spiritual meaning, and the allegiance He sought was one of unforced faith and love. His enemies repeatedly asked for "a sign," but with no sincerity: "The Pharisees came and began to argue with him, seeking from him a sign from heaven, to test him. And he sighed deeply in his spirit, and said, 'Why does this generation seek a sign? Truly, I say to you, no sign shall be given to this generation.' " (Mark 8.11–12) St. Luke gives the following report: "When the crowds were increasing, he began to say, 'This generation is an evil generation; it seeks a sign, but no sign shall be given it except the sign of Jonah. For as Jonah became a sign to the men of Nineveh so will the Son of man be to this generation . . . The men of Nineveh will arise at the judgment with this generation and condemn it; for they repented at the preaching of Jonah, and behold, something greater than Jonah is here. ' " (Luke 11.29–30, 32) The word "generation" has a very special meaning; something akin to "brood" or species." [1] We come close to it when we say, "This breed of men." Jesus here refers to the unrepentant who make up the present evil age, the era of sin that will be destroyed at the judgment. Without repentance, no sign can be seen. Elsewhere Jesus calls the Pharisees "blind guides." [2] We note that Jesus spoke about the sign of Jonah "when the crowds were increasing." This may indicate His concern over popular misconceptions that He was promising a quick and easy panacea without penitence, a Kingdom of God without godliness.

Though Jesus offered no sign to the impenitent, the Gospels give us no reason to assume that Jesus did not make use of signs. His words were never intended to stand without His

[1] cf. "brood of vipers," Matthew 23.33.

[2] e.g. Matthew 15.14. The signs of the Kingdom are visible only to those who have spiritual perception. When the Pharisees asked Jesus when the Kingdom was coming, He answered, "The kingdom of God is not coming with signs to be observed; nor will they say, 'Lo, here it is!' or 'There!' for behold, the kingdom of God is in the midst of you." (Luke 17.20–21.) He is saying, in effect, "Look, the kingdom is here, right in front of you, in your very midst. No Messiah is going to set up an earthly capital here, or there, to conquer the world by force and usher in the Millennium." (cf. Luke 17.22–37, where Jesus leaves the forcible conquest of the world to the sudden, unexpected Day of Judgment. cf. also Mark 13.21–22.) An alternative translation of "the kingdom of God is in the midst of you" is "the kingdom of God is within you." This would emphasize the crucial importance of the spiritual life within. "The key to observing the kingdom lies in your inner life."

works. "The words that I say to you I do not speak on my own authority; but the Father who dwells in me does his works. Believe me that I am in the Father and the Father in me; or else believe me for the sake of the works themselves." (John 14.10b–11) Again, "If it is by the Spirit of God that I cast out demons, then the kingdom of God has come upon you." (Matthew 12.28) When John the Baptist sincerely sought to know whether Jesus was the Christ, the Lord did not hesitate to refer to signs:

And John, calling to him two of his disciples, sent them to the Lord, saying, "Are you he who is to come, or shall we look for another?" And when the men had come to him, they said, "John the Baptist has sent us to you, saying, 'Are you he who is to come, or shall we look for another?' " In that hour he cured many of diseases and plagues and evil spirits, and on many that were blind he bestowed sight. And he answered them, "Go and tell John what you have seen and heard: the blind receive their sight, the lame walk, lepers are cleansed, and the deaf hear, the dead are raised up, the poor have good news preached to them. And blessed is he who takes no offense at me." (Luke 7.19–23)

The Meaning of the Signs

Signs were of crucial importance to the Jews because they knew God through His acts in history. Moses' work had been profusely attested with signs. The prophets were accredited by the events of history that had confirmed their words, just as the false prophets were known by the failure of their easy promises to come to pass. The rise and fall of the nation was considered in the hands of God and revealed His moral judgment. Too easily, no doubt, the prosperity or adversity of individuals was directly attributed to the favor or disfavor of God. Yahweh was the God of history and made Himself known in events. That was why there had to be a sign.

St. Paul knew this well. "The Jews demand signs," he wrote.

(I Corinthians 1.22) Then he said, "But we preach Christ crucified, a stumbling block to Jews . . ." (I Corinthians 1.23) This did not mean that he disapproved of the Jews' desire for signs, for as a Jew he shared the same desire. The cross was a stumbling block because it was an *unfavorable* sign: "If a man has committed a crime punishable by death and he is put to death, and you hang him on a tree, his body shall not remain all night upon the tree, but you shall bury him the same day, for a hanged man is accursed by God." (Deuteronomy 21.22–23) So ran the Jewish Law. Paul accepted it, but realized that with Jesus this sign of a curse had an unexpected meaning: that Christ took on Himself the curse of our sins, so that we might be set free from sin's curse.[3]

To Paul words were not enough. The Gospel must be demonstrated. He went on to write to the Church at Corinth:

When I came to you, brethren, I did not come proclaiming to you the testimony of God in lofty words or wisdom. For I decided to know nothing among you except Jesus Christ and him crucified. And I was with you in weakness and in much fear and trembling; and my speech and my message were not in plausible words or wisdom, but in demonstration of the Spirit and power, that your faith might not rest in the wisdom of men but in the power of God. (I Corinthians 2.1–5)

St. Peter also knew that signs were part of God's work. In his first sermon on the day of Pentecost he spoke of "Jesus of Nazareth, a man attested to you by God with mighty works and wonders and signs which God did through him in your midst, as you yourselves know." (Acts 2.22) The fourth Gospel puts great emphasis on Christ's miracles, saying near the end:

Now Jesus did many other signs in the presence of the disciples, which are not written in this book; but these are written that you

[3] cf. Galatians 3.10–14.

may believe that Jesus is the Christ, the Son of God, and that believing you may have life in his name. (John 20.30–31)

In view of the essential part played by miraculous signs in both the Old and the New Testaments, and considering the integral place that they hold in the entire Hebrew and early Christian thought, it is astonishing that so many modern Christians are embarrassed by them. Shall we bow in grovelling deference to certain twentieth-century patterns of thinking that have come unbaptized from ancient pagan Greece? Or shall we present the Gospel with the courage that comes from Christ's commission to bring the world to His feet? "Greeks seek wisdom," said Paul, "but we preach Christ crucified . . . folly to Gentiles, but to those who are called, both Jews and Greeks, Christ the power of God and the wisdom of God. For the foolishness of God is wiser than men, and the weakness of God is stronger than men." (I Corinthians 1.22–25)

The crowds that followed Jesus came mostly because of His miraculous healing. The first instance of healing told in the Gospel of St. Mark is the casting out of an unclean spirit from a possessed man in the synagogue at Capernaum. Mark says:

And they were all amazed, so that they questioned among themselves, saying, "What is this? A new teaching! With authority he commands even the unclean spirits, and they obey him." (Mark 1.27–28)

If we take our attention away from the details of each healing and instead observe the whole sweep and setting of Christ's healing ministry, we begin to get a perspective on its meaning. Mark tells next of the immediate healing of Peter's mother-in-law from a fever, then goes on:

That evening, at sundown, they brought to him all who were sick or possessed with demons. And the whole city was gathered together about the door. And he healed many who were sick

with various diseases, and cast out many demons; and he would
not permit the demons to speak, because they knew him.

And in the morning, a great while before day, he rose and went
out to a lonely place, and there he prayed. And Simon and those
who were with him followed him, and they found him and said
to him, "Every one is searching for you." And he said to them,
"Let us go on to the next towns, that I may preach there also;
for that is why I came out." And he went throughout all Galilee,
preaching in their synagogues and casting out demons. (Mark
1.32–39)

We note the tremendous throngs that are attracted at once
by His power to heal. This is no physician waiting patiently for
normal, gradual recovery. The sudden gathering of masses of
the sick would make no sense unless the healings were obvious,
immediate, and effective.[4]

Mark then tells of the instant healing of a leper.

And he sternly charged him, and sent him away at once, and
said to him, "See that you say nothing to any one; but go, show
yourself to the priest, and offer for your cleansing what Moses
commanded, for a proof to the people." But he went out and began
to talk freely about it, and to spread the news, so that Jesus
could no longer openly enter a town, but was out in the country;
and people came to him from every quarter.

And when he returned to Capernaum after some days, it was
reported that he was at home. And many were gathered together,
so that there was no longer room for them, not even about the
door; and he was preaching the word to them. (Mark 1.43–2.2)

Now a paralytic is brought. "And when they could not get
near him because of the crowd, they removed the roof above

[4] Dr. Boggs claims that in certain passages concerning Jesus' healing, the
Greek does not mean "healed," but "treated," "began to heal," or "tried
to heal." A discussion of this remarkable argument is found in Appendix
B, pp. 245–48.

him; and when they had made an opening, they let down the pallet on which the paralytic lay." (Mark 2.4) Jesus heals him at once. "And he rose, and immediately took up the pallet and went out before them all; so that they were all amazed and glorified God, saying, 'We never saw anything like this!' " (Mark 2.12)

Wherever He goes, the crowds follow. The reason Mark gives for their coming is always the same: "a great multitude, hearing all that he did, came to him" (Mark 3.8); "he had healed many, so that all who had diseases pressed upon him to touch him" (Mark 3.10); "immediately the people recognized him, and ran about the whole neighborhood and began to bring sick people . . ." [5] The multitudes come because Jesus does more than talk about the Kingdom of God. He demonstrates it by healing.

Why, then, does He so often command silence when He heals? [6] Is He trying to keep His healing a secret? If so, He is not very successful. The reaction to the healing of the deaf man who had an impediment in his speech, told in Mark 7.31–37, is instructive: "And he charged them to tell no one; but the more he charged them, the more zealously they proclaimed it."

The orders to be silent become more intelligible, however, when we examine them more closely. First, we notice that not only the people who are involved are told to be silent. The demons, too, are commanded to say nothing. (Mark 1.25, 34) This is surely not because the demons are likely to go around publicizing Him as a wonder-worker! St. Mark gives the reason. "He would not permit the demons to speak, because they knew him." (Mark 1.34) They were identifying Him! At the synagogue at Capernaum, the unclean spirit said, "I know who you are, the Holy One of God." (Mark 1.24) Mark 3.11 says, "And whenever the unclean spirits beheld him, they fell

[5] Mark 6.54–55. Read also through verse 56.
[6] Mark 1.25, 34, 44; 3.12; 5.43; 7.36.

down before him and cried out, 'You are the Son of God.' And he strictly ordered them not to make him known." The demon-possessed man at Gerasa [7] cried loudly, "What have you to do with me, Jesus, Son of the Most High God?" (Mark 5.7)

Silence was also commanded on occasions where there were no healings. When Peter identified Jesus, saying, "You are the Christ," Jesus "charged them to tell no one about him." (Mark 8.29–30) After the transfiguration, when the voice came out of the cloud, "This is my beloved Son; listen to him," Jesus "charged them to tell no one what they had seen, until the Son of man should have risen from the dead." (Mark 9.2–13) Although Matthew pictures the voice from heaven at Christ's baptism as saying, "This is my beloved Son" (Matthew 3.17) the earlier Gospel according to Mark, which Matthew used as a source, tells that the voice at the baptism said, "Thou art my beloved Son," [8] a private rather than a public message.

The reason, then, for the commands of silence was what has been called the "Messianic Secret." Jesus did not wish to be identified prematurely as the Messiah. Small wonder, considering how different was the popular conception of the Messiah from His. The Gospel of the Kingdom of Christ could not be revealed in its fullness or in its true perspective until after His death and resurrection. Another factor besides the problem of misinterpretation would be the danger of His ministry being prematurely cut short by His enemies. The cross was to come; but in due time, when His work was done.

St. John's Gospel, with its distinctive interpretation of Christ, gives no hint of any Messianic secret. Right at the beginning it pictures John the Baptist identifying Jesus as "the Lamb of God, who takes away the sin of the world." (John 1.29) And nowhere does the fourth Gospel suggest that Jesus commanded silence regarding His miracles.

[7] Or most likely, as Weatherhead believes, at Khersa.
[8] Mark 1:11. Luke 3:22 follows Mark in this.

Everywhere in the Gospels, though, the healing work of Christ is understood as providing signs that point to the Messiah and His Kingdom. God confirmed His message with the signs. Some have considered that when Jesus was told, "Every one is searching for you," and when He replied, "Let us go on to the next towns, that I may preach there also; for that is why I came out," (Mark 1.37–38) He felt that the burden of the crowds coming for healing was hindering His preaching. The implication is that He considered the preaching as His real ministry. This may be comforting to twentieth-century preachers, but it is a false antithesis. As Jesus went on to the next towns, He healed continuously right along with the preaching.[9] The two aspects of His work were inseparable. Jesus preached and God spoke His approval through the signs. "The words that I say to you I do not speak on my own authority; but the Father who dwells in me does his works. Believe me that I am in the Father and the Father in me; or else believe me for the sake of the works themselves." (John 14.10–11)

The Earthly Leads to the Heavenly

Although the purpose of the healing miracles was to signify the Kingdom of God, we ought not to assume that the crowds were motivated primarily by a hunger for spiritual things. Sickness had created the need for wholeness, and they flocked to Jesus in order to meet that immediate desire. Whether a man was ill himself, or one of his family was sick, or a friend, the great common motive was the relief of suffering. Even Jesus' closest disciples did not yet discern the profundity of the spiritual transformation which it was His purpose to give. It is a psychological impossibility for the multitudes to have been attracted by those spiritual depths with which they were far less acquainted. They were simple people coming for a simple reason: to be healed of their infirmities. Jesus did not hesitate

[9] cf. Mark 1:39.

to accept them on the only possible level that He could find them. He welcomed them just where they were and healed them.

This does not mean that Christ was content to leave people in the same spiritual state in which they came. He was concerned that they should see beyond the immediate need to the filling of their ultimate need, the healing of the spirit. After the miraculous feeding of the multitude, John's Gospel says that "they were about to take him by force to make him king" (John 6.15) thus twisting a heavenly kingdom into an earthly one. Jesus withdrew to be by Himself. The next day the people found Him.

When they found him on the other side of the sea, they said to him, "Rabbi, when did you come here?" Jesus answered them, "Truly, truly, I say to you, you seek me, not because you saw signs, but because you ate your fill of the loaves. Do not labor for the food which perishes, but for the food which endures to eternal life, which the Son of man will give to you; for on him has God the Father set his seal." (John 6.25–27)

The same lifting of spiritual relationships above the level of physical or mental restoration alone is to be seen in the healing ministry of Jesus. The curing of disease is meant to raise those who are involved to a new closeness to God,[10] and the overcoming of mental disorder is understood as a triumph over Satan.[11] Physical and mental wholeness are instruments of spiritual wholeness. In Jesus' ministry they are never isolated from His establishment of the Reign of God.

The Unity of Human Nature

In order to appreciate just how closely the physical, the mental, and the spiritual aspects of man's life are linked in the ministry of Jesus, we must realize that He was a Jew preaching

[10] cf. Luke 17.11–19, where only the leper who returned to give thanks showed the signs of spiritual wholeness.
[11] cf. Luke 10.17–18, Mark 3.22–26.

almost exclusively to Jews. Human nature as understood by the Hebrew mind is well summed up in Genesis 2.7: "then Yahweh God formed man of dust from the ground, and breathed into his nostrils the breath of life; and man became a living being." "Breath" and "spirit" are the same root word in Hebrew as in the Greek of the New Testament—and for that matter in Latin, from which we get the English "respiration," with the "spir" in common with the word "spirit." Man is a material body with the spirit of life. The body without the spirit is dead. The human spirit without the body is almost incomprehensible to the ancient Hebrew mind. Most of the Old Testament is very hazy about the possibility of life after death. On the one hand, "Sheol," the abode of the dead, seems inhabited by rather colorless, ineffective shades of the departed. Or else no hope at all is offered for personal survival; for example, Ecclesiastes 9.5–6 says, "the dead know nothing, and they have no reward . . . they have no more for ever any share in all that is done under the sun." When belief in life after death gained acceptance (as it did, particularly in the second century B.C.), the typical Jewish way to imagine it was as the resurrection of the body on the Day of Judgment. The immortality of the soul apart from the body was a Greek, not a Hebrew, concept. At the time of Jesus, there were two major schools of thought: that of the Sadducees, who denied life after death; and that of the Pharisees, who believed in the resurrection of the body. Christ and His disciples agreed with the latter.[12] The Christian belief also included a substantial life after death before the resurrection on the Day of Judgment.[13] Any separation of body and spirit other than during this intermediate state of waiting for the Judgment at the "end of the age" is unheard of in the Bible. Even in this state there almost seems to be some sort of body involved; at least the form of the body is there.

[12] cf. Mark 12.18–27.
[13] e.g., cf. Mark 12.27; 9.2–5; Luke 16.19–31; 23.43.

St. Paul, writing Greek to Christians outside Palestine, uses certain terms that may cause misunderstanding if they are removed from their setting. For instance, he frequently contrasts "the flesh" (e.g. Romans 8.3–8) or "the sinful body" (e.g. Romans 6.6) with "the spirit." But a careful study of his usage shows that by "the flesh" he does not mean the physical body, but human nature in its unregenerate and sinful state. What Paul is saying is seen in his letter to the Galatians:

But I say, walk by the Spirit, and do not gratify the desires of the flesh. For the desires of the flesh are against the Spirit, and the desires of the Spirit are against the flesh; for these are opposed to each other, to prevent you from doing what you would. But if you are led by the Spirit you are not under the law. Now the works of the flesh are plain: immorality, impurity, licentiousness, idolatry, sorcery, enmity, strife, jealousy, anger, selfishness, dissension, party spirit, envy, drunkenness, carousing, and the like. I warn you, as I warned you before, that those who do such things shall not inherit the kingdom of God. But the fruit of the Spirit is love, joy, peace, patience, kindness, goodness, faithfulness, gentleness, self-control; against such there is no law. And those who belong to Christ Jesus have crucified the flesh with its passion and desires (Galatians 5.16–24)

He does not condemn sex, but the misuse of sex. He does not condemn the normal physical appetite to eat and drink, but the misuse of drink. Most of what he calls "the works of the flesh" are not what we commonly refer to as sins of the flesh, but are indeed sins of the spirit: "idolatry, sorcery, enmity, strife, jealousy, anger, selfishness, dissension, party spirit, envy." That Paul does not identify "the flesh" (in his special sense) with the physical body is further seen in his discussion of sexual immorality in I Corinthians 6.12–20, which ends with these words: "Do you not know that your body is a temple of the Holy Spirit within you, which you have from

God? You are not your own; you were bought with a price. So glorify God in your body."

Another misunderstanding concerns his teaching about the resurrection body. This teaching is developed in I Corinthians 15. The translation of verses 44 and 46 in the Revised Standard Version of the New Testament contrasts the "physical" body which dies, with the "spiritual" body of the resurrection. However, the Greek word is not "physical," but would be literally rendered "soul-ish." [14] Here "soul" is used to designate the life-principle which man has in common with the animals. In fact, we derive the word "animal" from the Latin "anima," which means "soul." The Greek "psyche," to which Paul refers, has the same meaning. What Paul is really contrasting is the perishable "animal" body, which dies, with the imperishable spiritual body which rises. In the resurrection, a transformation of the physical body occurs, not its negation. This is one implication of the empty tomb of Jesus. Paul does not picture (if such a picture were possible) the risen man as a disembodied spirit, but as a union of the spirit with a changed and immortal body. "If the spirit of him who raised Jesus from the dead dwells in you, he who raised Christ Jesus from the dead will give life to your mortal bodies also through his Spirit which dwells in you." (Romans 8.11)

Thus we see that Paul shares the Hebrew view of the unity of body and spirit to make human nature. The prayer at the end of his first letter to the Thessalonians expresses this unity: "May the God of peace himself sanctify you wholly; and may your spirit and soul and body be kept sound and blameless at the coming of our Lord Jesus Christ." (I Thessalonians 5.23) It is hard to be certain of Paul's exact meaning in using the word "soul" [15] here, or even if he intended a precise mean-

[14] The Greek word is ψυχικόν (psychikon).

[15] ψυχή, psyche. Paul is probably following the Greek three-fold division of human nature: here "soul" means the vital force which animates the body, while "spirit" (πνεῦμα, pneuma) is the rational part of man, through which he perceives and understands divine and eternal things, and

ing. We can be sure, nevertheless, that the prayer affirms the unity of the different aspects of human nature, and that the holiness which comes from God is intended for every one of these aspects, leaving nothing to be exempted from the rule of Christ.

The phenomena of demon-possession, which seem so strange to modern Western man, are actually a logical conclusion from the Hebrew view of human nature. They serve as an additional illustration of that view. If man is a body into which God has breathed the spirit of life, we see that the living functions of the body depend on the spirit within it. But suppose there is (to use a modern term) a functional disturbance; that is, an illness with psychological rather than physical causes.[16] In Biblical thought, the disturbance would be in the spirit, since the body's functions express the activity of the spirit within. Our modern deduction would be that the spirit is sick, disordered in some way. But this is not the only way to look at it. Since this is a disturbance of normal activity and opposed to it, an equally natural conclusion is that a spirit which is evil has intruded itself, expressing itself in the body. The man's own spirit is now unable to control his body. He is possessed by an evil spirit.

If it is possible to be possessed by an evil spirit, it is also possible to be possessed by the Holy Spirit of God. Such possession is to be found in various forms in both the Old and the New Testament. One of the most memorable instances in the New Testament is the gift of tongues at Pentecost. (Acts 2.1–21)

---

through which the Holy Spirit acts. In this sense, man has a "soul" in common with the animals, but has a "spirit" which they lack. In this sense, too, the study of the "soul" is the province of *psychology*, while *theology* concerns the things of the "spirit." Psychology's realm is commonly called the "mind," and it is by this definition of "mind" that the Greek three-fold division can also be translated into modern English as "body, mind, and spirit." Perhaps this rendering is the easiest for us to understand.

[16] This oversimplifies psychosomatic relationships, no doubt, but we are concentrating on the general concepts, not the fine points.

Usually, however, the Holy Spirit does not take possession, in the sense of taking control over from the man's own spirit. He rules through the voluntary cooperation of the spirit of the individual. This is the typical case of "inspiration," the Holy Spirit dwelling within. St. Paul describes it in I Corinthians 12, where, for example, verses 4–7 say, "Now there are varieties of gifts, but the same Spirit; and there are varieties of service, but the same Lord; and there are varieties of working, but it is the same God who inspires them all in every one. To each is given the manifestation of the Spirit for the common good."

It should now be evident that the Biblical picture of human nature demands that spiritual purification be reflected in examples of mental and bodily wholeness. If a man is to be filled with the Holy Spirit, he must be emptied of evil spirits.[17] If his body is to be most effectively used for spiritual service, it should be freed from physical infirmity.[18] Christ's healing work not only provided signs of the Kingdom of God. It also carried out that renewal of mind and body that is implied in God's Reign. Spiritual wholeness leads to total wholeness.

Healing as an Expression of Christ's Love

Another important factor in the healing ministry of Jesus was His compassion toward the suffering. "God is love, and he who abides in love abides in God, and God abides in him." (I John 4.16) Nothing could characterize Jesus more than love. He could not fail to be moved by human misery. "As he went ashore he saw a great throng; and he had compassion on them, and healed their sick." (Matthew 14.14) "And a leper came to him, beseeching him, and kneeling said to him,

---

[17] And on the other hand if he is to be protected from evil spirits, he must be filled with the Holy Spirit. This is one implication of Matthew 12.43–45.

[18] This is not to deny, to be sure, that physical handicaps may be used redemptively and be the occasion of spiritual growth and service.

'If you will, you can make me clean.' Moved with pity, he stretched out his hand and touched him, and said to him 'I will; be clean.'" (Mark 1.40–41) These explicit references to His compassion only hint at the outpouring of love which He demonstrated in action over and over again.

The New Testament gives no hint of any occasion in the earthly ministry of Jesus when He was asked to heal and either refused or failed to do so. "Many followed him, and he healed them all . . ." [19] There were, of course, many who did not meet the conditions for healing. We cannot be sure why Jesus singled out one of the invalids at the pool of Bethzatha (John 5.2–9) to be healed by Him; but we also have no reason to suppose that anyone there sought healing from Jesus. A definite spiritual impediment is mentioned at Nazareth: "He could do no mighty work there, except that he laid his hands upon a few sick people and healed them. And he marveled because of their unbelief." (Mark 6.1–6) The barrier lay in their unwillingness to receive, not in His refusal to give. Although Mark 1:32 speaks of *all* who were sick or demon-possessed as being brought to Jesus at Capernaum, while verse 34 says only that He healed *many* who were sick or possessed, no explanation is given as to why this difference of expression is used. However, it is not unreasonable to suppose that when "the whole city was gathered about the door" with their sick (verse 33), and since they did not gather until sundown (verse 32), there was not time enough for Jesus to deal with each individual case, as was His custom, during that one evening. Verse 35 tells us that He rose long before daylight the next morning, so the time available for healing would have been very limited that evening. This, again, suggests no unwillingness of Jesus to heal. Christ's love reached out to all. His desire was to heal each sufferer. Those who sought Him in humble faith and were able to come into His presence were healed. Can any one imagine His saying to some sufferer who has come with ex-

[19] Matthew 12.15b. cf. Luke 4.40; 6.19.

pectant hope, "It is the Father's will that you remain sick. I will not heal you"?

Death and the Fall

If the cause of a disease is known, its cure may be more readily found. If the Biblical understanding of the fundamental cause of the dissolution of human life is known, the Biblical cure may be easier to understand.

The first story of Creation (Genesis 1.1–2.3) says, "God created man in his own image" (Genesis 1.27) and "God saw everything that he had made, and behold, it was very good." (Genesis 1.31) In the second story (Genesis 2.4–3.24), God breathes into man's nostrils "the breath of life" (Genesis 2.7), and puts him into the Garden of Eden which contains the "tree of life" and the "tree of the knowledge of good and evil." (Genesis 2.9) Through disobeying God's command not to eat of the tree of the knowledge of good and evil, Adam [20] (who symbolizes all mankind) and Eve [21] his wife, not only come to know good and evil, but lose the paradise with its tree of life. Adam is cast out of the garden "lest he put forth his hand and take also of the tree of life, and eat, and live for ever." (Genesis 3.22)

The meaning of this is that God has created human nature as something essentially good, for a life in which all needs would be provided. But through disobeying God, life's difficulties and suffering ensue and the opportunity to live forever is lost. Human nature is not what God created it to be. Man is fallen. He is sinful. He is destined to die.

Paul considers Adam to be a particular individual, and says, ". . . sin came into the world through one man and death through sin, and so death spread to all men because all men sinned" (Romans 5.12) and "For as by a man came death, by

[20] Which means "man."
[21] A word related in Hebrew to "living."

a man has come also the resurrection of the dead. For as in Adam all die, so also in Christ shall all be made alive." (I Corinthians 15.21–22)

Since Dr. Boggs claims that these quotes from Paul are insufficient to support the teaching that sin is the ultimate cause of disease and physical death, we should consider the passages that he claims set forth "other conceptions of death." To be sure, Isaiah 40.6 reminds us that "all flesh is grass," Deuteronomy 32.39 says, "I kill and I make alive," and Matthew 10.29 quotes Jesus' words that not one sparrow "will fall to the ground without your Father's will." But such words fit in perfectly with the doctrine that death is the consequence of the Fall. "All flesh is grass," and this is no less true if the death of man is due to the Fall. If life and death were not in God's hands, man would prefer to sin and live, too; "I kill and I make alive" is a prerequisite for the story of the Fall. The quote concerning the sparrows also agrees that life and death are regulated by God. When I Corinthians 15.26 says, "The last enemy to be destroyed is death," the obvious reference is to the redemptive work of Christ, which reverses the consequences of the Fall. Surely God does not rejoice at the destruction of man, His own image; death *is* Christ's enemy. Hebrews 2.14 speaks of the Devil as having the power of death, but this is plainly not in the ultimate sense of God's power over death, but means that falling under Satan's power leads to death— exactly what the story of the Fall would imply. Romans 5.14 says that death reigned over those who sinned, from Adam to Moses; that is, before the Mosaic Law was given. This is not an extraordinary observation. Romans 5.21 says that "sin reigned in death"; that is, sin reigned through the death it caused. The rule of sin is confirmed in its consequence of death. The turn of the phrase may be unusual, but the meaning is a repetition of everything we have said. No doubt a medley of these scattered quotes does produce the "somewhat confused picture" of which Dr. Boggs writes. But by understanding each passage in its context, we find harmony, not confusion. Everything is quite agreeable to the idea that death is the consequence of the sin of mankind. We may accept this idea, modify it, reinterpret it, or reject it. But it is what the Bible teaches.

We must agree with Dr. Boggs, however, that the meaning of "death" is not simply the death of the body. The Biblical revelation came over a long period of time, and a real transformation of understanding took place as the revelation unfolded. The earlier writers give little consideration to anything beyond this life. To them, death is simply physical. In the New Testament, on the other hand, death is primarily a spiritual matter and only secondarily physical. St. Paul, writing about the sin that dwells within, says, "Who will deliver me from this body of death?" (Romans 7.24) Without Christ, physical life is already "dead":

And you he made alive, when you were dead through the trespasses and sins in which you once walked, following the course of this world, following the prince of the power of the air, the spirit that is now at work in the sons of disobedience. (Ephesians 2.1–3)

Sin leads to condemnation and death; (cf. Romans 5.12–21) but for the Christian that death occurs when the old sinful self is "crucified" and "buried" in union with Christ's death, so that we may "walk in newness of life" with the risen Lord. (cf. Romans 6.1–11) Death and resurrection, in other words, take place spiritually in this life. "If we have died with Christ, we believe that we shall also live with him. (Romans 6.8) We are likewise reminded of the words of Jesus in John 5.24: "Truly, truly, I say to you, he who hears my word and believes him who sent me, has eternal life; he does not come into judgment, but has passed from death to life"; and in John 11.25: "I am the resurrection and the life; he who believes in me, though he die, yet shall he live, and whoever lives and believes in me shall never die." There are many other similar teachings. For the Christian, physical death is merely an incident. "For me to live is Christ, and to die is gain." (Philippians 1.21)

This does not mean, however, that physical death is ignored in the New Testament. The unity of the spiritual and the bodily in man's nature is never forgotten. But the ultimate destiny of the body is seen in terms that transcend the present order of things. This present world is passing, and a new order will take its place on the Day of Judgment.[22] Then the dead are to be raised, either to eternal life [23] or to a second and eternal death.[24] The final life or death of the body is determined by whether God or sin reigns in it.

The Causes of Suffering

The Scriptures do not give a complete explanation of sickness and suffering, but several strands of Biblical thought do lead to a further understanding of illness and healing. We have spoken of man's sinful state as the cause of death. The connection between illness and death should be plain enough. The conclusion is that sin causes sickness. Deuteronomy 28.58–68 gives a clear-cut version of this; a little too clear-cut, we might say. The suffering resulting from the sins of the nation is repeatedly proclaimed by the prophets, and Jesus Himself foretold God's judgment against Jerusalem. (cf. Matthew 23.29–24.2)

The teaching that sin causes death was applied to each individual in Ezekiel 18: "The soul that sins shall die." This principle was commonly used in the interpretation of the sickness of individuals as well, as Job's "comforters" show.

[22] cf. II Corinthians 4.7–18; also Mark 13, II Peter 3.1–13, Revelation 20.4–21.8, etc.

[23] cf. Matthew 24 and 25, Revelation 20.5–6; 21.1–22.5, etc.

[24] cf. Matthew 10.28, Revelation 20.7–15, etc.

"Know then that God exacts of you less than your guilt deserves." (Job 11.6)

The book of Job is a protest against this easy identification of all suffering with a judgment on sin. The only answer the innocent Job gets is that there is no complete answer. God's ways are beyond man's comprehension, and we cannot understand why He permits suffering as He does. We are consoled, however, when God finally heals Job and restores to him double of all that he had. And we are given to understand that God does not cause the affliction of the innocent: though God allowed it, Satan caused Job's misery and temptation.

Jesus knew that a man's sin could bring illness (cf. John 5.4), but He refused to ascribe all sickness to sin. Before He healed the man born blind (John 9.1–11), the disciples asked, "Rabbi, who sinned, this man or his parents, that he was born blind?" He answered, "It was not that this man sinned, or his parents, but that the works of God might be made manifest in him." This is one of the two places in the Gospels which some might reasonably interpret to indicate a source of suffering which is not inherently evil.[25] Yet even this passage does not say that God caused the blindness. It may mean only that God permitted it. As a matter of fact, since ancient Greek was not punctuated, the translation could just as well have been rendered: "It was not that this man sinned or his parents. But that the works of God might be made manifest in him, we must work the works of him who sent me, while it is day . . ." In any case, it is obvious that God's purpose was to overcome the blindness.

Although the demons or unclean spirits mentioned in the Gospels are considered part of Satan's work,[26] no clue is given

---

[25] The other possibility is John 15.2, where Jesus says, "Every branch that does bear fruit [my Father] prunes, that it may bear more fruit." However, this does not say that God sends disease, but only that He disciplines and purifies His imperfect servants.

[26] e.g. Mark 3.22–27; Luke 10.17–18; Luke 13.16. Note in the latter case that the woman had a "*spirit* of infirmity."

as to their ultimate origin. They are, of course, considered the evil cause of what we would term psychogenic illness. Demon-possession is connected with the sin of "this evil generation" in Matthew 12.43–45, but not enough is said there to allow us to decide whether or not every case of possession is considered as due to human sin.[27] Nowhere are we told why any particular individual has become possessed. This much is certain: the Devil, not God, is held responsible.

An example of Satan's work which has often been misinterpreted is St. Paul's affliction. He writes:

And to keep me from being too elated by the abundance of revelations, a thorn was given me in the flesh, a messenger of Satan, to harass me, to keep me from being too elated. Three times I besought the Lord about this, that it should leave me; but he said to me, "My grace is sufficient for you, for my power is made perfect in weakness." (II Corinthians 12.7–9)

Some have imagined this "thorn in the flesh" to have been sent by God, but Paul says it was "a messenger of Satan." Whatever the "thorn" was, God had not removed it at the time this epistle was written. He did answer Paul's prayers, though, in giving him the grace to carry on despite his handicap. Paul also gives a reason why it was not removed: "to keep me from being too elated by the abundance of revelations." Is he saying that he was too much inclined to spiritual pride? If so, we may wonder whether he might not have been healed if humility had come easier. We may wonder, too, whether later on he might not have been healed. We cannot judge these things. But it would be most unjust to make God responsible for Paul's infirmity.

Another passage which has been misunderstood as implying

---

[27] The quote from Jesus is tied to "this evil generation" in Matthew 12.45. But the same quote in Luke 11.24 makes no such reference. This suggests that perhaps the author of Matthew, rather than Jesus, applied the quote to "this evil generation."

a divine source of suffering is Luke 13.1–5, which refers to Galileans whom Pilate had killed and to those who were killed when a tower fell in Siloam. Jesus denies that they were worse sinners than their neighbors, thus relieving them of any special personal blame. But He adds, "Unless you repent you will all likewise perish." The implication is that all are involved in sin. Pilate's bloodiness and the careless work of the tower builders were the major sins in these examples, and their sins caused the suffering of others. Again, we have no reason to hold God responsible.

Some, apparently grasping at straws, have considered the death of the Gerasene swine (Mark 5.11–13) and the cursing of the fig tree by Jesus (Mark 11.14, 20) as showing a divine source of suffering. But the first was due to the demon-possession of the man whom Jesus healed and the second did not cause suffering.

Now we come to a most important reason for suffering. This is the opposition of the sinful world to the redemptive love of God.[28] It affects the innocent. (e.g. Matthew 2.16–18) It is seen in the persecution of the saints. It is seen supremely in the cross of Christ. "If any man would come after me," Jesus said, "let him deny himself and take up his cross and follow me. For whoever would save his life will lose it; and whoever loses his life for my sake and the gospel's will save it." (Mark 8.34–35) "Behold, I send you out as sheep in the midst of wolves; so be wise as serpents and as innocent as doves. Beware of men; for they will deliver you up to councils, and flog you in their synagogues, and you will be dragged before governors and kings for my sake . . . Brother will deliver up brother to death, and the father his child, and children will rise against parents and have them put to death; and you will be hated by all for my name's sake . . . A disciple is not above his teacher, nor a servant above his master . . ." (Matthew 10.16–18, 21–22, 24) Thus Jesus commissioned His Apostles.

[28] Isaiah 52.7–53.12 was written by one who knew this well.

Though the cause of such suffering is the wickedness of men, it is God's will for the Christian to contend against it, and it can be transformed into a useful discipline of the soul. "Beloved, do not be surprised at the fiery ordeal which comes upon you to prove you . . . If you are reproached for the name of Christ you are blessed . . . But let none of you suffer as a . . . wrongdoer . . . For the time has come for judgment to begin with the household of God . . . Therefore let those who suffer according to God's will do right and entrust their souls to a faithful creator." (I Peter 4.12–19) Here suffering comes to some through the sins of the world; to others, as judgment on their own sins. The same judgment upon Christians for their sins is seen in I Corinthians 11.28–32. Weakness, illness, and death have resulted from it . . ."But when we are judged by the Lord, we are chastened so that we may not be condemned along with the world." Hebrews 12.5–6 expresses the thought of Proverbs 3.11–12 when it says,

"My son, do not regard lightly the discipline of the Lord, nor lose courage when you are punished by him. For the Lord disciplines him whom he loves, and chastises every son whom he receives."

This has nothing to do with resigned acceptance of sickness, however. It is a bugle call to the army of God to rejoice in discipline in its battle against persecution. (cf. Hebrews 12.1–4, 12–13)

"Put on the whole armor of God," says the letter to the Ephesians, "that you may be able to stand against the wiles of the devil. For we are not contending against flesh and blood, but against the principalities, against the powers, against the world rulers of this present darkness, against the spiritual hosts of wickedness in the heavenly places." (Ephesians 6.11–12)

It was Jesus Himself Who fought the crucial battle against the evil forces of cosmic darkness. His path to the cross was in freely chosen obedience to God. His suffering was brought about because of His attack upon evil. Christ chose the cross because He chose to obey His Father, whatever the consequences.

In the garden of Gethsemane He prayed in agony of soul, "Father, all things are possible to thee; remove this cup from me; yet not what I will, but what thou wilt." (Mark 14.36) Does this compare with that easy, resigned "If it be Thy will" that too often marks our prayers for the sick? Christ's prayer is not resignation. It is the courageous entry into the battle for the world's salvation.

The revulsion against everything wicked and sinful and terrible; the monstrous agony of God in a human life about to draw into Himself the outrageous rebelliousness of all mankind, its black evil; the dark vision of His broken body, a sacrament ripped and bleeding under barbaric torments—all this and more in the unfathomable depths of His spirit led to that tortured cry, "Remove this cup from me!" And the fortitude to endure what was beyond human endurance causes Him to reply to His own request: "yet not what I will, but what thou wilt." He knew, He did not doubt, He did not waver in knowing His Father's will.

His steadfast love was as pure as His enemies' hate was vicious. His role alone was God-sent. The rest was straight from Hell. God permitted it in order to conquer it.[29]

Jesus went through the suffering to the eternal victory. That is the way of the cross—it leads to the Resurrection. The final word of Jesus is not the agony, but salvation. "Men of Israel, hear these words," said Peter. ". . . This Jesus, delivered up according to the definite plan and foreknowledge of God, you killed by the hands of lawless men. But God raised him up, having loosed the pangs of death, because it was not possible for him to be held by it . . . Let all the house of Israel there-

---

[29] Such passages as Philippians 2.5–11, Hebrews 2.10, and Hebrews 5.8 speak of the blessings that came to Christ through His suffering. But it would be improper to interpret these to mean that God inflicted that suffering.

fore know assuredly that God has made him both Lord and Christ . . ." (Acts 2.22, 23–24, 36)

There would be a certain intellectual comfort in saying that the Bible gives a perfectly rational account of all the reasons for suffering. But the Scriptures offer no such comfort. The comfort they do give is in the power of Christ to conquer sin, disease and death; to forgive the penitent, to cast out the demons, and to heal the sick.

The New Creation

The major theme of the New Testament is not pain but triumph. The Gospels rise to their climax in Christ's resurrection. The book of Acts and the Epistles evidence the power of the Holy Spirit to produce a new kind of man. And Revelation concludes with God's ultimate victory.

St. Paul puts suffering and its conquest in a cosmic setting:

I consider that the sufferings of this present time are not worth comparing with the glory that is to be revealed to us. For the creation waits with eager longing for the revealing of the sons of God; for the creation was subjected to futility, not of its own will but by the will of him who subjected it in hope; because the creation itself will be set free from its bondage to decay and obtain the glorious liberty of the children of God.

We know that the whole creation has been groaning in travail together until now; and not only the creation, but we ourselves, who have the first fruits of the Spirit, groan inwardly as we wait for adoption as sons, the redemption of our bodies. For in this hope we were saved. (Romans 8.18–24a)

Paul also says, "Therefore if any one is in Christ, he is a new creation; the old has passed away, behold, the new has come." (II Corinthians 5.17)

We are reminded here of the words of Jesus, "Unless one is born anew, he cannot see the kingdom of God . . . Truly,

truly, I say to you, unless one is born of water and the Spirit, he cannot enter the kingdom of God. That which is born of the flesh is flesh, and that which is born of the Spirit is spirit." (John 3.3, 5–6) And St. John's Gospel also says earlier, "But to all who received him, who believed in his name, he gave power to become children of God; who were born, not of blood nor of the will of the flesh nor of the will of man, but of God." (John 1.12–13)

The fountainhead of this new creation is Jesus Christ. He is the Word of God Who is God, Who "became flesh and dwelt among us." (John 1.1, 14) He reverses the Fall: "Christ has been raised from the dead, the first fruits of those that have fallen asleep. For as by a man came death, by a man has come also the resurrection of the dead. For as in Adam all die, so also in Christ shall all be made alive." (1 Corinthians 15.20–22)

Now the healing work of Christ is seen in a fuller light. It is part of God's new creation. His healing is a token and sample of the power of God incarnate in human flesh, the resurrection from the dead, of the victory of Jesus. It is a manifestation of the new birth to be sons of God. "If the Spirit of him who raised Jesus from the dead dwells in you, he who raised Christ Jesus from the dead will give life to your mortal bodies also through his Spirit which dwells in you." (Romans 8.11) Is this only a future hope? Or do Christ's works of healing provide instances of resurrection power in this world also?

In Jesus' healing ministry we see the beginnings of the new creation of man. When the paralytic was brought to Him at Capernaum (Mark 2.1–12), Jesus said, "My son, your sins are forgiven." In this the man's new life began. Then " 'that you may know that the Son of man has authority on earth to forgive sins'—he said to the paralytic—'I say to you, rise, take up your pallet and go home.' And he rose, and immediately took up the pallet and went out before them all . . ." In this the new life was demonstrated. Both forgiveness and physical healing were by grace, as a gift, received by faith, we notice. (cf. Romans 3.21–26) The man could neither find forgiveness nor walk by his own power. But through the healing love of Jesus he did both. He became a new creature.

Speculations have been made concerning the psychological and psychosomatic laws followed by Jesus in His healing.[30] Without intending any disrepect to modern psychological studies, we will keep our attention centered on spiritual implications in this review of the Biblical basis for healing.

Instead of analyzing here each case of healing by Jesus, it seems better to use them as illustrations whenever the occasion arises. Our main concern has been to give the over-all sweep, to see how healing is integrated into the whole Christian Gospel. We can say in summary, though, that the various instances of healing in the Gospels confirm and illuminate the whole New Testament outlook.

The new creation is made possible through the atoning death of Christ. "For if we have been united with him in a death like his, we shall certainly be united with him in a resurrection like his. We know that our old self was crucified with him so that the sinful body might be destroyed, and we might be no longer enslaved to sin." (Romans 6.5–6)

The most meaningful Old Testament passage that sheds light on the Atonement is Isaiah 52.7–53.12. There we read of the suffering Servant of God, Who "was wounded for our transgressions, . . . bruised for our iniquities; upon him was the chastisement that made us whole, and with his stripes we are healed." The Hebrew has a fascinating double meaning in verses 3 and 4 of chapter 53: "He was despised and rejected of men; a man of sorrows and acquainted with grief . . . Surely he hath borne our griefs and carried our sorrows" can also be translated, "He was despised and rejected of men; a man of pains and acquainted with sickness . . . Surely he

---

[30] A discussion of the psychological analysis of Jesus' healing is found in Appendix A.

hath borne our sicknesses and carried our pains." Our griefs, our sorrows, our pains, our sicknesses: all of these are borne along with our transgressions and iniquities.

Matthew 8.16–17 applies these words directly to the healing ministry of Jesus:

That evening they brought to him many who were possessed with demons; and he cast out the spirits with a word, and healed all who were sick. This was to fulfil what was spoken by the prophet Isaiah, "He took our infirmities and bore our diseases."

Christ lived and died and rose again to restore men to God, to renew the relationship broken by sin. What He accomplished was a new creation. It means not only the forgiveness of sins but the elimination of sin. It means both the casting out of demons and the fullness of the Holy Spirit. It means both the healing and the resurrection of the body. It means a Kingdom of God that far surpasses lost Eden, in which the whole man, body, mind, and spirit, may eat of the fruit of the tree of life.

If the Kingdom awaits its full perfection until Christ returns on the Day of Judgment, at least we can partake of its advance installments in this life. And if in this life we have the consolation of sin forgiven and sin overcome, we may also be consoled in this life with demons cast out and bodies renewed. If we are not discouraged even though sin remains in the world—and, alas, in the lives of Christians—until the Judgment, we should likewise not lose courage if all sickness is not removed or if all physical death is not averted. The perfection of God's new creation is yet to come.

Christ's Commission to Heal

From what has been said, it should be apparent that spiritual healing is solidly imbedded in the faith and works of New Testament Christianity. This realization gives full force to Christ's command to His disciples to heal the sick:

And he called the twelve together and gave them power and authority over all demons and to cure diseases, and he sent them out to preach the kingdom of God and to heal . . .

And they departed and went through the villages, preaching the gospel and healing everywhere . . .

On their return the apostles told him what they had done. And he took them and withdrew apart to a city called Bethsaida. When the crowds learned it, they followed him; and he welcomed them and spoke to them of the kingdom of God, and cured those who had need of healing. (Luke 9.1–2, 6, 10–11)

Not only were the Twelve empowered to heal, but

After this the Lord appointed seventy others, and sent them on ahead of him, two by two, into every town and place where he himself was about to come. . . . Whenever you enter a town and they receive you, eat what is set before you; heal the sick in it and say to them, "The kingdom of God has come near to you . . ."

The seventy returned with joy, saying, "Lord, even the demons are subject to us in your name!" And he said to them, "I saw Satan fall like lightning from heaven. Behold, I have given you authority to tread upon serpents and scorpions, and over all the power of the enemy; and nothing shall hurt you. Nevertheless do not rejoice in this, that the spirits are subject to you; but rejoice that your names are written in heaven." (Luke 10.1, 8–9, 17–20)

That the commission was understood as extending to the Church as a whole is shown by such passages as these:

"Truly, truly, I say to you, he who believes in me will also do the works that I do; and greater works than these will he do, because I go to the Father. Whatever you ask in my name, I will do it, that the Father may be glorified in the Son; if you ask anything in my name, I will do it." (John 14.12–14)

And he said to them, "Go into all the world and preach the gospel to the whole creation." . . . "And these signs will accompany those who believe: in my name they will cast out demons; they will speak in new tongues; they will pick up serpents, and if they drink any deadly thing, it will not hurt them; they will lay their hands on the sick; and they will recover" . . . And they went forth and preached everywhere, while the Lord worked with them and confirmed the message by the signs that attended it. Amen.[31]

In the one instance recorded in the Gospels where the disciples failed to heal (Mark 9.14–29), Jesus' reply was, "O faithless generation, how long am I to be with you?" It is not easy to tell exactly how He assigned the blame. The crowd was present, with His enemies, the scribes. The man whose son was possessed was there. So were the disciples. It would seem that everyone lacked faith. The father described the affliction, then said, " 'If you can do anything, have pity on us and help us.' And Jesus said to him, 'If you can! All things are possible to him who believes.' Immediately the father of the child cried out and said, 'I believe; help my unbelief!' " Apparently most of the crowd still did not believe, for when the boy lay still after the convulsion, looking like a corpse, they said, "He is dead." When the disciples asked Him privately why they could not cast the demon out, Jesus replied, "This kind cannot be driven out by anything but prayer." But in Matthew's version (Matthew 17.14–20), Jesus says, "Because of your little faith . . ." It may well have been that they neglected to pray because they lacked faith. In any case, Jesus considered this failure to heal as a sin.

Examples in the book of Acts [32] show that the Apostles continued their healing ministry after Pentecost. In the healing of Saul through Ananias (Acts 9.17–18), God chooses one who is merely called "a disciple" to be an instrument of healing. Acts 14.3 says of Paul and Barnabas, "So they remained for a long time, speaking boldly for the Lord, who

[31] Mark 16.15, 17–18, 20. Although this was not in the original text, it conveys the understanding of the Church in very early times.

[32] Acts 3.1–10; 5.12–16; 9.32–42; etc.

bore witness to the word of his grace, granting signs and wonders to be done by their hands." Neither of these men were among the Twelve Apostles, and we know that Paul had opposed the Church in the earlier days after Penetcost. Paul wrote to the Corinthians, speaking of himself, "The signs of a true apostle were performed among you in all patience, with signs and wonders and mighty works." (II Corinthians 12.12) Acts 14.8–10 tells of the healing of a cripple through Paul, and Acts 19.11–12 says that "God did extraordinary miracles by the hands of Paul," and indicates that they were healings.

The epistle of James speaks of the healing ministry of "the elders of the church," saying,

Is any among you sick? Let him call for the elders of the church, and let them pray over him, anointing him with oil in the name of the Lord; and the prayer of faith will save the sick man, and the Lord will raise him up; and if he has committed sins, he will be forgiven. Therefore confess your sins to one another, and pray for one another, that you may be healed. The prayer of a righteous man has great power in its effects. (James 5.14–16)

We see here that prayer for the sick is certainly not to be limited to the elders, but is for all Christians. St. James connects its effectiveness with righteousness.

St. Paul writes of the gifts of the Spirit, and says that some Christians have "gifts of healing." (I Corinthians 12.9, 28, 30) This is the sort of gift that could come to any Christian in any age.

Finally, spiritual healing is the inevitable consequence of Jesus' teaching about faith and prayer and love. Can a Christian be so loveless as to fail to pray for sufferers? As he prays, these words of Jesus cannot be forgotten:

Ask, and it will be given you; seek, and you will find; knock, and it will be opened to you. For every one who asks receives, and he who seeks finds, and to him who knocks it will be opened. Or what man of you, if his son asks him for a loaf, will give him a stone? Or if he asks for a fish, will give him a serpent? If you then, who are evil, know how to give good gifts to your children, how much more will your Father who is in heaven give good things to those who ask him. (Matthew 7.7–11)

Truly, truly, I say to you, if you ask anything of the Father, he will give it to you in my name. Hitherto you have asked nothing in my name; ask, and you will receive, that your joy may be full. (John 16.23–24)

✑ CHAPTER VII ✑

The Place of Spiritual Healing in the Church

Those who are in truth His disciples, receiving grace from Him, do in His Name perform miracles, so as to promote the welfare of other men, according to the gift which each one has received from Him. For some do certainly and truly drive out devils, so that those who have thus been cleansed from evil spirits frequently both believe in Christ and join themselves to the Church . . . others still, heal the sick by laying hands on them, and they are made whole. Yea, moreover, as I have said, the dead even have been raised up, and remained with us for many years.

St. Irenaeus, c. 180 A.D.

Thus Irenaeus explodes the notion that the age of miracles passed with the Apostles. The Church of the earliest centuries is replete with signs and wonders, exorcisms, healings, raisings of the dead. The evidence from the first three-hundred years has been beautifully collected by Evelyn Frost in her book, *Christian Healing.*[1] We can trace here only a few of the high points of the story she has pieced together.

Justin Martyr (c. 150–155 A.D.) in his *Second Apology— To The Senate*, vi., said, "For numberless demoniacs throughout the whole world, and in your city, many of our Christian men exorcizing them in the Name of Jesus Christ . . . have healed and do heal, rendering helpless and driving the pos-

[1] Mowbray, London, 2nd ed., 1949, 376 pp.

sessing devils out of the men, though they could not be cured by all the other exorcists, and those who use incantations and drugs."

Even the Roman advocates who accused Christians knew of healings through exorcism. Tertullian tells us that "the clerk of one of them who was liable to be thrown upon the ground by an evil spirit, was set free from his affliction; as was also the relative of another, and the little boy of a third. And how many men of rank (to say nothing of common people) have been delivered from devils and healed of diseases! Even Severus himself, the father of Antonine, was graciously mindful of the Christians. For he sought out the Christian Proculus . . . and in gratitude for his once having cured him by anointing, he kept him in his palace till the day of his death . . ." [2] Apparently Tertullian was well acquainted with these cases.

The great variety of afflictions that were healed in the early Church is seen in Irenaeus' comparison of Christian healing with the weakness of the heretics: "For they can neither confer sight on the blind, nor hearing on the deaf, nor chase away all sorts of demons—none indeed, except those that are sent into others by themselves, if they can do so much as this. Nor can they cure the weak, or the lame, or the paralytic, or those who are distressed in any other part of the body, as has often been done in regard to bodily infirmity. Nor can they furnish effective remedies for those external accidents that may occur. And so far are they from being able to raise the dead, as the Lord raised them, and the Apostles did by means of prayer, and as has been done in the brotherhood on account of some necessity—the entire Church in that particular locality entreating the boon with much fasting and prayer, the spirit of the dead man has returned, and has been bestowed in answer to the prayers of the saints . . ." [3]

[2] *Ad Scapulam,* iv., c. 210 A.D.
[3] *Against Heresies,* II, xxxi.2.

By the time of Origen, who was martyred about 253 A.D., there are signs of decline. He says, "There are still preserved among Christians traces of that Holy Spirit which appeared in the form of a dove." Note the word "traces." He goes on, "They expel evil spirits, and perform many cures, and foresee certain events . . ." [4] In another place, he writes that the Jews "have no longer prophets nor miracles, traces of which to a considerable extent are still found among Christians, and some of them more remarkable than that existed among the Jews; and these we ourselves have witnessed." Here is clear testimony to the continuing healing ministry, but there are signs that the fire is beginning to die.

Cyprian wrote around 250 A.D. The years before the persecution by Decius had been peaceful for the Church. As a result it was becoming soft and flabby. He speaks of Christians as being "eager about our patrimony and our gain, seeking to satisfy our pride, yielding ourselves wholly to emulation and to strife, and not in deeds, every one of us pleasing himself and displeasing all others . . ." [5] He feels that if moral laxity and division had not crept in, persecution would either not have arisen or else it would have immediately ended through the power released through the united witness and prayer of the Church. Cyprian notes dissonance and disagreement in prayer, and this is most displeasing to God. Now we find very little evidence of physical healing, although there are striking individual victories in persecution and there are references to many exorcisms. A class of exorcists now appears on the scene, channelling what was previously a free gift of the Spirit. When Lactantius writes in about the year 315, he puts great emphasis on exorcizing through objective symbols, the divine Name and the sign of the cross, as though these had inherent power,[6] though in one place he says that Christians have power

[4] *Against Celsus*, I. xlvi.
[5] Epistle 6, 1 and 4.
[6] Divine Institutes, iv. 27. This idea is also found in Irenaeus.

over demons "as long as there is peace among the people of God." Laxity and division are cooling the fire still further.

The cold blast of the world hit the Church full force with the Edict of Milan in 325. Constantine's favor toward Christianity brought that torrential influx of half-converted pagans that have been with the Church ever since. "Nominal" Christianity became the rule, true saintliness the exception. The spiritual hearth contained a fierce fire no longer. Its glowing embers have lasted only through the new heat of repeated reform and revival. They have been fragmented into patches of coals that no longer blister the world. When Christians repent and learn true love and reunite in their Lord, the fire may blaze again. Or perhaps it is just as accurate to say that a new blaze will tend to weld the parted embers.

As time passed, miracles of healing were associated only with most extraordinary individuals. They became part of the evidence in the canonization of those rare souls who were to be called Saints with a capital "S." Shrines and relics and prayers to the departed became the major channels of healing because the living were so impotent in their supplications. Anointing for healing was turned into "last rites" in the West, and the theology of this Extreme Unction almost implied surprise if perchance the sick were healed by it. Charms and amulets and all sorts of superstitions directed attention away from the state of the heart, where the key to healing lay.

There were exceptions, of course, and the commission to heal was never completely forgotten. Healing directly by the power of God was seen in the work of St. John of Beverly, St. Bernard, St. Francis of Assisi, St. Catherine of Siena, St. Philip Neri, George Fox, John Wesley, and many others. Yet they were the unusual, not the mainstream.

The Church's growing impotence in the face of disease led in two directions. One was constructive. It was the provision for hospitals and medical care which we have discussed in

Chapter V. Christian love was shown by providing healing in these ways. Thank God for that. And if it is done in His service, it becomes a supernatural act and a form of spiritual healing in its own way. More about this later.

The other reaction to the loss of miraculous healing was destructive. Instead of repenting, Christians rationalized. They invented excuses to justify themselves in their beloved habit patterns. They decided that "heal the sick" did not apply to them in the same way that it applied to early Christians. They told the suffering to be content with their lot and resign themselves to "God's will"; God had given them a "cross" to bear. They interpreted sickness as God's chastening, and too often they would not lift a finger spiritually to remove the burden of it. Inconsistently, they were glad enough to call the doctor if he was to be had. Apparently the strain on the purse to pay the physician and hospital was not so unpleasant as the strain on the soul to come to repentance. They should have called the doctor; they should not have ignored their Lord.

This is not to blame every individual Christian for this sad state of affairs. It has been a corporate sin for centuries, one generation mis-teaching the next. The heaviest weight of guilt falls on the clergy, whose special business it is to hear their Lord and teach their people. The duty of repentance likewise mostly falls to them. Impatient laymen who understand this, however, should remember that the parson has more wrong theology to unlearn than the layman has!

The result of the Church's failure to express Christ's healing power was that medical healing came to monopolize the field. Some of the experiences of scientific medicine with medieval Church decrees were not too happy, and medical science developed largely in isolation from Church leadership. Its growing effectiveness won it the widespread support it deserved. It became the mainstay of healing in Church as well as secular hospitals. And its methods have been applied in Church-supported clinics for the combination of psychotherapy with spiritual help.

But the healing that comes through modern medicine and psychiatry is based upon human skill. Scarcely anyone cares whether or not the doctor or nurse is a Christian. From the point of view of an individual physician's vocation, his healing may be a spiritual expression of obedience to God. But from the point of view of the typical patient, it is the doctor's mastery of the art and science of medicine, not his faith, that is uppermost. The physician may show love, but his work cannot be the same sort of sign of the Kingdom of God as were the miracles of Jesus. Our social order minimizes the spiritual significance of medical care. It is generally as secularly oriented as possible. Perhaps in some ways the most effective Christian witness is seen in hospitals where crucifixes, religious pictures and statues, a chapel, and Sisters are obviously on the scene. A chaplain is a witness, too, but he is easily interpreted as a sort of "extra" sent by the Church for religious purposes, but not vitally related to healing. The doctor heals. The chaplain builds morale; or else he consoles the suffering and prepares the dying. "Religion" is considered a matter of the soul, not the mind or the body. Many hospitals have negligible spiritual activities; each patient must depend on his own Church. Many ill Church members have lost almost all contact with both their clergy and congregations, and many pastors do little indeed for those who are sick or in trouble. True spiritual healing is too rare even in Church hospitals; complete spiritual neglect is too common elsewhere.

Once the Church healed the sick by the supernatural power of the risen Christ. Now it leaves healing to secular skills.

Unfortunately, many Christians have been unable to distinguish between these two methods of healing, and imagine that the Church is actually carrying on the same type of healing ministry that Jesus did. Dr. Boggs, for instance, says:

Our conclusion that Christian people are under a continuing obligation to heal the sick is supported finally by our surrender of the "supernatural" label so often attached to New Testament miracles. Only so can the presumption that others may learn to emulate Jesus in His use of the laws of healing be justified. We may now understand that the techniques employed by Jesus and the disciples in the treatment of sickness are from God in the same way the healing drugs, herbs, and chemicals are from Him. All alike are graciously provided by God, and are available for man's discovery and use. "He impressed the mind with its laws . . . It belongs to human wisdom to systematize the laws which govern spiritual healing, and these laws must be learned from the study of Christ's methods and from experience gleaned in the use of the knowledge so obtained." [7]

In surrendering the "supernatural" label, Dr. Boggs also surrenders the distinction between a Christian and a non-Christian perception of things. This blur is typical of a society whose Christianity is so nominal within the Chruch and so diffused throughout the surrounding secular culture that its Christianity can no longer be distinguished from non-Christianity. But it scarcely fits the New Testament or the early Church. Early Christianity was noted for turning the world upside down. We spend our time congratulating the world for its accomplishments.

The laws of healing that emulate Jesus operate on a plane that natural science cannot penetrate. It cannot perceive them because it is limited to a level of understanding that all men, Christian or not, share in common. Secular healing is based on that sort of understanding. I say this without any intention to criticize. One of the outstanding characteristics of the art and science of modern medical practice is that it is independent of creed. But Christian spiritual healing is witness and testi-

[7] Boggs, *Faith Healing and the Christian Faith*, p. 75. He quotes from Dawson, *Healing: Pagan and Christian*, p. 122. My criticism does not apply to Dawson's words in their own context, but to the sense in which Boggs uses them.

mony to one faith and that faith only: faith in Jesus as the Christ. Its signs and wonders point unmistakably to the reign of Jesus. They are bodily and mental expressions of the Spirit. They convey that wholeness that only God's new creation of man can produce. They express the love of God in Jesus in a way that cannot be replaced by secular medicine. Jesus' healing can be fully emulated by others *only* on the supernatural level, the level of faith and grace, of revelation and spiritual power.

While healing drugs, herbs, and chemicals are from God, and we thank Him for them, it is not true "that the techniques employed by Jesus and the disciples in the treatment of sickness are from God in the same way." They are from God in a radically different way. They do not merely express compassion. They lead directly to Christ and faith in Him. They are samples of the Incarnation, the Atonement, and the Resurrection, re-creating men to be sons of God. Can drugs, herbs, and chemicals do this?

Tatian wrote in the middle of the second century, "If any one is healed by matter, through trusting to it, much more will he be healed by having recourse to the power of God . . . Why is he who trusts in the system of matter not willing to trust in God? For what reason do you not approach the more powerful Lord, but rather seek to cure yourself, like the dog with grass, or the stag with a viper? . . . Why do you deify the objects of nature? . . . Yield to the power of the Logos!" [8] ("Logos" is Greek for "Word" or "Reason," and means the Word of God, the Divine Self-Expression, the Word which became flesh as Jesus.) Christians value medical help—was not St. Luke a physician?—but why do we rely so exclusively on medical help that we neglect supernatural healing? We talk like Christians and act like pagans.

The natural laws of healing are indeed "available for man's discovery and use." They are accessible to the mind through

[8] *To the Greeks*, Chapters xvii, xviii, xx.

study and experience. But is the knowledge of the senses and the intellect all we have? If so, why not be a consistent agnostic? Or are spiritual things discerned by senses and intellect alone? Are non-Christians simply unobserving and stupid? What has become of faith? Have we exhausted the possibilities by saying, "It belongs to human wisdom to systematize the laws which govern spiritual healing . . ."? How different from St. Paul, who said, ". . . my speech and my message were not in plausible words of wisdom, but in demonstration of the Spirit and power, that your faith might not rest in the wisdom of men but in the power of God." (I Corinthians 2.4–5)

Dr. Boggs goes on: "There is no reason why we should not explore by scientific methods the limits and laws of mind over matter, learning in the process all that can be known from the record of New Testament cures." *All*? Ah! We are in the Presence of Science! Let us pray.

Once we discard the supernatural there is, of course, no place for spiritual healing. All arguments about the causes of sickness or God's will in regard to it are then beside the point. The Church is left only with natural healing, and scientific medicine and psychiatry hold the field alone. The word "alone" should be taken seriously. Even Church-directed clinics become out-stations for secular healing, a social service happily made more available to the people. This is because in giving up the supernatural we have given away the Christian faith itself. Dr. Boggs retains his faith by holding that "the Christian is . . . always a 'supernaturalist'—even with reference to 'nature'—for all of the events of nature are 'supernatural' in their causality." But he defines his terms in such a way that the significance of God's revelation and man's response of faith are obscured. In this confusion he cannot see the distinctive contribution of spiritual healing to the Christian life.

Christians have long excused their spiritual ineffectiveness in the face of disease by the argument that illness is God's will. We shall now give this excuse further attention. Our examination of the Biblical record reveals the Scriptural teaching that all sorts of suffering, and death as well, come as God's judgment on human sin. Satan and his demons are held responsible for mental illness, though here, too, sin can play its part. The sins of an individual can cause him to suffer, but much suffering results instead from the sins of others. The latter is seen clearly in persecution and supremely in the cross. We find no statement that God afflicts the innocent, though He does permit the innocent to suffer. The reason for this may often be beyond our understanding. Following God's will in opposing evil may lead to suffering, as the cross shows, but the sins of God's enemies are responsible. God may always turn suffering to good account, as a discipline for spiritual growth. It is always God's will to win a victory over suffering, to come through the cross to the resurrection triumph. So much for the Bible.

Evidence outside the Scriptures gives us a somewhat different perspective. Disease afflicted animal life long before humans evolved. Illness and physical death were the lot of mankind from the beginning. There is no scientific reason to believe in a literal historical "Fall" of man. On the contrary, there appears to have been an evolutionary rise. How are we to fit such scientific conclusions into the Biblical teaching?

In the light of the Christian revelation, it cannot be said that any of these events is purely accidental. God is in control of His creation. The scientific account of that creation shows God to have been an exceedingly patient Master-builder. The process was complex beyond imagination. Multitudes of living creatures fell by the wayside, and others developed into all sorts of variations. Some of them were monstrosities that perished. Others were the novelties with whom the future lay. Out of this welter, God made man. Only certain milestones on the way are known. Most of the story lies shrouded in mystery.

At first the *mass* of animals was everything, the individual nothing but a part of the swarm. But God was working toward the crown of creation on earth—man: man, to be made in His image, to share in His creativity, to choose good or evil, to converse with God, to know and love the Almighty! In this creature, the individual must have the dignity of a son of God. If individuals were to develop from lower forms of life, generation had to follow generation. And for life to exist upon the limited resources of earth, individuals could not live forever. Death is a biological necessity.

The Fall could be pinpointed at the almost unimaginable time that the first true humans sinned. In fact, the earliest man could be defined as the first of earth's creatures to sin. Yet this is not really the point of the story of the Fall. As we examine the account in Genesis, it reveals itself as symbolism, not history. It signifies man's *present* condition. Adam is Man personified. His Fall is the state of sinful Man as he now is. We know ourselves to be not what God intends us to be.

The New Testament transmutes the issue of life or death into a realm beyond this mortal span of years. Physical death becomes but an incident in a greater drama. The penalty of the Fall is eternal death at the Day of Judgment. The release into the New Creation begins with faith in Christ and continues in eternity.

We can say that sickness is a natural consequence of the development of life on this earth. But the only human life we know, other than our Lord's,[9] is that which is tainted with sin. Who knows what powers perfect humanity has to resist the onslaught of disease? If the life of Jesus is a guide, all external attacks might be overcome by a completely holy man—even death. This is because the life of the Spirit is not contained in the evolutionary process. The New Creation transcends the old. "To all who received him, who believed in his name, he gave power to become children of God; who were born, not of

[9] Many Christians would add His Mother's life as sinless.

blood nor of the will of the flesh nor of the will of man, but of God." [10]

If this is so, as Christians believe, the conditions of life of sinless humanity are vastly different from human experience as we know it. If man had never sinned, the supernatural power released in him would have immediately lifted him above the natural limitations of his existence. The Fall is his loss of that condition of life that might have been. The New Creation is his restoration as a son of God. As St. Paul wrote, "When we cry, 'Abba! Father!' it is the Spirit himself bearing witness with our spirit that we are children of God, and if children, then heirs, heirs of God and fellow heirs with Christ, provided we suffer with him in order that we may also be glorified with him." (Romans 8.15–17)

The suffering with Christ that comes upon the children of God is caused by the enmity of the sin-dominated world. It is the Christian's share in the cross, and is to be expected until God's complete triumph when Christ comes again as Judge.

When all this has been said, though, human sin is not the only cause of suffering. Neither the sin of the individual nor his sharing in the sin of mankind nor his conflict with persecution are sufficient to account for all suffering. The book of Job points to this truth. It witnesses to some unfathomable mystery in suffering.

The trouble with many explanations of suffering is that they blame too much on God. They do not take enough account of the evil aspect of suffering. We testify to our sense of this evil by our struggle against suffering—a struggle always undertaken in good conscience. The Bible witnesses that God's final triumph eliminates this evil:

[10] John 1.12–13. It should be added that Jesus is God's Son in another way: He is God, the only-begotten of the Father. Just how much of His dominion over the created world is due to His divine nature and how much can be traced to His perfect human nature, is hard to say. Yet the Apostles, who were only imperfect humans, show an amazing ability, through God's help, to transcend natural limitations.

And I saw the holy city, new Jerusalem, coming down out of heaven from God, prepared as a bride adorned for her husband; and I heard a great voice from the throne saying, "Behold, the dwelling of God is with men. He will dwell with them, and they shall be his people, and God himself will be with them; he will wipe away every tear from their eyes, and death shall be no more, neither shall there be mourning nor crying nor pain any more, for the former things have passed away." (Revelation 21.2–4)

By trying to show how all suffering is, after all, so very rational, we only succeed in showing its fittingness, its ultimate goodness. Sometimes it is better to say, "There is evil here, and evil is irrational. We cannot perfectly explain it without explaining it away. Our task is not to explain it all, but to overcome it."

The questions that finally decide the place of spiritual healing in the Church are not whether God ever sends sickness or whether the innocent ever suffer. The crucial questions are:

1. Does God ever will that we shall merely accept sickness in resignation? Is it ever God's will that regardless of conditions an individual is to remain sick? Or is it always God's will to work toward a victory over sickness?

2. Can spiritual therapy meet the conditions for the removal of sickness?

3. Is the healing of the body or mind apart from the restoration of a true spiritual relationship with God an adequate expression of the love of Christ?

The distinction has been made between God's will that mankind be restored to Him and made whole, and His will "under the circumstances" that the restoration and wholeness await the fulfillment of necessary conditions. Dr. Weatherhead calls the first God's "primary" will and the second His "secondary" will. Dr. Boggs suspects that the distinction lies in Weatherhead's mind, not God's. This may be so, but it still preserves an important truth. This truth is that God's love extends to all men in whatever condition, and it is His will that they repent, believe, and be forgiven and renewed. God wills the salvation of all men. Otherwise some poor reprobate would be going against God's will if perchance he were saved! Yet without penitence and faith, forgiveness is impossible. Therefore, "under the circumstances" of impenitence, it is God's will that the sinner be condemned. Exactly the same reasoning can be applied to healing, though often the circumstances are different from the prerequisites of salvation. The conditions for spiritual healing will be discussed in later chapters.

Although under particular circumstances God may not relieve the sick, is it ever His will unconditionally that humans suffer? If it were, then, and then alone, would we be justified in calling off the struggle against an illness. If it is not God's will unconditionally, we would always be obliged to seek the conditions for healing and do our utmost to meet them. Any normal Christian knows that God wills healing, and this is why he does not hesitate to call the doctor in case of need. Who would stop to pray for God's guidance, saying, "Lord, show me Thy will. If it be Thy will that John recover, I will call the doctor. If it be Thy will that he remain sick, I will not call the doctor. Thy will be done." This would be about as silly as praying, "Lord, if it be Thy will, forgive Mary her sins." Yet many people doubt whether it is God's will for them to apply spiritual principles to heal the sick.

By our unhesitating acceptance of medical help, we show in our actions that we believe that God is on the side of health. What is to prevent us from an equally unhesitating application of spiritual therapy?

If a man dies after medical care, we may say that it was God's will to take him. But it is not our business to help the decision by refusing to provide the medical care. Similarly, we may pray for someone who then dies. We might conclude in this case, too, that it was God's will to take him. But are we any more justified in refusing spiritual healing than we would have been in refusing medical healing? Are we not guilty of negligence in either case?

In advocating the practice of spiritual healing in the Church, we affirm these principles:

1. That action which accomplishes the eradication of sickness is always God's will.

2. That sickness can be removed and overcome through the spiritual therapy which Christ gives in His Church.

3. That the most perfect form of Christian healing involves the whole man: body, mind, and spirit.

When we get down to bedrock, the first and the third of these principles find relatively easy acceptance. The real stumblingblock is the second. The record of the Church in overcoming sickness through spiritual therapy has been so poor for so long that people have taken this poverty for granted as the normal state of things. They have had so little experience with spiritual healing that they simply do not expect it. Often the clergy, who are more familiar with the habits of the Church, have a less expectant attitude than the laity. More than once we have seen the flock leading the shepherd. On the other hand, a vast number of laymen still know next to nothing about spiritual healing and associate it purely with odd fly-by-night religion. Unless some responsible Church leaders help them to realize the possibilities, they are not likely to give the matter serious thought. The medical profession is also largely unaware of the healing potential of spiritual therapy. They have been so plagued with the bad results of the unbalanced teaching of Christian Science and many faith healers that they are usually inclined to shy away from spiritual healing in any form. The basic responsibility for this problem, however, lies with the leaders of the more orthodox Churches. They have been so wanting in a positive and constructive program of spiritual healing that effective therapy has usually been divided between the medical profession and the minority religious "fringe." It is the hope of this book to give guidance to Church leaders so that the Christian Church may be helped to return to its God-given commission to be a center of spiritual healing.

We can do this if we can demonstrate that spiritual healing works, and if we can help Church leaders to find out how to do it. By "leaders" I do not mean just clergy, but anyone who can help others to share in the blessings of Christ's healing ministry.

If healing is so firmly imbedded in the Gospel as our study of the Bible indicates, it should play some part in the ministry of every clergyman. It should be found in some form in every congregation. Some will give it more emphasis than others, some will have special public services for healing while others will not, some will work with centers for specialized therapy —God will lead each individual in the way that is best for him to serve. But spiritual healing has some place in each local Church. As long as people are sick as well as sinful, they need healing united with forgiveness. Their pastoral care should open the door to both.

George Dawson wrote the following about the practice of the early Church:

The bishops and presbyters took over the entire pastoral care of the sick, and ultimately established hospitals and infirmaries where serious cases might be nursed. The "charisma of healing" belonged to them not by reason of a special gift or endowment,[11] whether original or acquired, but because of their official position. References to this are to be found in many early writings and in Ordinals. The 17th Canon of Hippolytus [12] orders the following prayer to be used at the ordination of bishops and presbyters. "Grant him,

[11] He might more accurately have said "*personal* gift or endowment."
[12] His footnote here explains that this is a "*Church Order* based on the *Apostolic Tradition of Hippolytus.* It dates from the end of the fourth century. The *Apostolic Tradition* . . . dates from the third century . . ."

O Lord, a mild spirit, and power to remit sins, and grant him to loose all bonds of the iniquity of demons, and to heal all diseases, and quickly to beat down Satan under his feet". . . The *Apostolic Constitutions* [13] direct the bishop to pray that all candidates for priesthood may be "filled with gifts of healing." [14]

Can we be satisfied with less?

[13] Dawson's footnote here says the eighth book of the *Apostolical Constitutions,* from which this quote is drawn, "is called the *Clementine Liturgy* and claims to be the *ipsissima verba* of the Apostles which were written down by Clement. It probably emanated from Antioch in the fourth century."

[14] Dawson, *Healing: Pagan and Christian*, pp. 146–147.

CHAPTER VIII

How God Led Me into a Healing Ministry

"Bless Yahweh, O my soul;
and all that is within me,
*   bless his holy name!*
*   Bless Yahweh, O my soul,*
and forget not all his benefits,
*   who forgives all your iniquity,*
who heals all your diseases . . ."

Psalm 103.1–3

All the theory in the world is no substitute for down-to-earth experience. With all their rough edges and imperfections, with their errors and blunderings, living and concrete events still incarnate the truth. Truth is always expressed in a limited way in real life, but there is no other way. Both Christianity and science testify to this. The Christian faith is that God makes Himself known in history, in what has come to pass. Man's response is seen in his actions. The scientific view is that truth is derived from observation and experience. Idealistic philosophizing is not enough for the Christian or for the scientist. That is why both are known by their fruits.[1]

Not because of outstanding fruits, but as an example of actual experience, I would like to tell the story of my own healing

[1] cf. the words of Jesus about distinguishing true and false prophets: "You will know them by their fruits." (Matthew 7.20)

ministry. The reader may be encouraged by seeing that an ordinary pastor, endowed with no particular personal "gifts of healing," can conduct a healing ministry in an average parish. He may also see how the laymen can play their essential part. Spiritual healing is practical in a typical, normal Church. I hope my experience will show that. May I share it?

My father would have been glad if I had been a doctor. But I was never knowingly influenced by that thought, because he died when I was four. What did impress me, though, was his absorbing interest in his hobby, which was building radios. He was an automobile repairman, and the long hours of physical labor were not enough to satisfy the yearning for some greater challenge to his mind. So he fell in love with radio, working with it often far into the night.

My mother carried on with great courage and tenacity after his death, working as a secretary in a bank each weekday and doing her best to be both mother and father to me in the time she had at home. The years only begin to reveal to me how much her love and understanding, coupled at times with her proper red-headed discipline, have meant to me.

Somehow I caught my father's fascination with the world of science and technology. My heroes became men like Edison and Steinmetz, Koch and Pasteur. At the age of twelve I too was bitten by the radio bug, and I have never recovered. Inventions, research, scientific discoveries filled my dreams for the future.

I had been raised in the Church, but never vitally interested in it. I did give more than usual attention to Church when I was instructed and presented for Confirmation. I remember, however, that the thought that I was then "on my own" in regard to Church responsibilities gave me a sense of relief from parental pressure; now I could skip Sunday School easier. It was usually a bore. I did pray, especially in times of trouble, but I always thought of religion as just one of life's many activities. It had never occurred to me that God could be central in anyone's thinking. Four of my father's brothers were Lutheran pastors, and my mother's father had been an Episcopal priest, but *why* any normal person would want to go into the ministry was completely beyond my understanding.

Around fourteen and fifteen I went through my doubting, agnostic days. I came through this with a vague sort of mystical feeling that God really does exist. This gave me comfort. It also offered no particular challenge. The "god" that truly stirred my soul was Science; it had captured and kept the devotion of my heart.

At sixteen I went through the shattering experience of what we called a "nervous breakdown." It was characterized by extreme anxiety, all sorts of odd sensations, and a haunting notion that at any moment my heart was going to stop. Our physician assured us (without convincing me emotionally) that my heart was normal, and prescribed rest, quiet, and mild sedation. No psychiatric care was given, but a fairly recent conversation with a friend who is a psychiatrist revealed some possible underlying causes—principally the unhealed emotional wound of my father's death and the emotional strain of the responsibilities of coming into adulthood. The known immediate causes were overwork in studies and the instability that attends adolescence. A deep unknown cause was revealed as the illness progressed. This was an unfilled hunger for God.

This unfed yearning made itself felt both in emotional upheaval and in hard, cold logic. If a person's minutes on this earth are numbered, what does the love of science offer for his future? The whole aim and purpose of my life was uprooted in the face of death. It did not matter that the danger of death was not real. It was the *meaning* of death that bore in upon me in vivid blackness. The hopelessness, the futility of my world came to me in perfect clarity. I had been following a road that led nowhere, dropping off into the darkness of nothing. My little two-dimensional "scientific" philosophy had no place for this third dimension. I was peering into the abyss. The abyss was waiting to annihilate the whole world, to swallow it into the void of nothingness.

It would be easy to analyze such an experience psychologically, to sit as a disinterested philosopher. It would be easy to be "objective" about it—and in doing so completely miss the point. When a person is so conscious of his own being that he literally feels every heartbeat, he may be in an advantageous position to see clearly the implications of life and death. He may see these implications inwardly, for each individual human soul—for each *person*, that precious entity that completely eludes armchair objectivity.

I had discovered the abyss, and I had discovered my soul. I could look down below the bottom of the universe now. Why not try looking up?

The heaven above turned out to be as majestic and as life-giving as the abyss was black below. The sense of the love and the presence of God that finally came to me were overwhelming. It did not appear in a day or a week or a month, but at last I knew "the peace of God that passeth understanding." God was my healing. God was my new life. How truly St. Augustine said, "Thou hast made us for Thyself, and our heart is restless, until it rests in Thee."

Without ever having heard the term "spiritual healing," I had received it. I had passed from death to life.

What a blessing I had been missing! What a privilege it would be to share it with others, to help them find God, too! For the first time in my life I caught a vision of the work of the ministry and sought to know whether God wanted me to enter it.

I began in a new way to bring not only my actions and my words but even my thoughts under God's dominion. I found forgiveness and strength for every time of need. I thank God that my religion and my parental teaching had never been based on force, but on love and persuasion. It made it so much easier to follow Christ in love, to see His reasons for things, to be persuaded and led by Him. I was also greatly helped by the young woman who finally became my wife, and by her family. Their Christian love and devotion were exemplary.

I repeatedly sought the Lord's guidance for the decisions that lay ahead, and I believe that I have received it. Without going into the details, I took my undergraduate work in physics, served as a technical radar officer in the Navy, and then felt guided to go to seminary and into the ministry. I still loved science, but I had long since stopped worshipping it. My struggle against the "this-world" philosophies in college and beyond only served to temper my spiritual sword.

I loved theological school. I loved it dearly, except for one thing. While in our theology courses we learned the value and true significance of the miraculous, our Bible courses denied that anything miraculous was historical! Our school was suffering from theological double-vision. Its effect on me was to strengthen my sense of the supernatural and the miraculous. In this I had the encouragement of my bishop.

I saw the "pooh-poohing" of the miraculous as an attempt to domesticate the life of the Son of God. I traced the source of negative criticism of the Gospels to scholars whose intention had been to destroy orthodox Christianity.[2] Yet my New Testament professors were more outspoken in disagreeing with the writers of the Gospels than they were in disagreeing with the negative critics! I almost despaired. What could I do? I expressed myself the best I could and wrote some strong letters of protest, but with little effect.

God showed me a better way. Jesus said, "Do not resist one who is evil." (Matthew 5.39) St. Paul wrote, "Do not be overcome by evil, but overcome evil with good." (Romans 12.21) God provided the good that will overcome the evil. No need to argue about miracles. The better way is to demonstrate

[2] cf. the quote from Schweitzer in Chapter IV.

them. Better yet, teach others also to demonstrate them. The sickness of the Church is healed by the healing power of God, not by contention. This did not dawn on me in a day, but came through God's persistent leading during several years in the ministry.

I was graduated from seminary in 1949. Providentially, the first clergy conference I attended (in September) was led by Dr. Alfred Price and the theme of the conference was spiritual healing. Several of the priests of our diocese had been investigating the subject, and reported on the work of such people as Agnes Sanford and Albert Cliffe. I was fascinated and set about at once to read such things as Mrs. Sanford's book, *The Healing Light*.

My interest was spurred by my belief in the supernatural. But a more urgent circumstance was the fact that I was visiting seriously sick members of my Church. If spiritual therapy could help them, I must try to bring it to them. I can still remember driving to see a woman who was slowly dying of a blood cancer, and praying fervently as I went that I might be a channel of God's power to heal. It turned out that she had been reading Unity literature for a long time, but this was the first she had heard of healing in her own Church. I visited her regularly, praying with her and laying on hands. I gave her literature on healing, which she enjoyed. When I was ordained Priest I took her the Holy Communion. We became warm friends. She gradually weakened, then died. I feel sure that she benefited spiritually from these ministrations. Her family was most grateful. I still sense her prayers for my work, as she continues her life closer to our Lord.

In my two years in that first pastorate at Rochester, Pa., I visited the sick, prayed, laid on hands for healing, brought the Sacrament to the ill, and distributed reading material as the opportunity arose. The indications were that in all cases the patients and their families benefited spiritually. I cannot say there were striking miracles, though I did expect one older man to die before I next saw him, and found him instead on the mend. We never know just what factors are responsible in such a case, but we did not hesitate to thank God for his recuperation. I preached on spiritual healing several times. But the people were not yet prepared for healing services or prayer groups. Some time after I left, my successor did begin weekly healing services.

In November, 1950, the healing of Dr. B. occurred. This is the case reported in detail in Chapter II. It was the first miraculous healing I had seen first-hand, and I was thrilled. When I was in college I was young and foolish enough to try to prove the existence of God to an agnostic professor. As I gathered my evidence, I read accounts of the healings at Lourdes. I used to think, "If only some day I could visit Lourdes and see such a thing with my own eyes." Now here was Dr. B., before my eyes! I was reminded of the words of our Lord: "Blessed are your eyes, for they see, and your ears, for they hear. Truly, I say to you, many prophets and righteous men longed to see what you see, and did not see it, and to hear what you hear, and did not hear it." (Matthew 13.16–17) The passage refers to the works of Jesus—but was not this one of His works in our day?

I began to listen to Miss Kuhlman's radio program, and attended her services a number of times. Though there was much that I did not particularly care for, I was fascinated to see about two dozen people claiming to be healed during each service! I did not investigate any of these, but the healing of Dr. B. led me to believe that what I was witnessing included genuine cures.

On August 1, 1951 I began a work that was to continue for almost six years as Rector of St. Peter's Episcopal Church, Brentwood, a suburb of Pittsburgh. This was a medium-sized congregation in a growing community. Its people were typical of suburbia—a good proportion were young with small children. They were responsive and energetic. It was an active parish. It had its problems of finances, of becoming self-supporting, of building, of integrating newcomers into the congregation. Its like is to be found in many communities across our land.

One of my first sermons in that Church was on spiritual healing. So little was said at the door that I had a feeling that this one "went over like a lead balloon." But the following week one person, then another, came to me or called me up and said, "What is this about spiritual healing? We want to know more." I said, "Fine, let's get together and talk about it." So we did.

A group of about a half-dozen met with me in one of the ladies' homes. I told them as much as I could, and answered their questions. We arranged for further meetings, and each person brought a couple of names of the sick whom they knew, with a brief description of the illness. If anything was confidential, a first name or initial only was used. In this way we began our prayer list. We each promised to pray for everyone on the list day by day. Thus we became a prayer group as well as a study group.

Interest was shown in healing services, so we visited several as a group. One couple began to attend one of these in an Episcopal Church in another part of the city, in order to pray for their daughter. They said that they were going to go every week in Lent as a special discipline. Some of the other members of our group were beginning to ask why we didn't have healing services in our parish, and now that I knew at least two people who would attend regularly, I invited them to come to our parish and began weekly healing services there. These services continued for the remaining five-and-a-half years of my pastorate at St. Peter's. Attendance was not large, but never was a service announced without someone coming.

A desire to participate in the healing ministry of the Church grew among our people with great rapidity. Books and pamphlets circulated. The prayer list grew until a system had to be worked out to eliminate those who had not kept in touch with us, and to divide the names among members of the prayer group. It developed so that we would normally be praying for about 150 sick people at any one time.

All this time I was continuing my pastoral ministry to individuals who were sick or troubled. But the more the people realized that we were interested in healing, the more they came with both illnesses and problems. Many requests were for prayer or help or visits for friends or relatives. Probably the majority of those who came to the healing services were interceding for someone else.

It was our custom to have midweek evening services during Lent. We took advantage of this, and followed the regular Lenten Services with a short healing service for those who wished to remain. In this way we introduced the healing ministry to a wider cross-section of our people. My predecessor had held one or two healing services in this manner shortly before I came to St. Peter's and this had helped to "break the ice." Every so often a Sunday morning sermon would present healing (though not so frequently as to sound like one-note music).

As time went on, I began to sense a change in the whole balance of my ministry. I found myself spending less time in small talk and more time as a spiritual physician. When people are in need of substantial help and a pastor can lead them to God to find that help, this work of mercy must take priority over casual social contacts. It was not unusual for a serious illness or pastoral problem to take one or two hours. If definite improvement results, the time is worth it. Compared to many forms of medical and psychiatric treatment, it is not inefficient. Nor was it so time-consuming that the over-all program of the parish suffered. In a large Church it would probably be necessary, however, to have someone on the staff specializing in spiritual healing.

While describing some of the main events in the healing work at St. Peter's, we must not overlook some of the spiritual factors involved. I remember, for instance, beginning my ministry there with a strong sense of the *power* [3] promised by Christ to His Apostles. If ours is a ministry in the Apostolic Succession, if our Bishops carry on the pastoral work of the Apostles, and if our Priests represent the Bishop in the local congregation, then the power to heal is ours by the same promise that Christ gave to the Apostles. This thought inspired me with great confidence. All I had to do was to get *myself* out of the way and let the Lord's promised power come through.

Then I was challenged. If Miss Kuhlman can provide a service in which Dr. B. could be healed, why can't the same healing grace be found in our own parish Church? Some of our people saw this, too.

Certain particular experiences were unusually significant in the development of the healing gifts. They may have added to, or they may merely have brought out, the gift of healing that belongs to the Apostolic Ministry; which, I do not know. The first incident occurred early in my ministry at St. Peter's and involved a mother who had had two miscarriages and was having trouble in another pregnancy. I visited her regularly, taught her and her husband as much as possible about spiritual healing (though they had doubts about it), brought her Communion and laid on hands for healing. She carried the baby for the full term but he was born with a deformity in the intestinal tract which required an operation almost immediately.

My sympathy and personal interest were considerably involved by now. I remember fasting all one day and attending Miss Kuhlman's service that same day especially for the child's healing. I felt it was God's will for the baby to live, so I bent every effort in prayer and fasting in order to open the way for healing. Further complications developed in the child's condition. But one evening I prayed at the altar for the child

[3] Greek: δύναμις (*Dynamis*).

with a devout member of my congregation, and we each felt a strong assurance that he would be healed. I sensed also some faint vibrations across the muscles of my chest, which were similar to what Miss Kuhlman referred to as "the power of God." With a great sense of relief and uplifted with joy, I went home. Shortly afterward, strong uncontrollable vibrations swept through various parts of my body in intermittent waves. They seemed to center in my arms and legs—a sort of rapidly pulsating contracture. I had never experienced this before, but interpreted it as God's healing power. It increased even more my confidence that the baby was being healed. I decided to telephone the hospital to confirm the baby's condition.

However, as I approached the phone, this new power seized my muscles more and more. The closer I went, the more I was held in an iron grip, so that it was impossible for me to touch it. I decided that the Lord didn't want me to call, and went to bed. Though less severe, the vibrations continued to come from time to time, and included motions that I would have been unable to produce voluntarily. I remember, particularly, small areas at the lower front of my neck that would tremble intermittently, as though the surface of a pool were being disturbed by falling drops of water. I awoke in the night and then in the morning, and the vibrations were continuing, though gradually weakening in intensity and coming less frequently. I felt as though a sort of "break-through" to a higher level of healing power had occurred.

In the morning I called the hospital. What I learned was an almost unbelievable blow. The baby had died the night before —at the precise time that I had tried to phone the hospital. During the previous day it had developed a new complication which finally stopped its breathing. I do not really know what it was. I went at once to the hospital to see the parents. Their attitude was excellent. The mother was grateful for the hope she had had. She felt that otherwise the anxiety would have been much more difficult.

I was greatly relieved, since I was concerned that my assurance that the baby would recover might only have added to the parents' disappointment. My own conviction was that on the other side of death the child had truly been healed and had entered into a new and eternal life. From that time on my healing ministry seemed to be on a new and higher plane of effectiveness.

Another notable step was associated with a healing mission conducted in our area by the Rev. and Mrs. Edgar Sanford. I brought members of my wife's family to Agnes Sanford for special prayers for healing. She laid on hands privately with each individual, asking the patient to lie down. As he relaxed, she laid her hands over the affected part of the body. She asked me to participate with her. She said she wanted to "connect" me "with the same current" that flowed through her. She said I would be able to do the same things she was doing. One of these prayers was for my father-in-law's heart. His pulse had been around 120 for a dangerously long period. Mrs. Sanford put one of her hands behind his back and the other on top of his chest, on either side of his heart. She told me to put my hands on his shoulder, where he had been having some bursitis. As she quietly prayed, a slow pulsation developed all across his chest, so that I could feel it through his shoulder. After she stopped speaking, the pulsation continued for some time. She waited until it stopped before removing her hands. She told my father-in-law to rest the next couple of days because the restoration of the heart would drain his energy. He was actually kept quite busy the next two days and was unable to rest as she had said. But within three days his pulse was 78, lower than it had been for weeks. The heart was not completely or permanently healed. However, I discovered that whenever I prayed with him in the same manner, a similar reaction would invariably occur, and the condition of his heart would noticeably improve at once. I have done this many times.

Since this experience with Mrs. Sanford, I have frequently

used the same method. I recall the first day that I read *The Healing Light*, sitting on the shore of Lake Erie at that first clergy conference. Agnes Sanford said that anyone could be a channel for healing as she was. This was a challenge and a puzzle. It was not so simple as the words made it sound. Yet once I had participated with her, it seemed to be simplicity itself. I felt as though I had "caught" something. It is not just taught and learned; it is more like something contagious.

I used Mrs. Sanford's approach one day on a pastoral visit. I had expected to make a routine call on a woman in my parish. When I arrived I found that her husband was also at home, recuperating from a mild heart attack. We will call him Mr. Jones. He had had a heart condition for some time, but was able to continue at work until this attack occurred. After my visit with them, as I was preparing to leave, I felt impelled to pray for his healing. I asked Mr. Jones to lie down on the living-room couch. As his wife was a very devout person and had previously shown an active interest in spiritual healing, I suggested that she kneel beside me. We both placed our hands on his back and on his chest, in the region of his heart. As I prayed aloud, all three of us felt a slow pulsation where our hands touched him. He then noticed a painful sensation which moved from the region of his heart to the left side of his neck, where a small area of perspiration developed. I also felt heat in my body. We all sensed that something was happening. Within the next couple of days he visited his doctor, who was surprised to find no trace of heart trouble. The indications are that this is a permanent healing. Mr. Jones does not hesitate to tell other people about it. His wife quoted him as saying, "I'll never doubt again."

Several years passed when he was stricken with an excruciating gall bladder attack while on vacation. He was moved to a hospital near his home, where I visited him. Mrs. Jones and one of their two daughters were also present. I asked Mrs. Jones to join me in laying on hands over the painful region, and as I led in prayer, we thanked God that the healing was taking place. Mrs. Jones felt a motion as though something were shifting position inside her husband's body; I noticed a vibration. The whole family had been under a great strain for several days, and had been quite concerned about the outcome. The visit and prayer broke the strain and the eyes of all three were filled with tears. That evening Mrs. Jones phoned her other daughter. When told what had happened, the daughter was overcome with emotion. As soon as she was able, she asked, "When was Father Gross there?" Her mother told her. It developed that at that time the daughter was praying alone at home for her father, and suddenly sensed a light and a Presence and felt a strong assurance: "Don't worry. He will be all right."

Two days later, I went to the hospital again. Mrs. Jones told me about her telephone conversation. The pain had not left, so prayer was offered, with hands imposed as before.

An infection had caused a fever. When the temperature returned to normal, an operation was planned to remove the gall bladder. Arrangements were made for me to bring Holy Communion, but I was unable to go until late in the evening before the operation. Mr. Jones had been very fearful throughout the day. He had undergone several previous operations, including some dangerous complications, and he did not relish any more surgery.

After receiving Communion, followed once more by the Laying on of Hands, Mr. Jones relaxed and said, "Now I know it will be all right."

The gall bladder was removed, and Mr. Jones gradually regained his strength. On a subsequent visit, I was introduced to Mr. Jones' new hospital roommate, Mr. Smith, who was there due to a heart attack. The two men had known each other years before. Mr. Jones had told him about the healing of his heart, and wanted me to pray for his roommate in a similar way. As Mr. Jones prayed silently, I laid on hands. Both the

Jones family and Mr. Smith felt that his condition improved from that time.

Instance could be added to instance, including the healing of relatively small things such as warts or a smoking habit or overeating; or painful distress like bursitis and headaches; or physical illness such as tuberculosis or thyroid trouble or injury; or the emotional stress of psychoneurosis; or the spiritual sickness of unforgiven sin. In all these things and more, I have witnessed the power of Jesus Christ to heal today.

Only a small fraction of those who came seeking healing received that healing suddenly. A larger proportion were helped in a gradual process. The sickness of some was not visibly improved. But in all cases, all of us sensed that spiritual strength was found through our ministrations.

Those who were under medical care were encouraged to continue and to let the doctor be their guide as to changes in treatment or in their condition. There was usually no occasion for direct consultation with individual doctors, since we were not in any way modifying medical therapy. If God healed, it was God's business and the physician would soon enough find it out and deal with it in the way he knew best. There were, of course, exceptions to this rule: for instance, in psychiatric treatment active cooperation was important. I referred a number of cases to a doctor's care, though as a rule the sick were already being treated medically. Doctors and hospitals have invariably been most cooperative in allowing my spiritual ministrations. I have yet to hear any objection to what we have been doing from anyone involved in the medical care of the sick for whom we have prayed. Indeed the attitude is always one of appreciation of our interest.

We found that the effectiveness of the healing service depended on two particular factors: the devotions and careful preparation that I gave to the work, and the active support and especially the prayers of our laymen. When I tended to neglect the healing services, they tended to fall off in attendance and results. When I gave them more time and effort, they were strengthened.

The importance of the spiritual support of the laymen cannot be overemphasized. Without it a healing ministry is impossible. Several of our people finally became active in the Order of St. Luke. With this they took on themselves a definite responsibility for furthering Christ's healing ministry. One of them organized a telephone prayer chain made up of about fifty people. She divided the names of those to be prayed for among the members of the prayer chain, so that each name was prayed for each day. In case of emergency, a call to any member of the prayer chain activates the whole group, who immediately begin special intercessions. Everyone who was in any kind of close association with our congregation knew and appreciated our concern for the sick. Many were involved who had no other contact with our Church. After a while we began to receive prayer requests from people in distant parts of the country. All the sick were in our prayers day by day.[4] A number of our women also derived great satisfaction from volunteer work for hospitals. Several served as nurses' aides at our own St. Margaret's Hospital.

So it is that what started out as the story of how God led me into a healing ministry has developed into a bigger story that includes many faithful Christians whom God has also led. No one ever knows where the direction of the Holy Spirit will take him. No one can set limits to His power. We ask forgiveness for those times when we have failed Him; we praise God's Name for giving us a share in the spread of His Kingdom. May His Name be praised for ever more. Amen.

[4] Dr. Alfred Price has a well organized and extremely devoted prayer group supporting his work. They volunteer to pray in shifts twenty-four hours a day.

❦ CHAPTER IX ❧

Principles of Spiritual Healing

"Make love your aim, and earnestly desire the spiritual gifts . . ."
I Corinthians 14.1

The *Treasury of Exorcisms* published in Cologne in 1626 contained a remarkable collection of vile epithets to be used in casting out devils. It was reasoned that since Satan's basic sin was pride, enough insults to his pride would drive him out. Here is a sample:

Thou lustful and stupid one, . . . thou lean sow, famine-striken and most impure, . . . thou wrinkled beast, thou mangy beast, thou beast of all beasts the most beastly, . . . thou mad spirit, . . . thou bestial and foolish drunkard, . . . most greedy wolf, . . . most abominable whisperer, . . . thou sooty spirit from Tartarus! . . . I cast thee down, O Tartarean boor, into the infernal kitchen! . . . Loathsome cobbler, . . . dingy collier, . . . filthy sow, . . . perfidious boar, . . . envious crocidile, . . . malodorous drudge, . . . wounded basilisk, . . . rust-coloured asp, . . . swollen toad, . . . entangled spider, . . . lousy swineherd, . . . lowest of the low, . . . cudgelled ass . . .[1]

Dr. White, who is quoted, goes on:

But, in addition to this attempt to disgust Satan's pride with blackguardism, there was another to scare him with tremendous

[1] *History of the Warfare of Science with Theology*, by Andrew Dickson White (Appleton, N. Y., 1900) Vol. II, p. 107. The *Treasury of Exorcisms* was not prohibited by the *Index* until 1709.

144

words. For this purpose, thunderous names, from Hebrew and Greek, were imported, such as Acharon, Eheye, Schemhamphora, Tetragrammaton, Homoousion, Athanatos, Ischiros, Æcodes, and the like.

Efforts were also made to drive him out with filthy and rank-smelling drugs; and among those which can be mentioned in a printed article, we may name asafoetida, sulphur, squills, etc., which were to be burned under his nose.

Whipping and torture were commonly applied to make the demon so uncomfortable that he would leave. We can imagine the effect of all this upon the mentally ill. If they survived the exorcisms and still did not recover, they were likely to be imprisoned under terrible conditions of neglect. At certain times and places they were in danger of losing their lives by being accused of witchcraft.

What a marvelous example of how not to do spiritual healing! Perhaps those who were eccentric in order to gain attention were discouraged, and perhaps some were jarred back to reality by this medieval "shock treatment," but the majority of seriously ill mental cases would only have retreated further into their misery.

The Church of the Middle Ages did not differ from the early Church in the fact that exorcism was used. Where it differed was in the *spirit* in which the exorcism was used.

Consider the simplicity of Jesus:

And immediately there was in their synagogue a man with an unclean spirit; and he cried out, "What have you to do with us, Jesus of Nazareth? Have you come to destroy us? I know who you are, the Holy One of God." But Jesus rebuked him, saying, "Be silent, and come out of him!" And the unclean spirit, convulsing him and crying with a loud voice, came out of him. And they were all amazed, so that they questioned among themselves, saying, "What is this? A new teaching! With authority he commands even the unclean spirits, and they obey him. (Mark 1.23–27)

There is not a breath of a hint in the Gospels that Jesus ever approached a possessed man with anything but kindness, gentleness, and love. Here was the love of God, and He touched these poor sufferers in the very depths of their being. By the Spirit of God He conquered the demons. (Matthew 12.28)

In this we see one of the most basic principles of spiritual healing. The key to this healing is not in externals or techniques, but in the condition of our hearts and souls. The visible world may be used to develop the proper spiritual attitudes, but it is these attitudes that are the main point.

I remember listening intently to Alfred Price the first time I heard him speak about healing. I was listening for the techniques, the art of it, the "things to do," and the technology, "the things to know about what to do." Perhaps that was because I had a technological education. I suspect, however, that all of us (and especially the men) are influenced by our culture to search for technique. We want to know how to manipulate the natural world so that we can conquer it.

Spiritual healing comes through an almost opposite process. The object is not complex technique, but something very simple—so simple that it is easily missed. It consists in this: *letting God use us.*

Some critics compare religion to magic. There are forms of religion which are magical. But magic is more the ancestor of scientific technology than it is of Christianity.[2] Both of them attempt to bring nature under man's control. Christianity attempts to bring humanity under God's control. This is a fundamental difference between scientific healing and spiritual healing. Our primary attention is not on manipulating the external world, but on surrendering ourselves to God. We are not looking for conquest; we are seeking to be conquered.

In the measure that God lovingly conquers us, we become

[2] Magic developed into science through the intermediate stage of alchemy. At least this is the historical mainstream of it. The influence of ancient Greek scientific beginnings was little felt until late in the age of alchemy.

His means for conquering sickness. In this way healing is not our act at all. It is God's act. Our business is to be a help and not a hindrance.

Medieval exorcism failed because it was an attempt at magic. By using the right words, the potent incantations, the painful acts of violence, the demon would be subjugated. The spiritual state of the exorcist was ignored.

Christ's exorcism succeeded because He was filled with the Holy Spirit and became the means of replacing the evil spirits in others with the Holy Spirit. He was under God's dominion; He reached out in love and faith so that the afflicted could also come under God's dominion.

Pinel was the great French pioneer of modern humane treatment of the menally ill. In this he furthered the progress of scientific enlightenment. But note: that is not all. He was motivated by love, and love is of God. It does not spring from science. It can move men to scientific endeavor, but love is not the offspring of science. Pinel was able to heal because he had allowed the Holy Spirit to arouse his compassion and because he became the means through which the response of love could be invoked in his patients. His work was truly God's work.

The dividing line between good modern psychotherapy and medieval practice is not only that medieval men believed in demons while moderns do not. It is also that modern therapists love the insane while the men of the Middle Ages usually did not. In this modern doctors and nurses are close to Jesus, Who believed in demons. They are far closer to Him in their healing work than were the Christians of the Middle Ages in their exorcisms.

A man whose life is given to God can be a means of healing in many different ways. It may be directly through faith and prayer. It may be through medical science, which now is transformed into a means of God's conquest of suffering. By "transformed" I mean that science without God can be used as a special form of magic, to bend the world to our proud ways;

but with God it becomes a tool in His hands to further His Kingdom. This is seen most clearly, for example, in medical missionary work.

It is also possible that a man may draw close to God and become a channel of healing even when he is mistaken in many of his ideas about God. God looks first at a man's heart, not his theology. And if Christians often fail to measure up to their theology, non-Christians also often exceed theirs!

Jesus gave no theological quizzes to those who came to Him to ask healing. When He said, "Your faith has made you whole," He was not speaking of a creed, but of an inner spiritual state. This is not to say that theology and creeds are unimportant, but it is to say that they merely symbolize and systematize religious experience, and that the door to healing lies in the experience itself.

Christian Scientists, spiritualists, and various sorts of faith healers all claim cases of healing through spiritual therapy. While many of these may be psychosomatic effects known to psychology, or the results of suggestion, or even due to unknown psychic influences, it is not necessary to assume that these categories explain everything. As a matter of fact, such descriptions are often nothing more than descriptions. The "psychosomatic principle," for instance, can be made so all-inclusive that it explains nothing at all, but is merely a technical term that says that the body and the mind somehow produce effects on one another—which is no news. However, what I am coming to is that God, Who searches the secrets of men's hearts, can still produce pure creative acts of healing in those whose intellectual formulations are confused.

Recently I heard a televised testimony of a Christian Scientist who said he was healed within a few days of severe injuries to his face and neck, caused by a clawing he had received from a lion when he got too close to the cage. I could not agree with his attitude in refusing medical care, and I knew I would utterly reject his theology, but he appeared to show the inner qualities

of faith, hope and love that could well have opened his spirit
to the healing power of the Holy Spirit. His own personal relationship to God could have done for him what his mistaken
conscious ideas could not. We should also note that it is not
necessary to agree with Christian Science as a whole to see
that many of its ideas and practices do have healing virtue.

Similarly, it is not necessary to believe that Harry Edwards
is not a channel of God's healing power just because he holds
the erroneous ideas of spiritualism. As we read his book *A
Guide to Spirit Healing,* for instance, we discover that his actions are very similar to those of some orthodox Christians, and
that much of his theory would receive general Christian acceptance. In Chapter 8, "The Healing Guides," he discusses
the trance state where "the healer is surrendered to a spirit
guide," and compares it with "the use of the gift of healing in
a natural manner." Though he accepts the validity of the
former, it is interesting to see that he has discarded it in his
own work and that his closest associates in the work have never
used it. The over-all impression from reading the book is that
he is actually healing without spiritualistic aid from the departed, but that his idea that he does have their help is not
preventing the exercise of his healing gift. As a matter of fact,
it may give him confidence which he would otherwise lack,
and this confidence may increase his effectiveness.

Healing done in the name of Jesus Christ has a spiritual
power that other types of religious healing lack. Christian
Science may seem to be Christ-centered, since it uses the words
"Christ Jesus," but even a glance at their Christmas hymns
reveals that they do not really mean that Christ has come in
the flesh [3] but merely that Jesus expressed a "Christ-principle."
Their "Christ" is no more than a "Divine Idea" that has nothing to do with first-century Christianity, but has some simi-
larities with ancient Docetic and Gnostic thought.

So far we have said that spiritual healing comes through the

[3] cf. I John 4.1–3.

proper inward state of the heart, whether or not the accompanying theology or outward expressions are entirely satisfactory. Now let us see what effect the objective expression of faith does have. Man is a wholeness that reaches beyond the heart to include the intellect, the body, and relations with God and with other people. Such things cannot be ignored.

The problem with those who engage in spiritual healing apart from the true Christian faith or outside the life of the Church is that their spiritual development is limited and partial. This is no doubt true of all of us. But error in faith or separation from the Church act as limiting barriers in themselves. And amid such limitations, confusions and self-contradictions develop. Spiritual healing becomes only partial healing and new factors that work against health enter in. Let us illustrate.

A woman had become seriously crippled with arthritis. She met some Christian Scientists who told her that her troubles did not exist, but were due to her wrong thinking. She became more and more interested and although she did not join the Christian Science Church, she read their literature, attended their church, and followed their discipline in most things. Her outlook on life became happier and more tranquil. Her arthritis finally disappeared, never to return. The inner change in her thinking had healed her when physical medicine could not.

All her children were trained as Christian Scientists. But many problems developed because of this faith. First, there was the withdrawal from reality. There was the pretense that pain and sickness did not exist. "You are God's perfect child" covered up both sin and suffering. A youngster could be severely injured and receive no comfort or sympathy—the injury did not exist. Then there was the hypocrisy that covered all selfishness; one simply acted as though nothing were wrong. Beneath the outward smile, self-centeredness was often nurtured without check. According to the theory, it wasn't there! The family could enjoy its wealth in undisturbed contentment because there were no suffering poor. Such things were just an error of "mortal mind."

In analyzing this case, we might say that the mother found relief for her arthritis by developing a new neurosis. Her spiritual problem was not solved; its symptoms were shifted to another area of life. Insofar as she had developed an inner peace, she was following Jesus' words, "Be not anxious . . . ," and insofar as she entered into a serious relationship with God, she had improved upon her previous half-hearted religion. As her emotions became more harmonious, her body was also restored to harmony. In these ways she was healed.

But the new religion also stultified her own spiritual growth, preventing her from coming nearer to Christ. Its neuroticism infected the next generation and who knows how many generations beyond that. It was fed by their continued religious training. It cut the family off from the benefits of medical aid. Worst of all, it made it impossible for most of the family to come to faith in Jesus Christ. With the partial cure came a worse sickness.

If only the orthodox Church to which she had once belonged had provided the loving concern and the spiritual therapy that Christ had commanded it to give, she might have been healed of her arthritis and found the answer to her spiritual needs, and those of her family as well. Was it necessary to abandon faith in Jesus as Saviour from sin and death in order to find Him as healer of the emotions and the body? Was it necessary to renounce God-given medicine in order to find God-given inner healing?

Another example of the adverse effects of Christian Science is the case of a young woman of a Christian Science family who cut her finger slightly while working in the garden. For several weeks after that she went into seclusion. When she returned to normal life, her thumb was gone. She had had a serious infection and had narrowly escaped dying. "It will come back," she said. "The whole hand was gone, and it grew back. The thumb will, too." All of this might have been prevented by a simple application of antiseptic—certainly by a doctor's care. Was it necessary for her to endanger her life and lose a thumb in order to keep God's healing love? Is healing to be found by denying it? [4]

In earlier chapters we have had frequent occasion to disagree with Wade Boggs' position in *Faith Healing and the Christian Faith*. The time has come now to commend him on many of his observations of the limitations of faith healers. They do often oversimplify and they do frequently make both theological and medical errors. When those errors are made, they harm the ministry of healing. That they can be a hindrance is seen in their effect on Dr. Boggs. If spiritual healing is to win wider acceptance, it must develop the most adequate theology possible.

The types of weakness that tend to afflict faith healers that work in isolation from the Church include the following: unbalanced presentation of the Gospel; egotism, fed by adulating admirers; discouragement of medical treatment or interference with it; insufficient instruction in the spiritual meaning of healing, leading to various problems related to spiritual immaturity, such as disillusionment if physical healing does not occur; aggravation of emotional disturbances due to a highly charged emotional "atmosphere"; hoaxes and spiritual quackery for the sake of money or attention; claims of healing unsupported by medical opinion or exaggerated by hysteria; and so on. Every time such evils occur they not only work against healing in the sick who are immediately involved, but tend to discredit spiritual healing in the eyes of others.

The conclusion from all this is that the fullness of spiritual healing can be found only where there is the fullness of Christian teaching and Church life. The Devil must be quite pleased that spiritual healing has been so largely associated with ques-

---

[4] cf. "Problem Patient: The Christian Scientist," by Lois Hoffman, *Medical Economics*, December, 1956.

tionable expressions of religion. The more the orthodox Christian Church develops the healing ministry, the less there will be any reason for unbalanced healing sects. The evil spirits of heresy and schism are cast out and kept out by the fullness of the life-giving Holy Spirit.

Now that we have considered some of the effects of theology and Church life on the ministry of healing, and now that we see more clearly that the inner emotions are not the *only* factors of importance in spiritual healing, we must now see how very important they really are.

The Bible continually draws our attention to the "heart." This is a man's true self, the center of his desires, the spring of his worship, the seat of both his sins and his godly obedience. It has been translated into modern terms as the unconscious mind. Since a man's motivation is both conscious and unconscious, his heart is not simply his unconscious, but it *mostly* is. Spiritual healing comes through the right condition of the heart. This means that healing comes when the attitude of the unconscious mind is favorable to it. As most of an iceberg lies hidden beneath the water, so the vastly greater part of our nature lies beneath the level of consciousness. Spiritual therapy depends on the cooperation of this gigantic unconscious, and its principles are largely shaped by the laws that govern the unconscious.

The unconscious mind reaches in several directions. It links together the conscious mind with the body and the spirit, and it either contains or touches a psychic function which is responsible for such things as telepathy. Figure 1 is a crude attempt to clarify how the unconscious mind and the other factors in human life link together.

This diagram makes a four-fold division in human nature:

1. The *spirit* (A), that which allows direct communication with the Holy Spirit of God. This is also responsible for man's creativity and free choice, and sets man apart as the one creature made "in God's image."

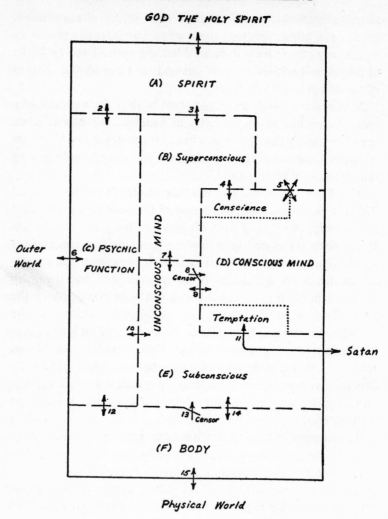

Physical World

2. The *mind* (B, D, and E), which is the concern of psychology. Its subdivisions will be discussed later.

3. A *psychic function* (C), which is studied in parapsychology. It is responsible for the so-called "psi" phenomena: telepathy, clairvoyance, precognition, post-

cognition, psychokinesis, etc. It is responsible for spiritualist phenomena, for certain healing effects, and may be the channel for spirit-possession.

4. The *body* (F). This is our contact with the physical world.

The size and shape of the various components in the diagram were chosen only for convenience and have no further meaning.

The mind is divided into two sections, the *unconscious* and the *conscious*. The *unconscious* is also divided, as follows:

1. The *superconscious,* which is a modification of Freud's "*Superego.*" It is an unconscious director of moral standards.

2. The *subconscious.* This is the psychological link between the *body* and the *conscious mind* for such things as sense-perception, memory, and exchange of messages and orders. It is the channel for psychological drives with a biological origin. It is a modification of Freud's "*Id.*"

The *unconscious* is largely irrational, and is generally taught by suggestion, not reason. It does have "reasons" of its own, which is to say that it follows certain laws. However, its impulses do not necessarily agree with the reasoning of the conscious mind; so it is that we say it is "irrational."

The *conscious mind* (D) is more rational, and is a modification of Freud's "*Ego.*" It includes two special subdivisions:

1. The *conscience,* which is the conscious provider of moral standards;

2. The area of *temptation,* which is the conscious pull toward sin.

The various numbered arrows show interaction between adjacent areas, as follows:

1. God's contact for spiritual purposes is through the *spirit.* This reaches into the depths of unconsciousness. The Holy Spirit's influence may often be seen in those who do not consciously acknowledge Him. On the

other hand, the outwardly pious have often chosen to cut off this contact. Of course, as Creator and Sustainer of His universe, God is also present in *every* aspect of the human personality.

2. The *spirit* and the *psychic-function* interact. Spiritual gifts may bring the *psychic-function* into operation, causing various kinds of extra-sensory knowledge or using the *psychic-function* as a channel for healing. (Of course, extra-sensory knowledge could also come directly from God.) Likewise, psychic influences may affect the spiritual life.

3. The *superconscious* is related to the *spirit* in a man's moral standards.

4. *Conscience* is influenced by the *superconscious* as well as by the reasoning of the *conscious mind*. This influence may be either good or evil. The *superconscious* may also be taught by the *conscience*.

5. *Conscience* is also influenced directly by the *spirit,* but it is not free of the influence of the irrational *superconscious.* The direct reaction between the *spirit* and the *conscious mind* indicates that reasoning, spiritual choices, etc., may take place without interference from the irrational *unconscious mind.*

6. The *psychic-function* may interact directly with any part of the outer world, physical or not, at any place or time.

7. The *superconscious* is related to the *subconscious.* Many of the influences of the *superconscious* on *conscience* have nothing to do with the *spirit,* but may be due to the memory of unfortunate circumstances which have produced irrational "guilt complexes."

8. The impulses arising from the *subsconscious* are often filtered through a *censor* controlled by the *conscious mind.* If they are objectionable, they may come to consciousness only in a disguised form.

9. This represents the continous interaction between the *subconscious* and the *conscious mind.*

10. The *psychic-function* is probably connected to consciousness through the *unconscious mind.* Frequently its messages are vague or in symbolic form.

11. *Temptation* comes through the *subconscious.* But since human nature as created by God is good, the ultimate source of *temptation* is outside, from Satan, an evil spiritual agent in rebellion against God. The *subconscious* cannot be held responsible for *temptation* even in sinful humanity, since it is no sin to be tempted, while it is a sin to tempt. If the tempter were the same individual as the tempted, he would be sinning and guiltless in the same action at the same time—an absurdity.

12. The *psychic-function* and the *body* may be directly interrelated, though perhaps the link to the *body* is always through the *unconscious mind.* In the latter case, this arrow should be omitted.

13. The *unconscious* can *censor* impulses coming in from the body. Though not shown, the *superconscious* also influences this censorship. An example is the refusal of a hypnotized subject to follow a suggestion to act against his moral code. Factors other than the *superconscious* may likewise operate this censor.

14. The *body* and the *subconscious* continually interact. In fact, many (or even all) things psychologically attributed to the *unconscious* may actually be pure biological functions. It is possible that the *psychic-function* actually mediates between the body and the mind. If so, our diagram should be modified.

15. Of course the *body* and the physical world affect each other.

This diagram is only a suggestion and might well be improved. It should not be pushed beyond its relatively simple significance. Human nature is actually a unity, and these sub-divisions are to help clarify our thinking, not to represent some hard and fast divisions separating us into parts! If at any point such a diagram becomes misleading, it should be ignored. It is merely a sort of parable or a hat-rack on which to hang our thought-hats.

We can see what a variety of channels are available for healing. Influences either for health or for sickness can flow in any direction symbolized by an arrow. The exceptions, of course, are that only health and holiness can be communicated between the Holy Spirit and man's spirit, and only evil can come from dealings with Satan. Spiritual healing turns out to be a complex activity which is tied in with many other influences. It is no wonder that individual case histories are difficult to interpret.

Using our diagram, we may, for example, trace some of the influences that work to heal the body. The numbers refer to the appropriate arrows. The diagram shows three ways in which the body may be influenced: by the physical world (15); by the unconscious mind (14); and by the psychic function (12). In addition to these, it is subject to direct action from God.[5] Healing can come physically by means of drugs, surgery, and other forms of medical care. It can come psychosomatically through the unconscious mind. The unconscious mind can be a middle link for bodily healing through any of the channels touching it (3, 4, 9, or 10). This means that the body may be healed through the proper cooperation of the spirit and the unconscious, the conscious and the unconscious mind, or the psychic function and the unconscious. Physical healing can also result from the influence of the psychic function. The psychic function could in turn mediate bodily healing by cooperating either with the spirit or with something from the

[5] By "direct action" I mean not mediated through the other parts of the person who is healed. I would also include in "direct action" an answer to the prayer of the person who is healed, as long as the bodily result is not channelled through the unconscious mind, the psychic function, or the physical world.

outer world. Finally, through prayer God could heal the body directly.

Similar distinctions can be made in the modes of healing for parts of human nature other than the body. The healing of the mind, for instance, is influenced by the spirit, the psychic function, the body, and the direct action of God. If we were to follow every possibility, we would see just what a complicated affair healing can be! Further complications arise when we realize that we do not know all the laws governing either the body or the mind, and we scarcely know anything about the psychic function.

In order not to become hopelessly confused, our attention must now be drawn to an understanding of the laws of the spirit. Yet this must be done without losing sight of the influence of the mind, the psychic function, and (indirectly) the body, on the working of the spirit. When our whole nature is cooperating in the greatest possible harmony, the opportunity for healing is the very best.

The unconscious mind is the great crossroads that links everything else together. That is why it is particularly important that spiritual laws hold sway in this vast domain. The Holy Spirit is often admitted into our spirits and His influence comes into our conscious minds, but too seldom is He allowed to penetrate far into our unconscious. The key to a holy and victorious life is the dominion of the Holy Spirit in the unconscious mind.

Medieval theology came close to this understanding in its idea of *virtue*. Virtue is expressed in a *habit*. When a habit is established, its pattern is followed *unconsciously,* as though it were merely "doing what comes naturally." Yet a habit does not come so "naturally," but by *repetition* and still more repetition.

The unconscious is modified by repetition of thought or action. It is also educated by *suggestion*. Generally speaking, it has no power of logic. It is moved by feelings that are "caught" from a surrounding emotional "atmosphere." Suggestion may come from outside, by way of the body's acts or observations, or it may come from the inside; for instance, from the conscious mind.

The wisdom of Catholic Christianity in using liturgy, ceremony, music, art, incense, beautiful architecture, and all the rest, is vindicated in its effect on the unconscious mind. These "externals" work through emotion, suggestion, and repetition to prepare the unconscious mind to be hospitable to the Holy Spirit. Much of Protestantism has been designed with no consciousness of the importance of the unconscious! Where Protestant practice is most effective in reaching the unconscious mind is in such things as congregational singing, the emotional impact of "revival" services, "altar calls," preaching that reaches the imagination and the emotions, and so on. But all this tends to be "toned down" in the more "respectable" forms of Protestantism. The perennial Protestant problem with stirring the unconscious is that the latter is irrational and Protestantism seldom has effective means of channelling its power. If, when the fire is lighted, there is no fireplace, the house will probably go up in smoke! The Catholic problem, on the other hand, is that the fireplace provided may be too small to contain the blaze; and when the firemen arrive to save the house they are likely to pour water in the fireplace too. The only answer seems to be in a wide fireplace.

An individual can consciously strive to bring the unconscious under the dominion of the Holy Spirit. But he must take care! He must not confuse enforced obedience with unforced love. The unconscious cannot be forced to obey. The Puritan approach to life tries to force the issue, but only succeeds in increasing the activity of the censor into the conscious mind (arrow 8) and aggravating the conflict between the superconscious and the subconscious. In other words, the conflict between moral standards and subconscious urges is intensified and at the same time the urges become more hidden from consciousness. This is what is called "*repression*." The conscious mind becomes caught between struggling emotions that it cannot understand, and emotional or mental illness can result.

True holiness, on the contrary, is approached when the unconscious changes its urges: when the superconscious becomes more God-like in its demands and when the subconscious begins to *want* to do God's will. Then the heart's motive is *love*, not forced conformity.

It was no mistake when the English word "holy" came down from the Anglo-Saxon word for "whole." It was no mistake when our word "heal" came from the same root. Holiness and health both come from a "whole" man—a man whose entire being is in harmony. That harmony can only come from God.

We will now consider the primary marks of holiness, which are also the principal doors to wholeness: faith, hope, and love.

Faith

> ". . . 'if you can do anything, have pity on us and help us.' And Jesus said to him, 'If you can! All things are possible to him who believes.' Immediately the father of the child cried out and said, 'I believe; help my unbelief!' "
>
> Mark 9.22b–24

The man who does not believe in miracles is the man who will see none. Faith is the doorway to God. It is the eyesight that reveals the vistas of the supernatural. It is the hand that reaches out to receive pardon from sin, the life-line that rescues from death. Faith brings the impossible to pass. Through faith the Word of God is heard and His new creation springs into being.

A leper came to Jesus. (Mark 1.40–45) He did not say, "Can you make me clean?" He said, "If you will, you can make me clean." Jesus did not hesitate or question. "Moved with pity, he stretched out his hand and touched him, and said to him, 'I will; be clean.' And immediately his leprosy left him . . ."

A centurion sent messengers to ask Jesus to heal his slave. (Luke 7.1–10) He did not say, "Can you do anything?" He said, "Lord, do not trouble yourself, for I am not worthy to have you come under my roof; therefore I did not presume to come to you. But say the word, and let my servant be healed. For I am a man set under authority, with soldiers under me:

and I say to one, 'Go,' and he goes; and to another 'Come,' and he comes; and to my slave, 'Do this,' and he does it." Jesus said, " 'I tell you, not even in Israel have I found such faith.' And when those who had been sent returned to the house, they found the slave well."

Again and again we hear His voice. "Rise and go your way; your faith has made you well." (Luke 17.19) "Daughter, your faith has made you well." (Mark 5.34) "Go your way; your faith has made you well." (Mark 10.52) "Go; be it done for you as you have believed." (Matthew 8.13) "All things are possible to him who believes." (Mark 9.23) "If you have faith as a grain of mustard seed, you could say to this sycamine tree, 'Be rooted up, and be planted in the sea,' and it would obey you." (Luke 17.6) "If you have faith as a grain of mustard seed, you will say to this mountain, 'Move hence to yonder place,' and it will move; and nothing will be impossible to you." (Matthew 17.20)

Faith is a magnet that draws its object to itself. William James has illustrated the power of faith by the example of a mountain-climber. The climber has come to the edge of a chasm which he must cross in order to save his life. With all the powers at his command, he can barely jump to the other side. If he does not believe he can make it, he will be fearful and hesitant. His muscles will not summon their full coordinated strength. He will fall, and thus prove his fear that he cannot succeed. On the other hand, if he believes without flinching that he can cross the chasm, all his powers will be summoned in perfect skill and strength, and he will land unhurt on the other side. By his faith he will prove his faith.

Doctors are well-acquainted with the effect of morale upon the sick. If the patient is discouraged and filled with negative thoughts, his faith in the power of the illness tends to reinforce the illness. "I can't. Nothing can be done. It is incurable. I won't live. How sick I am! How miserable I feel!" Thoughts such as these speak to the unconscious mind in the only language it understands: suggestion, repetition, imagination. It informs the body's cells and they share in the panic. If the cause is lost, why fight? Any army would react the same way, and so does the army of cells that makes up the body.

But the effect of faith can be just as strong—indeed, stronger. Is not God's power greater than that of sickness? Why not say, "I can. I will. God is healing. His loving power is reaching into every cell of my being, restoring, renewing. He made me. He is now re-creating me anew. Thank you, God, for bringing this to pass." By repetition, by suggestion, by exercise of the imagination, picturing health and strength as restored, the unconscious mind responds and the cells of the body respond. Even if at first you don't believe what you say, by working at it you come to believe it. Then faith proves itself by its results. "Your faith has made you well."

Jesus set no limits to the power released by faith. He knew well that most of us are not in danger of fanaticism, but of spiritual lethargy. Faith does have limits, but faith will never be found by concentrating first on all the reasons why it is dangerous. Some of the clergy, surprisingly, are guilty of this very thing—pulling out long lists of the pitfalls of spiritual healing long before they have taught anyone to do it. If they had filled their heads with all the dangers of falling when they were learning to walk, they would be spending their lives in wheelchairs! Even evil men prove the power of faith, as we see it help them carry out their evil schemes. Communist atheists conquer by faith in Communism. How much more should Christians seek faith!

In order to pray for healing, we must first of all believe that God *can* heal. What right have we to go around setting limits to God's power? Has His universe somehow gotten beyond Him? We are fond of imagining that God's experience is no bigger than ours. We take our limited experience, call it "the laws of nature," and decide that God must not transgress it! We dress it up a bit so it won't sound so crude, saying, "Of course, God *could* perform miracles. But He *doesn't*." How are we so *sure* He doesn't? Only because we have such faith in His limitations!

How much better to follow the example of Jesus and have faith in God's love and in His power to bring victory! The God of Israel is *Lord* of His creation. Who are we to decide that God can't heal physical diseases, or that He can't heal cancer, or that He finds certain illnesses to be "difficult"? Just because I may find difficulties in dealing with a certain ailment, I am not justified in passing my limitations on by planting the suggestion in someone else's unconscious that such-and-such cannot be healed. Perhaps that someone else is the very one that God can use to bring about the healing.

Speculation about Jesus' use of "psychosomatic healing" is a nice exercise. But Jesus never heard of the term. His insight and His method were not due to His study of psychology, but to His closeness to God, His love of men, and His inspired insight. "He knew all men and needed no one to bear witness of man; for he himself knew what was in man." (John 2.25)

Jesus did not say, "Believe that you can be healed of those illnesses that are influenced by your mind, and no more." He had faith enough to multiply loaves and fishes and to raise the dead to life! Enough of deciding that Jesus did not multiply loaves and fishes or raise the dead because we cannot understand how He did it! Why do we fail to understand? Do we not see that *God* did it? Will we not believe that God can create or annihilate matter at His will?

It has been quoted before, but one of the most striking illustrations of the power of God is written in *Everyman's Search*, by Rebecca Beard: [1]

Then we came to the great hurdle—the headless horseman—that frightening thing which still holds the majority of the people

---

[1] (Harper & Brothers, N. Y., 1950), pp. 13–15. Mrs. Beard, as E. Weaver Johnson, M.D. practiced medicine for twenty years.

of the world in the grip of fear—cancer. Our thought was—perhaps we can do everything through prayer but this, and yet, in our intuitive knowing we realized we dared not step out into the world of spiritual healing until we were absolutely sure that there was no barrier, and no hurdle that could not be overcome through God's healing power.

Because we had seen so many cancer sufferers we found this a tremendous hurdle to pass. We needed conviction, and we prayed, "Father, show us a condition that is unquestioned, about which no one can rationalize. We want to see something that is so evident in its outward manifestation that everyone can see it. We want to see something that is called incurable. We want to see an instantaneous healing, and we want to see it complete and made possible without any agency but prayer."

The answer to our prayer was the healing of our friend, Alice Newton of Leavenworth, Kansas. It was not many weeks after we had prayed that she came to us in Saint Louis. She had known me in Kansas City when I practiced there. This is what she said, "I come because I have faith in you, and because I know you have something beyond medicine. I am in great need. Tell me the truth." Her appearance when we first saw her shocked us. Her huge abdomen was larger than a woman at full term pregnancy. She had the dreaded cachexia. Her emaciated body was scarcely able to carry the great burden. Her question was, "Do you think that I can be healed with prayer and nothing else?" For just a moment I felt a sinking feeling. "This is it," I thought. "You have asked for it. You wanted it."

You see, I did believe with my conscious mind, but my subconscious said, "Help Thou mine unbelief." Then I heard myself saying, "Yes, Alice, I believe. But I want to see it. I need to see it." "All right," she replied, "I'll do it for you and for my husband. I will go home and map out a program and a schedule. I will follow it every day, and I have absolute faith now that our prayer will be answered, and the Lord will heal me." She went home, canceled all social obligations, did simple things about the house, rested, walked in the open air, read her Bible, sang hymns, and prayed.

Every day she repeated the same pattern. She wrote to us often and in none of her letters did she ever suggest failure. She confidently awaited the moment of her healing. You have no idea how this strengthened our faith. The unswerving faith of one person is a tremendous factor in building the certainty of God's power in one's life. "Nor knowest thou what argument thine own life to thy neighbor's creed hath lent."

Among Alice's friends was a wonderful doctor who visited her often, not as a doctor but as a friend. His medical knowledge made him insist that she permit him to tap her. It was curious, but the relationship of doctor and patient seemed to be reversed between them. It was she who would say to him, "Don't you worry about me, Doctor." She often consoled and encouraged him, but he would go on his way, sorry and unbelieving. A spiritual conviction and certainty such as hers is not easily gained. It is necessary to pay the price. Her constancy of purpose lasted over a period of two years. Finally, one night, with no special preparation, the miracle happened.

At the time, her husband, a guard at the Leavenworth prison, was working from midnight until early morning. Alice retired shortly after he left for work, and went to sleep as usual. As she slept she had a vision of the disciples asleep as Jesus came down the mountain side from His lone vigil of prayer. His face was full of sorrow as He looked at the sleeping men, then He glanced over and smiled at her. Immediately the scene changed. It was the day of the crucifixion. The cross was being lowered into the hole that had been dug for it, the Master's body already nailed upon it. Torn with the thought of how the jar would hurt Him, she cried out, "Oh my Jesus," putting up her hand to steady His body and ease the suffering. At that moment her hand dropped to her abdomen and she awoke. Turning on the light she saw that it was three o'clock. Only then she realized that her abdomen was perfectly flat. The huge accumulation was gone! Immediately she felt all around her for moisture, thinking surely something had passed, but the bed was dry. There was no pain. Her spirit rejoiced, and she knew something wonderful had happened. So she turned out the light and waited.

Her husband came home rather early that morning. He felt, somehow, that something had happened. His excitement was so great when he heard the news that, to relieve him, she asked him to go for her friend, the doctor, cautioning him not to tell. Alice was a woman with a marvelous sense of humor, so before the doctor came she slipped a pillow under the bed covers. She wanted to hear him scold. As he came in and stood at the foot of her bed, he shook a warning finger, saying, "Alice, I told you to let me tap you." She only smiled at first, then she said, "Yes, Doctor, and I told you that God was going to take care of me. See what He has done," and she pulled the pillow out and dropped it to the floor.

The doctor was speechless for a moment, then he rushed around the bed and knelt at her side. His questions came short and fast in his excitement. "What passed?" "What came away?" "Was there water?" "Was there blood?" "Did you perspire heavily?" "What was it?" To all she answered truthfully, "Nothing." Finally his questions ceased, for her answers continued to be "No, nothing passed—nothing came away." At last he said quietly, "No one but God could perform a miracle like that."

She stayed in bed for a week because they thought it wise. People passed through the house constantly to see her in the days that followed. At the end of the week she was weighed, and it was found that she had lost thirty-eight and a half pounds! That had disappeared overnight. And that was the answer to our prayer. That was a condition which no one could say had not existed. It could not be rationalized away. It was an instantaneous healing. No one could explain it. Where did thirty-eight and a half pounds of actual weight go in three hours? That was the miracle. I had wanted to see something which I could not explain. God had answered my prayer.

Later, Alice came to Saint Louis and asked if I wished to examine her. This I did, and found every organ fresh and virginal as though she had never been ill. She lives today. This happening has had a strange sequel. During the past twelve years the Leaven-

worth paper and the Kansas City Star have mentioned this remarkable recovery each January on the anniversary of Alice's healing! [2]

Once we believe that God *can* heal, we must go on to faith
that God *wills* healing. The leper said, "If you *will,* you can
make me clean." Can we imagine Jesus answering, "Sorry, but
it isn't God's will"? We have discussed God's will for healing
at some length in Chapter VII. It is our conviction that any
action which eradicates sickness is always God's will. It is
always God's will that we do all we can to overcome disease,
and this includes spiritual therapy. Jesus *never* refused a plea
for healing. And Jesus reveals God. If God does not heal, some
obstacle stands in His way, and we should seek to remove it.

Sometimes it is God's will that a loved one should be taken
into the fuller life beyond this world. Yet no one will imagine
that He takes any sickness along with that loved one. Some
healing is through the death of this perishable body. Life here
or life beyond is in God's hands, but we can always pray for
health and for release from suffering. Jesus did not hesitate to
pray that His own suffering would be taken away even though
it was the suffering of the cross. (Mark 14.36) Usually we
know that God's will is for health in this life. But if the healing
is to take place beyond, it is even greater health. We who have
already passed from death to life must learn not to dread our
promotion to be closer to our Lord!

God wills healing.

The father of the boy with the "dumb spirit" cried out to
Jesus, "I believe; help my unbelief!" (Mark 9.24) He should
be the patron saint of the faithful, because none of us are so
faithful that we cannot do with more belief. He should also be
the patron of the faithless, since no one is so lacking in faith
that he cannot make a beginning. How can we increase our
faith?

[2] For a discussion of this case and its implications in the physical world,
see Appendix C, "On the Creation and Annihilation of Matter."

If for some strange reason you wanted to catch a cold, you would go to someone who already had a cold. If you want to catch faith, go to someone who has lots of it. If you want faith for healing, find someone who has been healed through faith or someone through whom God heals. If you want faith in God, find Christians who have real faith. Faith is very infectious.

The great fountainhead of Christian faith is Jesus Christ. As you read of His work in the Gospels, take the time and trouble to visualize each scene. Use your imagination. Picture the colors, the voices, the smell of the sea, the touch of the cloth of coarse garments, the taste of fish or passover bread or wine. As you visualize with your senses, you become a part of the scene. Your unconscious mind travels with you into the Presence of the greatest source of faith in God the world can ever know. Read, reread, get the "feel" of it. If at first it seems strange and far away, live with it long enough so that you feel at home. Many people are helped with a modern English translation. The Revised Standard Version of the Bible is excellent. Less precise, but easiest to understand, is *The Gospels in Modern English,* translated by J. B. Phillips.[3] Use the help of a commentary or a Bible dictionary if you need it. If faith is worth anything, it is worth working to achieve!

Faith comes from the inside, too. With what faith you have, pray for more. It is God's gift. If you think you have no faith at all, act as though you did, and soon it will come. The important thing is to *act*. By doing, you demonstrate the faith you have, and from that sprout the tree begins to grow.

Your problem in prayer is not that God does not hear you. Your problem is that you do not hear God. His love is constant, His presence is unchanging. But we do not always accept His love nor are we always conscious of His presence.

---

[3] His translations of the rest of the New Testament are also very fine: *The Young Church in Action* (Acts); *Letters to Young Churches* (The Epistles); and *The Book of Revelation.*

Love involves links with one another, and it is His loving desire to accomplish His Kingdom with us and in us and through us, not bypassing any one of us. So it is that His Kingdom is partly stopped in its spread when we stop His entry into our hearts. When we open ourselves to Him, we become instruments for His Kingdom to go on spreading through us. Prayer is our coming into a loving, personal relationship with God. Prayer changes us. It does not change God's nature. But it does change God's action, since it is His will to accomplish through our prayer what He will not accomplish without it. That is His way of love. Prayer changes things because prayer is the expression of faith, hope, and love, and these qualities make a difference to God.[4]

Faith comes first, and is the gateway to all the rest. To be the most effective, faith must permeate our whole being. Our greatest difficulty is in getting our unconscious mind to accept faith in God. Repetitious prayers can be completely useless if they become meaningless words. They are then magical symbols as ineffective as a Buddhist prayer-wheel.[5] God doesn't have to be saturated with telegrams. But our unconscious *does* have to be saturated. That is why persistent prayer, as long as it is *meaningful* to us, *is* valuable. Importunity is unnecessary to get God's attention, but it may be absolutely essential in order to get the attention of our own unconscious!

And he said to them "Which of you who has a friend will go to him at midnight and say to him, 'Friend, lend me three loaves; for a friend of mine has arrived on a journey, and I have nothing to set before him'; and he will answer from within, 'Do not bother me; the door is now shut, and my children are with me in bed; I cannot get up and give you anything'? I tell you, though he will not get up and give him anything because he is his friend, yet because of his importunity he will rise and give him whatever he needs. And I tell you, Ask, and it will be given you; seek, and you

[4] cf. "Section III: Prayer," *Healing: Human and Divine*, pp. 131–182.
[5] cf. Matthew 6.7–8.

will find; knock, and it will be opened to you. For every one who asks receives, and he who seeks finds, and to him who knocks it will be opened. What father among you, if his son asks for a fish, will instead of a fish give him a serpent; or if he asks for an egg, will give him a scorpion? If you then, who are evil, know how to give good gifts to your children, how much more will the heavenly Father give the Holy Spirit to those who ask him?" (Luke 11.5–13)

A time often comes when prayer must end. When we have spoken with God with all that lies in us, we sense that now all is in His hands. God does not need to be pestered or persuaded, as though we had to convince Him to heal. "Thy will be done" can be a lazy man's excuse for doing nothing. It can be perverted into an expression of defeat and hopelessness, blaming God for every setback. But at the end of diligent prayer it has its place. Then its meaning is found from its context: "Thy Kingdom come, Thy will be done!" This is not resignation, but triumph. It is like the word "Amen"—"Let it be so—now it is happening, Thy reign is being established, Thy will is being accomplished." In this sense we stand back. We dare not hinder God's action. If we were to pray on, pleading in desperation, we would only prove our lack of faith, our inability to believe that God is fulfilling His promises.

Prayer in the Name of Jesus means not only that we seek to pattern ourselves after His love and obedience. It also means that we pray with *faith* like His. His words are, "Truly, I say to you, if you have faith and never doubt, . . . even if you say to this mountain, 'Be taken up and cast into the sea,' it will be done. And whatever you ask in prayer, you will receive, if you have faith." (Matthew 21.21–22) "Amen. Let it be so. Thy will be done!" We await God's act.

Sometimes we are too emotionally involved to pray effectively. It is often difficult to pray for one's self or for someone in the immediate family. Worries and anxieties crowd too closely in upon us. We often lack the perspective that would give us calm and composure. This is the time to turn to others for the support of their prayers, the kindness of their love, the expectancy of their hope, and the certainty of their faith. God intends that we bear one another's burdens—let God strengthen you through the help of your brothers and sisters in Christ.

If faith is mature, it will not only trust God for blessings, but continue to trust Him in disappointments. There are times when the obstacles to our prayers are too great for them to be answered in just the way we ask. Sometimes the reasons for our disappointments become clear in the course of time. Sometimes they remain obscure. In any case, we have the assurance of God's love, and His strength to bring a spiritual triumph out of every difficulty.

Prayer is not one-way conversation. Faith means careful listening for God's direction. It involves willingness to follow that direction, wherever it may lead. So often we complain that we cannot find faith when the truth is that we do not want to find it because of its consequences! In some ways, going to God for healing is like going to the dentist: you never can be sure where it is going to hurt before you get cured. We have to trust God far more than a dentist or even a surgeon. Sometimes He requires some severe spiritual surgery, but the results are worth it. In speaking of breaking off from the sin of adultery, for instance, Jesus says, "If your right eye causes you to sin, pluck it out and throw it away; it is better that you lose one of your members than that your whole body be thrown into hell. And if your right hand causes you to sin, cut it off and throw it away; it is better that you lose one of your members than that your whole body go into hell." (Matthew 5.29–30) Thus in rich and even shocking Oriental symbolism, Christ commands an end to sin, at whatever cost. This is the price of salvation. It is the consequence of faith. "He who does not take his cross and follow me is not worthy of me. He who finds his life will lose it, and he who loses his life for my sake will find it." (Matthew 10.38–39)

Christian faith does not come without a cross. Any substitute offer of cheap sentimentalism, as though Jesus did nothing but contemplate the world in a rosy glow, is not the path to wholeness, but a neurotic escape from reality. Faith in Christ is a conquering faith with a sword in the hand.[6]

If Christian faith leads to severe requirements, it is likewise the road to the most generous forgiveness. God's high standards and man's frailty can both be honestly acknowledged because through repentance and faith, Christ offers pardon. "For God so loved the world that he gave his only Son, that whoever believes in him should not perish but have eternal life. For God sent the Son into the world, not to condemn the world, but that the world might be saved through him. He who believes in him is not condemned . . ." (John 3.16–18)

How many psychological illnesses are due to unbearable guilt. And how many more normal lives are burdened with guilt. The problem of guilt is solved through faith. First of all, faith gives a perspective on guilt by relating it to an objective standard: God's will. By perceiving God's will, through faith, guilt separates itself into true and false guilt. False guilt is due to the *superconscious* or to a mistaken conscience wrongly accusing us. True guilt is seen as disobedience of God, and this is *sin*.

When faith transforms the problem of guilt into the problem of sin, faith also points the way to its solution. False guilt can be dealt with by bringing it to consciousness and by reorienting the superconscious to a healthy condition. It is a problem for psychological healing, and if it appears in serious enough "guilt complexes" it may require psychiatric treatment. Through the right kind of faith, however, spiritual therapy can cooperate with psychotherapy.

[6] cf. Matthew 10.34.

The guilt of sin, on the other hand, can only be relieved through forgiveness. If we have sinned against another person, it may be possible to find his forgiveness, and that will be a help. But it is not enough: first, because a sin against our neighbor is a sin against God, and also requires His forgiveness; secondly, because we cannot always receive forgiveness from another person. He may refuse it, or he may not be available, or the complications in seeking it may outweigh the benefits to be received. The only finally satisfactory source of forgiveness is our loving Lord God.

His only requirements: a willingness to change, to give ourselves anew to Him; and faith in our Saviour, Jesus Christ, Who died to take away our sins and rose to bring us to newness of life. Forgiveness is a free gift from Him. It cannot be bought or earned. It can be ours only through faith. As St. Paul wrote to the Christians at Rome:

What then shall we say about Abraham, our forefather according to the flesh? For if Abraham was justified by works, he has something to boast about, but not before God. For what does the scripture say? "Abraham believed God, and it was reckoned to him as righteousness." Now to one who works, his wages are not reckoned as a gift but as his due. And to one who does not work but trusts him who justifies the ungodly, his faith is reckoned as righteousness. So also David pronounces a blessing upon the man to whom God reckons righteousness apart from works:

> "Blessed are those whose iniquities
>   are forgiven, and whose sins are covered;
> blessed is the man against whom
>   the Lord will not reckon his sin."

Therefore, since we are justified by faith, we have peace with God through our Lord Jesus Christ. Through him we have obtained access to this grace in which we stand, and we rejoice in our hope of sharing the glory of God. (Romans 4.1–8; 5.1–2)

CHAPTER XI

Hope

"Now faith is the assurance of things hoped for, the conviction of things not seen."

Hebrews 11.1

I talked on the telephone one day to a mother in great distress. Her child had been born with Mongolism. The doctor's advice was to arrange to have the child sent to a State hospital for the mentally deficient. We began at once to pray for the child, and the mother, whom we will call Mrs. Smith, began to read *The Healing Light*. She wrote to Agnes Sanford, who told her to pray and lay on hands each day. Mr. Smith, who is a Roman Catholic, pinned a saint's medal on the child and prayed in his way

As hope lighted its warm blaze, Mrs. Smith began to smile and to talk to her child in a normal manner. For the first time the baby smiled back! At the beginning she was subject to respiratory infections, as is typical in these cases. But as she grew older, these diminished, then went away. She was slow in walking and in learning, but each year finds her less slow. More and more she looks more natural and acts more normally. She talks like a chatterbox. The doctor is surprised—and pleased, of course!

The parents plan to send her to a Roman Catholic school for retarded children. But there is no longer any thought of losing her to a hospital. Both Mr. and Mrs. Smith are wise,

educated and intelligent, and I have no doubt that they will
be able to help their little girl grow as normally as possible.
They can do it because they have hope.

Faith without hope is scarcely faith at all. Hope gives faith
its triumph. It is wonderful to have certain hope. Yet sometimes we are tempted to be presumptuous. Unless God gives us
most clear guidance, we must not put ourselves in the position
of a crystal-ball gazer, saying, "You will be healed at 2 P.M.
tomorrow." If two o'clock comes and there is no healing, hope
will be dampened. God cannot be pushed. Hope is not the absolute certainty of details; if it were, it would no longer be hope,
but sight.

On the other hand, there is no hope without genuine expectancy. Faith becomes effective when it is expectant. Hope
is like walking on top of a wall—you can fall off on either side.
One side is passive hopelessness. The other side is over-bold
fortune-telling. Expectancy without presumption—that is the
way to stay on the wall! Fortunately, this wall has a very wide
top.

Hope, like faith, is "caught." Gloominess suggests to the
unconscious mind, "Why fight? Why not give up? The cause
is lost." A cheerful manner, however, suggests triumph. "Keep
up the good work. However hard the battle, it will not be lost.
Christ conquers!" Our attitude speaks louder than our words.

Sometimes we hear a lot of negative thinking about "positive
thinking." Perhaps at times the advocates of positive thinking
have gone too far. But the modern Church as a whole could
scarcely be described as a hotbed of rabid positive thinkers!
We still need far more of it than most of us have. When the
critics of such people as Norman Vincent Peale begin to help
people with their real problems as much as he has, we will have
greater respect for their negative comments. It was Jesus, not
Dr. Peale, who first said, "If you have faith as a grain of mustard seed . . . nothing will be impossible to you." (Matthew
17.20)

Oh, for the triumphant attitude of the early Church! Will you have an example of positive thinking? Do you want to know what hope is? Imagine yourself bound in a slave labor camp with no chance of release. Imagine yourself where no America and no free world existed ever to challenge the power of tyranny. Imagine yourself in that helpless torment, and you could be a third-century Christian in the hands of pagan Rome. In the midst of that world of terror, read these words of a real third-century Christian, St. Cyprian:

A Christian body is not very greatly terrified at clubs, seeing all its hope is in the wood of the Cross. The servant of Christ acknowledges the sacrament of his salvation: redeemed by wood to life eternal, he is advanced by wood to the crown. But what wonder if, as golden and silver vessels, you have been committed to the mine that is the home of gold and silver, except that now the nature of the mines is changed, and the places which previously had been accustomed to yield gold and silver have begun to receive them? Moreover, they have put fetters on your feet, and have bound your blessed limbs, and the temples of God with disgraceful chains, as if the spirit also could be bound with the body, or your gold could be stained by the contact of iron. To men who are dedicated to God, and attesting their faith with religious courage, such things are ornaments, not chains; nor do they bind the feet of Christians for infamy, but glorify them for a crown. O feet blessedly bound, which are loosed, not by the smith but by the Lord! O feet blessedly bound, which are guided to paradise in the way of salvation! O feet bound for the present time in the world, that they may be always free with the Lord! O feet, lingering for a while among the fetters and crossbars, but to run quickly to Christ on a glorious road! Let cruelty, either envious to malignant, hold you here in bonds and chains as long as it will, from this earth and from these sufferings you shall speedily come to the kingdom of heaven. The body is not cherished in the mines with couch and cushions, but it is cherished with the refreshment and solace of Christ. The frame wearied with labours lies prostrate on the ground, but it is no penalty to lie down with Christ . . . You celebrate and offer a sacrifice to God equally precious and glorious, and that will greatly profit you for the retribution of heavenly rewards . . . You celebrate their sacrifice without intermission day and night, being made victims to God . . . Who would not bravely and unfalteringly receive a death precious in the sight of the Lord? . . . For that is His doing that we conquer, and that we attain by the subduing of the adversary to the palm of the greatest contest, the Lord declares and teaches in His Gospel. (Cyprian, Epistle lxxvi, 2–5)

Such is Christian hope.

Some of us do not find hope because we do not really want it. The words of Jesus to the man by the pool at Bethzatha (John 5.2–9) are to the point: "Do you want to be healed?" This man had been ill for thirty-eight years! We cannot be sure just how Jesus meant His question, but many who are sick have no hope of healing because they prefer their sickness. It may be that it gives them attention, relieves them of responsibility, or gives them a life with servants and a way of dominating other people's lives. Doctors can recognize such people, but can seldom cure them. Neither can God, until they are willing to give up their selfish hopelessness. If only they would see how much richer life could be with hope!

Other people have lost hope because they got tired of trying. They gave up too soon. Or they tried without God and have not yet seen that with God's help they can have new hope. Or else they were not led to expect much from God. Maybe their prayers were only for strength to endure when they should have also been for the power of God to heal. Perhaps they never found out how to pray with hope.

Once I was asked to pray for a child with a most uncomfortable skin condition. Her mother had the same trouble. I went to see them. Many Christian friends knew, and we had the strong backing of the prayers of a multitude. First I spent some time getting acquainted. I prayed with the youngster and laid on hands. Though no one in the family had suggested it, I then asked the girl if we shouldn't pray for her mother, too. We

did, and I laid my hands on her mother's head, asking for
God's healing. Tears came to the mother's eyes, and she began to tell me of her feelings of guilt about being responsible
for her child's illness as well as her own. They both had the
same weakness: a sensitivity to emotional stress that came out
in this itchy skin rash. The skin trouble made them more nervous, and that aggravated the skin—and so on, around and
around.

I could see that if the mother could regain her emotional
equilibrium, the atmosphere of the home would help the child
as well. Both could be helped simultaneously. We arranged for
another visit with the mother. I searched out every important
emotional conflict I could find, and sought for Christ's healing
answer to each one. She had been hospitalized for this condition a few years earlier, and from her treatment then and
from her continuing medical care, she realized very clearly
what her problem was. But I discovered that in her prayers
she had almost lost hope. She had been ill for so long, and
the strain had been so great, that she was no longer visualizing
herself as cured. I worked to restore hope, to renew the picture
of healing. She had confidence that through our prayers God
could help her, and from this beginning we were able to find
more hope. As I laid on hands again, we prayed for forgiveness, for release from tensions, and affirmed our faith that
God was healing. Within a few days there was a marked improvement in both mother and child. No new medical treatment was involved. The mother had renewed her hope.

Hope becomes established in the unconscious in various
ways. One is by drawing vivid pictures in the imagination.
There is scarcely any emotional impact in praying for the
ills of the whole world at once. But there is great emotional
content in picturing a miracle in some particular individual.
The imagination allows us almost to live through the scenes
it pictures. Some will find it easier to think this way and some
will find it more difficult. But those who can should use it.

Do not work against yourself by picturing the disease. That
suggests the wrong thing. Imagine in as clear detail as possible
the process of healing. Do not hesitate to think of organs, blood
vessels, muscles, nerves, bones, blood cells, or anything else
that you know would be involved in the healing. Picture them
working in perfect harmony, cooperating with one another as
health is restored. Imagine God's loving power filling them,
renewing and re-creating them. He has made them. He can
make them new once more. If you are praying for someone
and you are with them, and if it seems wise and comes
naturally, speak these thoughts aloud in a relaxed manner—
slowly, deliberately, confidently, in clear pictures, using suggestion to speak to the unconscious mind, and through it, the
body. Picture the person as well and strong again, able to
work and to be with his family once more, joyful and confi-
dent. Picture him close to God, strong in faith and love. Re-
dedicate yourself and lead him in rededication wholly to God.
Then thank God that He is bringing all this to pass. By giving thanks now you are affirming faith and hope. If you have
doubts about the outcome, express as much hope as you have,
not the doubts. Let hope grow on hope, not worries upon worries.

Another way hope is planted in the unconscious is through
action. We all know that a thought becomes clearly crystallized when we say it or write it. We can do mathematical
problems easier on paper than in our heads. This is because
we bring more of our whole make-up into action. Inner
thoughts send little abbreviated impulses through our nervous
system. For instance, as we think words, tiny signals go to the
muscles of our tongue, lips, mouth, and throat. We *almost*
speak out loud. Sometimes we catch ourselves doing it—talking to ourselves. There is nothing odd about it, because we
always talk to ourselves—only not quite out loud. If we think
of lifting a bucket of water, special electric impulses can be
measured in the nerves going to the muscles that would do the

lifting. They are abbreviations of the act of lifting. Even if we don't move a hair, our bodies are still involved in the thinking process. And the more fully we *act,* the clearer the thinking becomes. The unconscious mind and the body are reinforcing our conscious thoughts. Furthermore, as we consciously sense our actions—hearing the spoken words, or seeing the written words, and feeling the muscular action that makes the words, or seeing and feeling and hearing the bucket of water lifted—as we sense these actions, all the senses reinforce the thought that is acted out. Action establishes thought.

Therefore, if you wish to establish hope, act hopefully. Too often we preach pious generalities and suggest no path of action. We talk about *what* but do not say *how.* The ministry of healing is full of hows. God knows the infinite variety of them, and nothing I say should be interpreted as meaning this is the *only* way. All I mean to say is that these are some of the ways, some ways that have worked for us. Use what is helpful for you; don't use the rest.

Hope is expressed every time we lay on hands. You can keep a silent prayer within yourself, and no one will be the wiser if the person you pray for is not healed. The laying on of hands is different, as any outward act of faith is different. Now we are willing to "go out on a limb." We are willing, in a sense, to expose ourselves to the possibility of public failure. "What if nothing happens?" We lay on hands because we *expect* something to happen. We have hope. Our experience is that hope expressed in action is not disappointed. What happens may not always be just what we had hoped, but something always happens, and that something always carries God's blessing.

The same applies to healing services. "What if no one comes? What if no one comes up for the laying on of hands? What if nothing happens?" Never having had such an experience, I cannot say. We hoped. Someone always came. Someone always received the laying on of hands. Something always happened, some blessing was always received. Through hope, we proved the validity of hope. If you do not hope for healing, you are not ready to begin healing services.

Special services or appointments for spiritual healing provide a way for those who are praying to actively *do* something to express their faith. It is good to ask someone else to pray with you. It is better not to stop there, but to take the time and effort to add spiritual *action* to your prayers. By this action you strengthen hope. God does not honor laziness.

Hope is likewise affirmed every time we share the experiences of God's healing with one another. Many a person has found hope through hearing what God has done for someone else. They discover that it is real, after all!

Sharing experiences is often as helpful for the person who tells as it is for the one who is told. There is an old and true saying that the best way to learn is to teach. Similarly, a good way to develop faith and hope is to share them. The more you give the more you get. A member of our parish whom we will call Mrs. Johnson was visited one day by an elderly saleswoman who was struggling with obvious infirmities. Mrs. Johnson had been actively involved in spiritual healing, and had found help both physically and spiritually. One of her troubles of some long standing had been an enlarged thyroid, which was still visibly swollen. Out of concern for her visitor, she inquired about her health. One thing led to another, and she discovered that the older woman had already been interested in spiritual healing. So Mrs. Johnson began to tell without hesitation how she had been helped. When they finished talking she suddenly realized that the lump on her throat had almost disappeared. The swelling had gone down during their conversation. God honored her faithfulness and her love. Jesus said, "You are the light of the world. A city set on a hill cannot be hid. Nor do men light a lamp and put it under a bushel, but on a stand, and it gives light to all in the house. Let your light so shine before men, that they may see your

good works and give glory to your Father who is in heaven."
(Matthew 5.14–16)

Usually the greatest hope is to be found where there is the
greatest patience. I marvel as I see the patient love of a family
I know whose teen-age daughter has suffered mentally since
early childhood with deep emotional conflicts beyond the
doctors' understanding. Though her life has been one series of
doctors, hospitals, treatments, and special schooling, her family
never gives up hope. I bow my head in humility before a mother
who tenderly cares for her young spastic daughter who can
scarcely see or hear—day by day, week by week, year by year,
never losing hope, always a channel of God's blessings to
others. I am uplifted as I see hope rekindled in a young mother
whose son cannot properly assimilate his food, and whose
brain therefore has not been developing normally; I rejoice
when I see the strength her faith is giving to others. I am almost overwhelmed as I see the patient work in a hospital for
children with such afflictions as cerebral palsy and polio. One
new word or one new step may be the cause of great rejoicing.
See how the little blind girl claps her hands to the music!
Watch—Johnny caught the ball this time! Patience, and a
smile, and more patience, as month follows on month: if you
would learn hope, learn it from these people. Their lives cry out
that "suffering produces endurance, and endurance produces
character, and character produces hope, and hope does not
disappoint us, because God's love has been poured into our
hearts through the Holy Spirit which has been given to us."
(Romans 5.3–5)

✑ CHAPTER XII ❧

Love

So faith, hope, love abide, these three; but the greatest of these is love.
Corinthians 13.13

No one can foresee the marvels that pour forth from the love of God in human life. I know a young woman who specializes in therapy for cerebral palsied children. We shall call her Miss White. She is a vital, glowing person who throws herself into her work. She has a great love for these little ones.

Perhaps no child has been more on her heart than a little girl we shall call Susie. She is the child I told you about in my first chapter; the child whose mother came to Bishop Pardue for help; the child who has been so wonderfully used to bring healing to others. Because Susie's mother, Pat, is a part of this effort of love, Miss White and Pat have become close friends.

On Saturday, September 22, 1956, Miss White was skeet shooting with a group of friends when an accident occurred. Apparently she had a defective shell, for as the load went out of the gun, the back of the shell struck her face, embedding small particles of brass in her cheek and eye. The cornea was injured, and the eye was, of couse, painfully irritated. She was taken immediately to an eye specialist who removed the particles of dust from her eye, except for the cornea. He gave her a sedative to ease the pain, and put some medication on

185

her face. "My whole upper cheek was covered with little cuts —they actually looked like pock marks—as if I had had chicken pox." She was sent home and told to stay in bed for the rest of that day and the next. She did this. But Monday, two days later, in spite of the pain, she went to work.

The administrator at the hospital where Miss White is a therapist, felt when she had seen her that they should double-check with another eye specialist. They called an office in Pittsburgh, said it was an emergency, and had her go right in. In Miss White's words, "He examined my eye very thoroughly and gave the same diagnosis. And the same prognosis. He said that the powdered brass was embedded in the cornea, and he said, unfortunately, in the center, so that I would have impaired vision, and since they couldn't remove it, it was permanent damage, so that I would always have impaired vision."

This was said, not only to Miss White, but to Pat, who had accompanied her to the doctor's office. They were told that in time she would adjust to the condition but that there was nothing anyone could do about it.

"The damage was to the right eye and the type of vision I had was something like double vision. I saw an object and then the shadow of itself behind it. Like a ghost in television— that's the way everything appeared to me, so that there was con-fusion, and particularly in reading. It was annoying in every-thing else, but in reading it was impossible."

On Tuesday Miss White went to the University of Pitts-burgh where she was just starting to take classes and also teaching classes at night. When she went into her office on this first day of the semester, the assistant head of the department handed her a sheet with the names of the instructors in one column and the classes they were to teach in an opposite column. Miss White found her name, but she could not follow it over to the other column to see what her classes were. She took a sheet of paper and tried to line it up, but it was impossible for her to read her classrooms. "That's when I really felt it the heaviest," she said. She handed the paper back and asked to have it read to her. "It was sickening, horrible." Nevertheless, she went ahead as planned. At 4:30 that day she went to the first course where she was a student. When the assignment sheets were passed out, Miss White was unable to read hers. Nor could she read the print in her textbook. "I saw that I couldn't possibly take classes."

Next she went to the first class she was to teach. Her custom was to ask the students to write their name, address, and status in school on a piece of paper that first day. Then she would read them through, making sure she had the names pronounced correctly. This day, after she had collected the papers, she tried to carry out the reading of their names, but was unable. "I just laid it aside. It showed me that I couldn't study, neither could I teach because of the damage." After class she got into her car and as she drove along the boulevard, "it just struck me suddenly: I can't have impaired vision because I can't do my work. I just said out loud, 'Oh God, I can't do my work! Do something about it if You want me to work for You. I've promised that I would, now how can I? I can't do it, I simply can't do it with this impaired vision.' It wasn't a thing of, 'Please God, will You?' It was, 'It's simply got to be. I just simply can't do it.' It was different from anything I've ever experienced in my life. I felt it so firmly that I said out loud, 'God, I can't work with this kind of vision.' "

That night when Miss White got home she called another friend and told her how she felt about it. This friend belonged to a prayer group which met the following morning. Still another prayer group headed by a former pupil of Miss White's met in West Newton, Pa., on Wednesday morning at 10 o'clock and was in prayer for Miss White's eye at that time.

On Wednesday morning Miss White was in her office at the hospital with Susie and Pat. She picked up a textbook and read aloud from it. In Pat's words, "She stumbled through very badly, missing a lot of words and getting the wrong words in some places. It was obvious that she couldn't possibly study."

Miss White told Pat of her strong feelings as she drove along the boulevard the night before. Then she said, "I want to pray and we'll have a silent prayer and ask God to give me my vision." She told Pat, too, that "the power of love was there; the love that we have will do it."

The two women were sitting on low children's chairs beside a cot on which Susie was lying. Miss White took Susie's hand and held it. Then she prayed the same prayer she had prayed in the car. "God, I can't work with this vision. I have given my life to Your service and I just can't work with impaired vision. Give me back my vision."

Then Pat prayed. Pat had her hand over Miss White's right eye, but she felt no sensation, although she could feel Miss White begin to shake. "I started an uncontrollable shaking. I was holding Susie's hand, and I was shaking so hard, all over, that I had the feeling of wanting to hold on to something solid. This is the only feeling I had except that I had this feeling of absolute surety."

When Pat had finished praying, Miss White put a record on the player for Susie, turned to put the headphones on the child and placed the needle on the record. Pat spoke to her and as she turned to look at Pat, suddenly she could see clearly. "I just stared at her. She said, 'What do you see?' And I threw my arms around her and started to cry. 'Pat, I see you all right!' It was so sudden we just said, 'Amen'." Miss White took her textbook and was able to read it perfectly, no matter what distance she held it from her eyes. Moreover, the marks on her face from the brass were completely healed from that time on, to the amazement of her colleagues at the hospital. There are no scars. Her eyes are better than they have ever been, and she no longer wears glasses at all for any purpose.[1]

[1] The doctors did not feel that anything unusual had happened. See Chapter XIII for a discussion of this.

One thing was disturbing to Miss White and Pat. They found it difficult to believe that there was no thrilling sensation, that except for Miss White's shaking, there was nothing different or out of the ordinary. One moment her vision was impaired. The next, it was perfect. Miss White talked this over with her father who is a minister. He said, "This is what I love about God's way of working; the beautiful, quiet dignity of it."

He reminded his daughter that Pat often did favors for her and that when she did, Miss White simply accepted with thanks. Yet when God had done this, she had reacted with excitement and almost disbelief.

Miss White agrees with Pat, who said, "I think that the prayers of the prayer group created a proper climate, and then the power was concentrated at a particular moment and the healing was brought about at that time."

A minister friend commented: "It couldn't have happened any other way, because the situation was right. You and Pat and Susie have worked together, and had a prayerful life with Susie all of the time, and this is God's way of showing you that He has been hearing all this time. It had to happen with the three of you."

"Remember," Miss White told me, "I started out saying I have this feeling that love is going to heal my eye . . . It was presented to me this way . . . In that office we work with love. We talk love and we feel it. We know we have this beautiful love of God in us with Susie. We look at Susie and we share this very beautiful love together with her . . . I know no greater love than I have with Pat and Susie—it seems to me the epitome of love. And that's why I felt surely that the power of love could heal my eye."

In such ways the healing love of God is shared. God is love (I John 4.8) so if we want to come to Him, we must come with an attitude of love.

Sad to say, "love" is a confusing word in the English language. Its most common use is in popular songs that praise the kind of love "you fall in." Romantic love has its place, to be sure, but it is quite different from the special kind of love that comes from God.

Even some theories of psychology imagine that all love has a sexual root. Here we must choose between a materialistic view of human nature that teaches that the idea of God is spun out of our biological urges; or the spiritual view that sees human nature, including body, emotions, mind and spirit, as created by Almighty God. If, as we believe, sex is created by God, and not vice versa, then sexual love is the result of God's love. To imagine that either love for God or the sense of God's love for us derives purely from sex drives is to put the cart before the horse and to uproot any real faith in God.

God-like love is so distinctive that the Greek New Testament has a special word for it.[2] This was translated in the King James Version of the Bible as "charity," a word easily distinguished from "love." Unfortunately, "charity" has taken on another meaning in modern English: it now usually refers to external *actions* which should be (but might not be) motivated by God-like love. Yet Webster's first definition of "charity" is exactly on the track: "Christian love; specif.; a *Now Rare*. Divine love for man. b. Act of loving all men as brothers because they are sons of God."

The first Letter of John sums it up this way:

Beloved, let us love one another; for love is of God, and he who loves is born of God and knows God. He who does not love does not know God; for God is love. In this the love of God was made manifest among us, that God sent his only Son into the world, so that we might live through him. In this is love, not that we loved God but that he loved us and sent his Son to be the expiation for our sins. Beloved, if God so loved us, we also ought to love one another. No man has ever seen God; if we love one another, God abides in us and his love is perfected in us. (I John 4.7–12)

[2] ἀγάπη.

This is the kind of love that heals the whole man: body, mind, and spirit. Other types of love also heal, but they are limited in their effects.

Note that this love is a gift which comes from God as its source:

"We love, because he first loved us." (1 John 4:19)

And in the words of Christ:

This is my commandment, that you love one another as I have loved you. Greater love has no man than this, that a man lay down his life for his friends. You are my friends if you do what I command you . . . You did not choose me, but I chose you and appointed you that you should go and bear fruit and that your fruit should abide; so that whatever you ask the Father in my name, he may give it to you. This I command you, to love one another. (John 15.12–14, 16–17)

The way to obtain this gift is to seek it prayerfully, in faith and penitence of heart. But too many of us lock the door to God's love by cherishing hatreds and resentments.

A young woman once discussed some financial problems with me. I suggested that God would provide a way to meet the family bills if she would ask Him in real faith. "Of course," I said, "there are conditions. We have to be willing to do what He wants us to do."

A few days later, she told me that she had been thinking over what I had said, and she was not at all sure that she was fulfilling the conditions. "Every time I come to the place in the Lord's Prayer where it says, 'Forgive us our trespasses as we forgive those who trespass against us,' I get stuck. I can't get along with my brother." They each had an apartment in the same house, so they were unable to avoid one another, but they had been bitter against each other for a long, long time.

I told her about a "Ten-Day Plan" that has been prescribed by Dr. Alfred Price. "It's not a cure-all, but it has helped a lot of people. Why don't you try it?"

The plan works like this: take the person who aggravates you the most—whoever it is that you just can't stand—that really obnoxious person. If you can solve this biggest problem, the smaller ones will fall into place. For this young woman, the person would be her brother. The object is to pray for that person—that God will truly bless him. If he is a business competitor, ask God to give him a good year. If you work with him, ask God to make him a truly fine, wonderful, happy person. Don't concentrate on your own attitude; concentrate on him (or her), and seek God's richest gifts for him.

Ah, but there's a catch! You have to do this for ten days in a row, and you can't count day number one until you *really mean* it! You must be absolutely sure in your heart that you mean it before you begin counting. Then, if you should miss a day, or not mean it one day, you must begin counting all over again. You don't quit until you have prayed this way ten days in a row. Sometimes it may take three weeks to get to day number one. But that's part of the program.

The young lady tried it. She had only counted a few days when she came to me in jubilation. "Do you know what happened? My brother came down and sat in my living room and talked like he hasn't in months. I feel so much better about it—but I'm not the only one who has changed—so has he!"

At the end of the ten days, she said, "This is wonderful! I'm afraid to stop!" So she went on praying.

Not long after that, their father died. They were able to go through that difficult experience reconciled, with their days of bitterness behind them.

A number of other people have told me of similar good results from the "Ten-Day Plan." Definite prayer-projects are most worthwhile. The Catholic Novenas are another example of a sustained effort in prayer. Such things are much more effective than casual, half-hearted praying.

Whatever the approach, however, it is essential that we rid ourselves of the absurd burdens of resentment. They harm us more than they hurt our enemies. Unwillingness to forgive cuts us off from having our own sins forgiven by God. How can His love fill us as long as we refuse to express His love? If water is to stay fresh, it must run; if it is kept in, it becomes stagnant. Similarly, God's loving and forgiving grace must flow *through* us and be shared with others, or we become spiritually stagnant. If we would *keep* God's love, we must *give it away*.

As Jesus said, "For if you forgive men their trespasses, your heavenly Father also will forgive you; but if you do not forgive men their trespasses, neither will your Father forgive your trespasses." (Matthew 6.14–15)

The path to healing is made straight when we are willing to share God's love with others. Sometimes, however, we appear more generous with others than with ourselves. Some of us seem willing enough to forgive others and help them in their troubles, but we remain rigidly moralistic in our own lives. We accuse ourselves unmercifully, unwilling to tolerate human frailty and failure, stony-hearted and unforgiving of our own sins. The more we thus turn inward against ourselves, the more we prepare the conditions for sickness. Dr. Gotthard Booth, who has specialized in Parkinson's disease, believes it has an origin in such conflicts.[3]

God's commandment is, "Thou shalt love thy neighbor as *thyself*." If we hate ourselves, how can this commandment have any meaning? If Christ lived and died for each one of us, offering forgiveness as a free gift through faith in Him, will we raise ourselves to be more severe judges than God? Repent—turn away from sin, including the sin of hateful self-condemnation! Believe—*accept* Christ's forgiveness, *receive* it; unlatch the door to it; take down the burden of it from your back, leave it at God's altar and do not reach out again to pick it up. If *He* has forgiven you, you are restored as God's child, and

[3] The whole picture of Parkinsonism includes many other factors, of course. Dr. Booth has written a particularly revealing article, "Basic Concepts of Psychosomatic Medicine," included in *Healing: Human and Divine*, Edited by Simon Doniger.

you must not hate God's child. Now you are free to be objective about your sins, to seek God's power to overcome sinful habits. You have admitted the truth that you are a sinner. But who is not a sinner? We *all* live only by the grace and mercy of God. When we really understand that and accept it, we can love ourselves because we share Christ's love for sinners. Jesus said, "Those who are well have no need of a physician, but those who are sick. Go and learn what this means, 'I desire mercy, and not sacrifice.' For I came not to call the righteous, but sinners." (Matthew 9.12–13) You are God's child, not because you are perfect, but because He loves you. Love yourself.

And when you learn to love yourself, loving your neighbor will be easier.

Some people have the odd notion that it is wrong to pray for one's self. But Jesus not only prayed for Himself,[4] but taught us the Lord's Prayer which is full of petitions for "us." Selfishness does not consist in concern with the self, but in putting our own selves *above* other people. The prayer for "us" keeps that balance of equality with others.

It is often more difficult to pray for one's self, but this is no excuse for not doing our best at it. If we ask for necessities, not self-indulgence; if we ask for health so that we may most effectively serve God and our brothers; if we ask for the Holy Spirit so that each day of our lives may be devoted to God, why should we not pray for ourselves wholeheartedly?

Self-denial is not self-hatred. It is, rather, bringing ourselves to be loving servants of God, so that the center of life is in God, not ourselves. In doing this, we do not blot our own lives out of existence, but bring them into the only kind of existence that is truly good for us. In Christ's words, "Whoever would save his life will lose it; and whoever loses his life for my sake and the gospel's will save it." (Mark 8.35)

Our love for God finds its expression in humility. "If any

4 cf. Mark 14.35–36.

one would be first, he must be last of all and servant of all."
(Mark 9.35) "Every one who exalts himself will be humbled,
but he who humbles himself will be exalted." (Luke 18.14)
"Whoever does not receive the kingdom of God like a child
shall not enter it." (Luke 18.17) Openness to God, willingness to learn, a desire to grow spiritually, the wish to serve
others—such things are the marks of Christian humility.

Love is patient and kind; love is not jealous or boastful; it is not
arrogant or rude. Love does not insist on its own way; it is not
irritable or resentful; it does not rejoice at wrong, but rejoices in
the right. Love bears all things, believes all things, hopes all things,
endures all things. (I Corinthians 13.4–7)

One Good Friday several years ago, my wife, Anne, decided
to fast completely until three o'clock in the afternoon, the time
Our Lord died. She offered the fast as a thanksgiving to God
for His sacrifice, adding, almost casually, that if He cared to,
He might use it for her father, who had not been in good health.

As the day went on, she developed a severe headache, centering in the right eye. Since she had never fasted before she
assumed this was from not eating, and because our two children
were small, she had to take Empirin in order to keep going.
The pills had no effect on the pain, and she finally had to lie
down, taking the children to bed with her. When I came home
from the three-hour Church service, she was emphatic: "I'll
never do that again!"

Around supper time, her father called on the phone. He had
not said anything to anyone in the family, but three weeks
earlier he had been told by the eye doctor that a cataract was
beginning on his eye. That Good Friday afternoon at about
4.30 he had again seen the optometrist. The examination produced a surprise: the doctor searched for an hour, but he could
find no trace of the cataract.

"Which eye was it?" my wife asked.

"The right eye."

Then she told him of her experience. And we all thanked God.

This is the close bond of love that links us to one another and to God. Why do we ever hesitate to come to Him for healing?

Every so often someone will say to me, "I know my husband is seriously ill, but I can't single him out in my prayers. There are so many others with the same disease, and I can't be selfish about it. I think it's better to pray for all of them, and pray and contribute toward research to cure this thing."

And I will say, "It's fine to pray for research and to give for it, and it's fine to remember all the sick in your prayers. But God has also given you a *special* responsibility for one person: your husband. What if you decided that because all the others who are sick like this are equally loved by God and by their families, you could not single him out for physical care? What if you decided to divide your energies to nursing all these sick people equally? You would accomplish nothing at all but to break yourself down and you would completely neglect your own husband. We hope that each of these other people has someone like you who cares about him personally and individually, so that each may receive the best possible physical treatment.

"The same is true of spiritual care. God has given you—and no one else—the spiritual responsibility that is yours. As his priest, I also have a special responsibility that no one else shares. Each member of the family has his or her own part to play, too—and so it is with the neighbors, or people in our congregation. Their particular part depends on how close their responsibility is.

"Love is like that—a chain of many individual interwoven links; it's not a hazy blur that tries to take in the whole world at once and ends up meaning almost nothing.

"God wants you to give as much personal care to your husband in your prayers as you do in providing doctors, nurses, and medicine. You show your love for him by spending hours at his side, by reading to him, changing his pillow, fixing his tray, and a hundred other things. You don't have time to do that for anyone else. Pray for others; but God wants you to concentrate your prayers on him."

The prayer of love is centered on its object: on God and on the person we bring to God for healing. Through our love we link the two together. When we try to link too many at once, we weaken the force of love, because love is not abstract or generalized, but particular and concrete. Jesus never said, "Thou shalt love all men." He said, "Thou shalt love thy neighbor" or "Love one another." This is the way healing actually comes.

God's love for us is likewise individual and specific. He was not content to love us with an eternal love spread everywhere. His love became incarnate—expressed in the flesh of a single human life, the life of Jesus of Nazareth. He lived at one time —almost two thousand years ago; in one place—Palestine. He died on one cross and rose from one grave.

The Christian Church is made up of those who are individually baptized, and who are each given the Holy Spirit so that each may play his own special melody in God's harmonious symphony. The Church was never intended to submerge the individual in a faceless mass, nor was it to produce primadonnas who selfishly ignore their brethren. God means it to be a loving fellowship of real persons. In such love lies healing.

At the heart of Christian life lies the Feast of love—the Holy Communion. Here we are nourished and united with the love and life of Christ Himself, and from this altar radiates the healing of men and nations. This Sacrament is also called the "Eucharist," which is from the Greek for "Thanksgiving." In this one word, true Christian love is summed together.

"Let us give thanks unto our Lord God." [5] The prayer of

[5] American Book of Common Prayer, 1928, p. 76.

love will offer thanks—for God's mercies now and in times past, for particular answers to prayer (and we do well to picture them individually in our imagination), and above all for the life and death and resurrection of Jesus Christ. And out of gratitude for Thy mercies, we continually "offer and present unto thee, O Lord, our selves, our souls and bodies, to be a reasonable, holy, and living sacrifice unto thee . . ." [6] This is the path of love, the path of healing.

[6] Ibid., p. 81.

CHAPTER XIII

Difficulties

Beloved, do not believe every spirit, but test the spirits to see whether they are of God; for many false prophets have gone out into the world."

I John 4.1

The practice of spiritual healing is not all sweetness and light. It has its hardships and mysteries. And in addition there are a host of imaginary problems. If we are enthusiasts for healing we are likely to overlook the real difficulties; if we are shy of the subject we are liable to be frightened out of proportion by the dangers. Actually the dangers are not so fearful that we dare not whisper them. Neither are they so important that we talk of nothing else.

The timidity of some of the clergy regarding spiritual healing is a wonder. To think that they are supposed to be in the same spiritual family as prophets and martyrs! The first words on such people's tongues paint dark and gloomy portraits of the pitfalls and goblins waiting to swallow up whoever ventures too far. Like superstitious sailors invited by Columbus, they would rather stay on dry land than try to discover anything new—they might fall off the edge of the world!

At the risk of scaring nervous souls still further, it is only just to point out first that there are perils in *not* practicing spiritual healing. Here are a few:

Some Dangers in Failing to Practice
the Ministry of Healing

1. The danger of disobeying God. Christ's commission to heal is discussed in Chapter VI and Chapter VII.

2. The danger of indifference to God. If we do not consider God "a very present help in trouble" (Psalm 46.1), do we not show our disbelief in the effectiveness of prayer? Are we not expressing the notion that it is useless to develop a personal relationship with God? Is this not the end of living, God-centered religion? Is it not the end of spiritual power? Jesus said:

I am the vine, you are the branches. He who abides in me, and I in him, he it is that bears much fruit, for apart from me you can do nothing. If a man does not abide in me, he is cast forth as a branch and withers; and the branches are gathered, thrown into the fire and burned. If you abide in me, and my words abide in you, ask whatever you will, and it shall be done for you. By this my Father is glorified, that you bear much fruit, and so prove to be my disciples. (John 5.5–8)

3. "The danger of a sick person and his relative thinking only of physical recovery, and neglecting the matter of spiritual well-being." This was originally cited as a danger in the practice of spiritual healing! [1] It is, as a matter of fact, exactly what would happen if spiritual therapy were *neglected*. It is too easy to assume that "medical" or "purely psychological or psychiatric" healing exists apart from the healing power of God, and that such healing is just as effective without prayer as with prayer. How much better it is to see the doctor as God's agent! It is too easy to act as though human knowledge and skill can accomplish healing while a closeness to God in prayer cannot. How much better it is to thank God for both the blessings of

[1] By Dr. Harry B. Taylor at the Fifth Spiritual Healing Seminar sponsored by the Laymen's Movement. See p. 124 of the Wainwright House report on that seminar.

medicine and the inner healing power of the Holy Spirit! By separating the healing of the body and mind from the healing of the spirit, we deny the unity of man's nature and suggest that he can be whole by the doctor's skill alone. How much better it is to realize that wholeness includes holiness!

4. The danger of imagining that God is limited by the laws of nature known to man. This is considered in Chapter V. Along with this is the danger of interpreting only in the spiritually sterile terms of "natural law" that which God intends as a personal Word spoken to us to bring us closer to Him.

5. The danger of denying the Christian faith. If we never expect God to perform miracles of healing, do we not testify to our general disbelief in miracles? [2] Do we not likewise disagree with the New Testament point of view that God confirmed the Gospel from the beginning with miraculous signs? And if we deny that He so confirmed the Gospel, do we not say that the early Christians were wrong in believing the Gospel because of the signs? Do we not also disagree with Jesus Himself, Who referred to the signs as God's testimony to His work? [3] From a first-century point of view, denial of the miracles is denial that the Christian faith is from God. How can we justify ourselves for believing a faith that started with people who believed it themselves only because of what we consider a false premise? If we neglect spiritual healing, does our neglect not ultimately bear witness to the falseness of Christianity?

6. The danger of hopelessness and resignation in the face of disease. While the fainthearted worry lest we become too hopeful, the New Testament considers hope a virtue. "Who

[2] We might, instead, say that "the age of miracles is past." But we have shown in Chapters VI and VII that this view cannot be supported. Historically, the idea that "the age of miracles is past" seems to have developed with the rise of Rationalism in the 18th century. It agrees with the Rationalist denial of miracles, but makes an exception in the case of the Sacred Scriptures—for fear of the consequences of carrying Rationalist logic out to the bitter end.

[3] cf. Chapter VI.

shall separate us from the love of Christ? Shall tribulation, or distress, or persecution, or famine, or nakedness, or peril, or sword? . . . No, in all these things we are more than conquerors through him who loved us." (Romans 8.35, 37) This is the Christian note of victory, and spiritual healing expresses it.

7. The danger of refusing Christian love. If we really love the sick, will we not desire their healing? Will we not do all in our power to renew their strength? How can we condemn medical neglect and condone spiritual neglect? Do we show love to the suffering by ignoring Jesus? He said, "Ask, and it will be given you; seek, and you will find; knock, and it will be opened to you." (Matthew 7.7) And, as St. James wrote, "You do not have because you do not ask. You ask and do not receive because you ask wrongly . . ." (James 4.2–3) When we love enough, we will seek healing and find it.

Take care, O timid brethren—the dangers of healing are small alongside the dangers of not healing. Take heart, too— many of the dangers of the healing ministry are imaginary dragons easily slain, while others are not impossible to conquer.

Disappointment

One of the common problems of those to whom spiritual healing is new is the worry that the promised results will not materialize, and that the people who came in faith will leave in disillusionment. The curious thing is that in actual practice this feared despair is a rarity indeed. It is much more theoretical than real.

A great deal depends, of course, on what you promise. I have seen advertisements by a traveling evangelist which claimed that everybody would be healed—apparently during each of his tent meetings. The same man later got in trouble with the law. Naturally such things lead to the disillusionment of those foolish enough to believe wild claims. However, we must strain our imagination a bit to picture promises like this being made by clergy of our "respectable" churches. They are more likely to expect nothing at all.

This is the real root of the difficulty: not that our people are likely to lose heart, but that we clergy do not have the courage to step out on our faith—to try it and see.

We need never fear if we inspire hope and confidence in God, but then learn to leave the specific results in God's hands. If we do what we can in prayer, the answer is God's responsibility. Note the *if*; the trouble with most of us is that we tend to make God responsible *before* we have done our part. Of course, it is not always easy to know how close we have come to doing our part. In practice, prayer for healing is a process of striving to bring ourselves more and more under God's rule, so that His Kingdom may come and His will be done more fully through us.

Whenever we do this, we may be sure that God's healing blessings will flow through us. And all concerned will be thankful for these blessings. We may compare this with medical treatment. In no case is absolutely perfect medical knowledge and skill applied to the sick; all doctors are limited human beings. Even the best of scientific knowledge is limited knowledge, and even the greatest medical practitioners are not utterly flawless in their work. Nor do they have magical powers to overcome all obstacles to health. Yet doctors have the courage to go ahead, and we thank God for the help they give. We do not dwell on their limitations or become disillusioned with medicine because some treatments do not produce cures. We well know that our health is better with their help than without it.

The same is true with spiritual therapy. Miracles happen, but (unless God gives unusually clear guidance) none of us can promise to be such a perfect channel of grace that in such-and-such a case a complete healing will inevitably occur, or that healing will be within a certain time limit. What we can do is to work toward the spiritual conditions which appear to be the most favorable to health. As we do so, we must remember always that health is for the *whole* man, *body, mind,* and *spirit,* and that our prayers may be answered with improvement in any or all of these aspects of man's nature. Then we thank God for whatever help we receive.

Through serious spiritual therapy we can have the satisfaction of knowing that we not only provide the sick with the best medical care within our power, but also the best possible help through our relations with God. If a patient dies, for instance, his family does not become bitter and disillusioned, but thankful for the loving concern of Church people, and for the spiritual sustenance which they know God has given. This reaction is consistently reported by those who are responsibly undertaking the ministry of healing.

An illustration of this is a case recently brought to me where a woman was dying of cancer. A member of our parish felt strongly guided by God to ask me to visit the dying woman. I said I would go if the woman and her family clearly understood why I was coming and if they expressed a desire for me to come. I was especially careful to have their sympathetic understanding because they all belonged to a different denomination, and I did not want to seem like a stranger intruding into their affairs. They knew something about spiritual healing, so they did understand my purpose, and they were most happy to see me. I spoke with the woman's husband briefly in the hall before entering the sick woman's room, and in conversation with those who were at the hospital, I encouraged a positive and expectant attitude, but without attempting to predict whether or not she would be physically healed. She was in an oxygen tent, so I laid my hands on her side and prayed for healing. When I finished, the husband added a spoken prayer of his own in a very genuine manner. The sick woman and all those present expressed their gratitude for my coming, and I left.

The next day I received word that the woman had died. The lady who had first asked me to come later wrote me a letter. It said, in part:

I want you to know how much I appreciate your help in praying for my friend's friend. As you may know by now, Mrs. S. passed away at midnight that day you went to see her.

She had cancer but she did not know. She thought she had pleurisy. My friend said you gave wonderful help and comfort to Mrs. S. and were responsible in bringing father and son together again. The sister, Miss W., wanted you to come some time ago but she could not get the husband's consent until that last day. Something fine will come from your visit, I feel sure.

This was one of those circumstances that look like a complicated jig-saw puzzle put together by the Lord. I was merely one piece in the whole pattern, and did little enough. But with each piece in place, the picture could be seen. The picture was one of God's blessings, certainly not of disillusionment.

The letter was typical of those received by others who carry on the healing ministry.

Another case, earlier in my ministry, was much more difficult. A man who was hospitalized for another disease had developed pneumonia. As I drove to the hospital to see him one evening, praying as I went, I had a strong uplifted feeling, as though he were receiving healing strength. When I arrived, he seemed more clear of mind and more interested in his surroundings than he had been. In talking with his wife I had the impression that he seemed to improve only a few minutes earlier, which tended to confirm my feelings on the way down. He was in an oxygen tent, but disturbing things as little as possible, I put my arms under the edge of the tent and laid my hands on the front and back of his chest and prayed for healing. His wife stood by the side of the bed, praying silently with me. My arms felt as though healing power were going through them, and the wife also felt some sort of sensation, so that both of us had great confidence that he would be healed. I left, telling her that I would be in touch with her as to his progress.

I was shocked to hear that he suddenly died about a half hour after I had been there. Neither the wife nor I could fit this in with our expectations. At first our main concern was with the effect of his death on his family. But there were other emotional effects which persisted because of our application of spiritual therapy. These effects demanded of each of us a growth in spiritual maturity.

The first result was a somewhat depressing influence on my healing ministry. I did not doubt God's power to heal, but I did see more clearly that the practice of healing is not so neat as I had been told in books. I was impressed with how little we really do know about the subject. Then I began to wonder whether my laying on of hands could have made the patient worse. We do not know all the details of how and why the laying on of hands works just as it does.[4] And it has been said that in certain cases the laying on of hands should not be used for fear of increasing blood flow in an area which should be kept quiet. Yet this did not seem to apply to pneumonia, and it did not square too well with the idea that God is directly doing the healing: would He not know how to heal without stirring up new disturbances? I finally decided to rely on the conviction that it is God Who heals, and that the hands are merely His instrument, however they may fit into the picture. And what God does is constructive, not harmful. I decided this intellectually, but emotionally I was fearful—especially about laying hands on a vital organ like the heart.

I was put to the test before long when I was given the responsibility to care for several people with serious heart conditions. I had known what distinct improvements can result in heart cases through the laying on of hands. So in good conscience I was bound to do anything that might help

[4] This is discussed further in Chapter XIV.

heart patients. My mind drove me to visit these new heart cases, but by now I had become terrified emotionally at the thought of doing harm. So I simply steeled myself to do what I knew I must do, and I did it (as much as possible) as though I were not afraid. In each case there was an immediate and marked improvement in the functioning of the heart! After such experiences I lost my fear. One of the added lessons this taught me is that it is the basic attitude, not an uncontrollable emotional state, that is most effective in healing.

I have also come to realize that disappointments come when detailed predictions of healing fail to materialize, and the way to overcome such disappointments is to wait and see, open-mindedly, just what God will do. We can increase faith, hope, and expectancy by concentrating on what God *has* done, on His *promises*, on a clear visualization of the healing we desire, and by thanking Him for the healing He is giving in His perfect way. Then, unless He unmistakably reveals more to us, the time comes just to stand back and see what His way is.[5] In this way we can avoid disillusionment without diminishing the effectiveness of our prayers.

The wife of the man who died with pneumonia also had her spiritual problems. The emotional shock was, naturally, much greater on her, and her husband's death was so close to the time of the prayers for healing that the spiritual consequences might have been severe. She was not fully aware of the spiritual effect until some months later. She had realized that her spiritual life was not as it should be. But one day as she talked with a neighbor, she almost inadvertently expressed doubts as to whether it was any use to pray. She then became conscious of how she had been feeling. But she had the maturity to seek a perspective on herself. She came to me, and through expressing her feelings she gained insight and obtained mastery

[5] This assumes that every possible active step toward healing is being taken, but it avoids presumptuous attempts to "force God's hand." On the other hand, there is generally no need to emphasize or even mention the negative possibilities. This could easily discourage hope.

of them. As time went on, she became a concerned and effective participant in the healing ministry of the parish. She has not only been helped herself, but seeks and finds spiritual healing for her friends. I believe she is spiritually stronger now than she was before her husband's death.

The cynical and the disillusioned are not those whose prayers are answered in unexpected ways—even children soon learn that everything they ask is not given in the manner they desire. Children do not turn against their parents because of such things. They turn when they do not have their parents' love. So it is with those who turn against God—they have not perceived His *love*. What is greater evidence of the love of Christ: minimizing prayer for fear He will disappoint us, or maximizing prayer in confidence that He will not disappoint us? By ignoring spiritual healing we say, "God does not care." By practicing spiritual healing, we say, "We care because God cares."

The way of love is not easy. Paradoxically, it is the easiest way of life there is, because there is no other Way that goes anywhere. But Christ's love was shown through a crown of thorns, the hard-driven nails, and a life-giving cross. One must be willing to take a cross before sharing the resurrection. This is ultimately the only real difficulty of spiritual healing, because it is the difficulty of Christ-likeness itself. Do we have the humility to listen to God, the patience to hear Him through, the faith to follow His voice in the dark, the hope in Him that cannot be quenched, the single-minded love that dies to self in order to live with God?

Failure?

A common question about spiritual healing is, "How do you explain your failures?" The first response to this should be, "What do you mean by failure?" If we are concerned with the healing of the *whole* man, and if, as we believe, the life of the *spirit* is primary, the only true failure would be a failure to bring a sick person closer to God. My experience has been that only a small fraction of those who come for healing are restored miraculously; a majority are improved in physical or mental health in some way through spiritual ministrations; and practically everyone benefits spiritually. The "failures," those who do not improve spiritually, seem to be less than in almost any other ministration. At Baptism we completely renounce sin, profess our faith in Christ, and promise obedience to God's will and commandments the rest of our lives. How many of the baptized turn out to be "failures"? It is odd that clergy who never hesitate to baptize should be slow to try spiritual healing for fear of "failures."

I will tell now of a saintly young man whose spirit was healed while his pain was offered to God. It is an example of what some shallowly call a "failure" in spiritual healing. It is a failure that succeeded.

James (as we shall call him) was operated on for cancer. The surgery went well, but if even one cancerous cell is left in the body, there is a chance of recurrence. About a year later he complained of pains in the abdomen. He was taken to the hospital for examination. The first X-ray showed a sizeable shadow which the doctors felt to mean a new growth of cancer. I brought him Communion and laid on hands for healing. A special healing service was held on his behalf, and not only his friends, but his family physician came. As the hospital tests proceeded, no further evidence of cancer could be found. In about ten days he was discharged.

A year later there was new evidence of cancer. This time a lump about the size of an orange was identified in his abdomen. A series of X-ray treatments was started. Again we concentrated our prayers on James, and I laid my hands on the affected area. In just a few days the growth diminished to the size of a pea, then disappeared. The X-ray series was discontinued much earlier than the doctors had expected. We all rejoiced and gave God thanks.

Yet another year and the disease came back once more. The physicians did all they could, and we applied all the spiritual therapy we could, but James' condition went from bad to worse. Unfortunately, at this point, there were serious spiritual barriers to healing—not because of James' own attitude, but because of influences which cannot be described without breaking confidences.

Although James' bodily health rapidly deteriorated, his spiritual stature mounted from strength to strength. His physical pain was complicated by anguish of mind, but his patience and love showed like a beacon light. No one who knew him could remain unimpressed by his closeness to his Lord Jesus Christ. His victory and his healing were in the spirit. No one I have known has impressed me more with the resurrection life. As he lived, so he died. As he died, he lived anew. His healing was not perfected here, but it is surely perfected there in God's paradise beyond this life. His prayers and his love are still with us, and ours with him.

If healing is not complete in this life, shall we deny that it is healing? In James' case, we thank God that through medical skill and through prayer, his life was prolonged those extra years. Most of that time he was able to lead a normal, comfortable, useful life. Instead of complaining that the cancer was not removed once and for all, we rejoice that it was checked as much as it was. Instead of considering this a "failure," we see in it a triumph of the spirit. All the grace of God released through faith and prayer was finally concentrated in his spiritual development. As a result, though he lost the life which is for all men perishable and temporary, he gained strength in the life which is eternal.

This was his faith:

I know that my redeemer liveth, and that he shall stand at the latter day upon the earth: and though this body be destroyed, yet shall I see God: Whom I shall see for myself, and mine eyes shall behold, and not as a stranger.[6]

Death

Whether it is the matter of death or a host of other difficulties, the solution becomes apparent when spiritual healing is held, as it should be, in the context of the whole of Christian teaching. Seen in perspective, the healing of the body or the mind is always subordinate to the healing of the spirit, although perfect healing includes all three. And the only permanent and finally complete healing is in the resurrection to eternal life.

The time comes for each of us to leave this world; although, as Agnes Sanford says, the apple should fall when it is ripe, not because of a worm.

There are cases, especially involving older people, when it is not easy to know how to pray. We do not want to prolong the agony of dying. On the other hand, prayer for healing is not prayer for agonized existence, but for the removal of sickness. God can heal either by restoring health in this life or by restoring it in the next.

We would be wise to imitate the attitude of the doctors, who always strive for health, however, hopeless the case may seem. Too many "hopeless" cases have recovered. This is even more true in spiritual healing. Who could have been more "hopeless" or "incurable" than Lazarus? Yet Jesus raised him up.

Life and death are in God's hands, not ours. To pray for the death of those whose suffering is drawn-out seems to be a spiritual parallel to mercy killing. Why not simply pray for

[6] Job 19.25-27, as quoted in the American Book of Common Prayer of 1928, p. 324.

release from suffering? Let God decide whether it shall be in this life or the next.

Many a supposedly dying person has outlived his doctor and his pastor, so that the best prayer in most cases seems to be one that helps the person to come as close to God as possible, and that seeks healing for body, mind, and spirit. This is the best preparation for renewed health and it is also the best preparation for a new life beyond death. Of course, this does not mean a skirting around preparations for possible death—a man should keep his house in order in any case, doing his best to provide for his family, to make amends where he can to those whom he has harmed, and so on. However, such things are best taken care of in health, and should not be postponed to a death-bed. Once such matters are in hand, spiritual ministrations such as confession of sins and Absolution, the receiving of Holy Communion, and anointing or laying on of hands for healing, are at the same time an ideal preparation for physical healing or physical death. This is because they help unite the soul to Christ, and He conveys both healing and eternal life. Prayers to commend the soul to God are surely not out of place if death seems highly probable, but in deciding when such prayers should be used, we ought to seek God's guidance and do all we can to avoid planting the suggestion of death in the mind of someone who otherwise might live. There have been times when through negative suggestion, Last Rites have frightened the critically ill into a worse state.

Blame

Another problem in the practice of spiritual healing arises when we try to place blame when a healing is incomplete. There are times when obstacles are clearly seen. But more often the reasons remain a mystery. When they are, we must take care that we do not make up accusations of "lack of faith" or assume that some individual's sins are being punished. We are not God, to judge other people's sins, nor can we always be sure of our own. When we accuse ourselves or others without knowing the truth, we merely deepen a sense of guilt and hinder healing. It is better to seek forgiveness for our unconscious sinning and to look for guidance and spiritual strength for an improved future. It is better to accept God's power to overcome our frailties, and to go ahead without any unnecessary burden of guilt. "For God sent the Son into the world, not to condemn the world, but that the world might be saved through him." (John 3.17)

Neglect of Other Parts of the Ministry

The fear has often been expressed that the undertaking of a healing ministry might cause the clergy to "neglect other essential aspects of their total ministries." [7] This worry would carry more weight if we did not hear it so often from people who are neglecting the healing ministry.[8] Those who are engaged in healing can scarcely appreciate being told by bystanders what is and what is not essential to their ministry. That is a delicate question which can only be answered finally by God Himself.

This much is certain: Christ did not command a multitude of trivial activities with which we ministers all too often busy ourselves. He did command us to heal the sick. Those who seriously strive to obey that command find that the emphasis of their work inevitably shifts. It shifts in unforeseen ways— ways that are new to most people. A healing ministry is a new kind of ministry to modern Christians. Therefore, many do not grasp its implications. When they or someone near to them become sick, they appreciate it. But they may well think that

[7] I quote Dr. Harry B. Taylor, *Fifth Spiritual Healing Seminar* report, p. 124.

[8] In saying this, I intend no reflection on Dr. Taylor. I do not presume to judge his work in any way.

their pastor is neglecting other things which they think are essential. If this happens—I speak boldly—the time may have come when the pastor must choose between God and men. He has only twenty-four hours in the day, and he must resolutely determine to use them according to God's guidance, not men's opinions. Is it more important for him to spend an hour to make a nice social contact or to relieve suffering? Is it more fitting that he be an ecclesiastical salesman, or should he be first of all a spiritual physician? Which is more Christ-like? Does he serve his people most by following their inherited preconceptions of the ministry, or by seeking God's way, wherever it may lead? A recent article in *Life* magazine asked why so many of our ministers have breakdowns. The basic reason that emerged from a careful study of the article is that too many were trying to fulfill an artificial standard of impossible responsibilities—a standard derived from social pressures, not divine guidance.[9]

As in other emphases in the ministry, some individuals may find themselves called to give their major attention to spiritual healing. If so, they will find places where they can properly work with this understanding. But this should not be considered a *danger,* any more than any other specialized ministry, such as teaching or missionary work, is dangerous.

Many interests of a clergyman are personal and individual matters. But Jesus gave us three basic tasks: to preach, to teach, and to heal. We are set apart to minister God's Word and Sacraments. In doing this, healing is not optional, according to personal preference or development. It should be found in every Christian Church in the world. It is time we stopped shying away from God-given responsibilities by fears of over-doing. Too many of us are afraid to warm up ice-water in case it should boil.

[9] Unfortunately, some may use these words to fall into the opposite trap: ignoring what the Holy Spirit is saying through others in order to go one's own way instead of God's. True guidance is not always easily found.

Feelings

A seminarian once asked me, "What if I don't feel like praying for the sick?" My friend, what if you don't feel like loving God or your neighbor or going to Church—or if you are a clergyman, what if you don't feel like preaching a sermon or visiting someone? You do your best at it anyway.

We may, of course, be guided to choose wisely *how* we pray for the sick: when to pray silently, when to be vocal, when to bring sacramental helps, and so on. But this is another story and depends on each circumstance as we deal with those who are ill.

Over-Involvement

There is a danger lying in the opposite direction from "not feeling like praying." It is most likely to beset the conscientious and the enthusiastic. This is the danger of becoming too much involved in the problems and emotions of those we are trying to help. It is possible even to transfer many symptoms of the sick to ourselves. The end could well be that two are sick and none is well.

The answer lies in developing a perspective and a proper detachment. We can copy the example of the lifeguard. Unless he is willing to get himself wet and expose himself to danger, he cannot rescue the drowning man. On the other hand, he must take care that he is not drowned along with the man he came to save.

Expert Help

The lifeguard must also be trained in order to do his work safely. In spiritual healing, we must take care not to go beyond the depth that each of us is prepared to handle. This is especially true in dealing with people with deep emotional or mental problems. It is most important in such cases that we have guidance from doctors who have expert knowledge in the field. Some patients need psychiatric treatment, and in the hands of an amateur (however well-intentioned) they may grow worse instead of better.

We have repeatedly encouraged cooperation with physicians. This is fairly easy to establish in cases of physical disease. But psychological illness is far more difficult. It is not always easy to recognize. It may be aggravated by emotional strains: large, emotionally-charged healing services are especially dangerous for the psychologically ill. They are often in no position to meet necessary requirements for true spiritual healing, and their condition may break down further under strong currents of mass excitement. Healing services with a quiet and peaceful atmosphere are far more likely to be helpful.

For such reasons, the psychologically ill should be dealt with individually and by those skillful enough to be a help instead of a hindrance. We can always pray for them, and we can always have love for them. But we cannot always expect them to react normally. The help of a Christian doctor cooperating with a psychologically-trained pastor is the best thing we could find.

Medical Interpretations

At times we run into difficulty because of conflicting interpretations of a healing, one medical and the other spiritual. This can be very annoying to all concerned.

An example is the healing of Miss White recounted at the beginning of Chapter XII.

We will recall that she told of suddenly being healed through prayer of an eye injury caused by an exploding defective gun shell. I questioned both the eye specialists who had treated her without telling them of the extraordinary circumstances of her healing. Neither saw anything unusual in the fact that she had recovered her vision. Neither one had met her before. The accident was on Saturday, September 22nd. Dr. X. saw her that day, again on Monday the 24th, and a third time on Thursday the 27th. Dr. Y. saw her only once, on Monday the 24th. The healing was on the morning of Wednesday the 26th.

Both doctors agreed on the general diagnosis, and that the injury was neither deep nor severe. They also agreed that the best treatment was merely a topical anesthetic to keep down pain. A natural reaction after hearing either one of them would be to wonder whether under the emotional strain of the incident, Miss White had not exaggerated the whole thing. After all, a threat to eyesight is important enough to cause quite an upset.

However, further reflection on the details sheds a different light. True, Miss White is so emotionally involved that she cannot be completely objective. But the two physicians do not agree on every detail. Their major discrepancy is over whether or not there were brass particles in the cornea. Dr. X. said,[10] "In one area midway in the corneal stroma or the main substance of the cornea there was noted a small, flat, sheet-like disruption of stromal tissue. It was not felt that that was imbedded foreign material. But I could not be certain on the first visit . . . The breaks in the corneal epithelium were produced probably by tangential contact from the powder as it ricocheted off the cornea. The disruption in the stroma of the cornea was rather well localized and contained no foreign material and it was my feeling that it was produced merely by the closeness of the blast rather than having foreign material driven into the stroma itself." Dr. Y., on the other hand, said [11] that there were "many very minute small dust particles, brass, imbedded in the cornea of the right eye," and that the eye

[10] On April 1, 1957.
[11] On April 3, 1957.

had healed over these. He measured the vision in the right eye as 20/30 and in the left as 20/20. His prognosis had been that she would become accustomed to her condition.

According to Miss White,[12] on Saturday Dr. X. "removed the particles of dust from the section of my eye except for the part in the cornea, and this he said could not be removed because it was too finely powdered—and it couldn't be removed with a magnet." Next Thursday, she says, "He looked through this machine into my eye. When he first looked at me he put his hand on my face and said, 'Oh, your face is better, too, isn't it?' And then he looked into the machine, and looked away from the machine, and then looked back in the machine again. He was very puzzled and then he said, 'Well, this is wonderful. That certainly healed up fast.' He said, 'I can only detect a wee little tiny black spot in the middle of the cornea. I see no brass at all. There's nothing there except this . . . spot, which is probably a little bit of scar tissue.'_"

Dr. Y. definitely said there were brass dust particles in the cornea on Monday. Dr. X. said there were not, but added, "I could not be certain on the first visit." Miss White's recollection is that Dr. X. thought the dust was there on Saturday, but not the next Thursday. If it had been there and disappeared by Thursday, what would be more natural than for Dr. X. to assume it had never been there?

We have one piece of particularly significant objective evidence: the change in Miss White's eyesight. Previous to the accident she had worn glasses in order to help her reading. Her eyes focused properly at a distance (which was why her left eye was a normal 20/20 when Dr. Y. examined her on Monday). But when a printed page was held at a normal distance for reading, the eyeglasses were necessary to provide a sharp focus.

She tells how she could not read at all on Tuesday. Perhaps in time she could have adjusted herself to reading with the

[12] As she told me December 30, 1956.

left eye. Dr. Y.'s examination showed her right eye to be below normal on Monday; at close range, the vision would have been worse than with his relatively distant eye-chart.

At the time of the prayers Wednesday morning she could suddenly see clearly and read a book at any distance without her glasses. After that she discovered that the glasses were useless: they just blurred things. And Dr. X. examined the right eye on Thursday, when he discharged her. He said, "Its final vision upon discharge was 20/10, which is two lines better than what is accepted as average normal, though by no means uncommonly good vision." Dr. X. had not tested her vision previously, or perhaps he would have discovered that for *her* this was uncommonly good.

The important features of Miss White's story, I might add, were corroborated by her friend, Pat, who was with her when she was healed and when she visited Dr. Y.; and also by the Administrator of the hospital where she works, who was her supervisor during the period of the accident and the healing. Pat was present when I interviewed Miss White on December 30, 1956, and I visited the hospital Administrator for an interview on April 1, 1957.

Miss White's case has been discussed in detail, not only as an example of spiritual healing, but also as a sample of the typical difficulties in getting medical case histories. At this time only the most patient, thorough, and painstaking search is likely to reveal instances of spiritual healing which have clear medical documentation. We can often expect conflicting evidence, but it will not do to shrug off careful investigation by the lazy assumption that nothing will ever come of it, or by the narrow-minded dogma that such healings "don't happen." The kind of scientific study that needs so much to be undertaken will require hard full-time work by many qualified people. It will not be done until someone is willing to invest the time, money, effort, and prayer to bring it to pass. I cannot see how spiritual healing can ever be fully integrated with twentieth-century medical science unless the proper research is done.

The word of caution that needs to be given to those engaged in spiritual healing is that we should not overlook or in any way depreciate the part played by medical healing. Some distress resulted recently when a clergyman told of a miraculous healing of cancer, but omitted any mention of a series of X-ray treatments on that cancer. His version sounded as though prayer were effective while medical care was not. The truth was that prayer and medical care were effective together. When both are in the picture, it is a sin to fail to credit either one. But above all, we give credit to God, Who is the Giver of *all* good things.

Psychotherapy

We have given some thought to the relation between spiritual healing and psychotherapy in Chapter V. We have already noted how the theological and psychological realms overlap. Since this is true, it is useless to think of a complete isolation of "spiritual" from "purely psychological and psychiatric" healing. A boy was once healed of warts by coming to our healing services. Warts can be healed by suggestion. But this was not "any old kind" of suggestion—it was couched in a spiritual atmosphere. So it was that the boy not only got rid of his warts, but in the process came closer to God. That is psychological—or, more properly, psychosomatic—healing. But it was also spiritual healing. If God uses psychological principles to heal, will we fail to thank Him? I think not. In the case of the boy with the warts, He not only helped the body, but the spirit; so indeed we give Him double thanks.

Demons

Our final word is about evil spirits. Chapter VI included the New Testament view of mental illness as demon-possession.

The modern psychological outlook considers the same illnesses as having physical or emotional causes within the individual. In his *By the Finger of God*, S. Vernon McCasland takes pains to show that the accounts of first-century demon-possession are historically accurate, that they are paralleled by demon-possession today (especially in areas not penetrated by Western ideas) and that they are instances of well-known psychological illness which we merely label differently.

With the rise of natural science, causes of phenomena which seemed "supernatural" [13] in any way were discarded. Being conscious of the cruel medieval treatments of the possessed, and having seen the tragic foolishness of witch hunts, modern men had a strong motive for abolishing evil spirits from their thinking.

Some have suggested that the coming of Christianity abolished the devils. Historically, though, it was the "Enlightenment," beginning around the eighteenth century, that abolished them.

However, twentieth-century history suggests that demonic influences were not really abolished, but merely removed from consciousness. Jungian psychology recognizes the demonic element in human life, and so does much of recent theology. The powers of darkness that infest the depths of the human soul do not go away by being ignored. It is still true that "we are not contending against flesh and blood, but against the principalities, against the powers, against the world rulers of this present darkness, against the spiritual hosts of wickedness in the heavenly places." (Ephesians 6.12)

Yet when all this has been said, we still have not fully faced the problem of demon-possession. That problem has to do with our use of exorcism. This is the method used by Jesus to heal the possessed. It has been successful in many instances, and is finding growing acceptance among those practicing spiritual

[13] Note that this involved a somewhat different definition of "supernatural" than that of Chapter V.

healing. But the typical Protestant church makes no provision for it at all. The "Enlightenment" has prevailed.

It is hard to imagine a successful exorcist who does not believe that actual spirit-entities are in possession of those who are being treated. This is the crux of the matter. Are they? If so, when? How and when should we exorcise?

Such questions are liable to horrify a modern psychologist or psychiatrist. They would credit the success of exorcism (when it does work) to the principle of suggestion. But they would also consider it an inferior and misleading method.

Will exorcism develop in grand isolation from all modern knowledge of the mind? Or is there a way to bridge the gap? The bridge may yet come through "sensitives," people whose abilities in extra-sensory perception seem to allow them to perceive spirit-entities.[14] They may well prove a major avenue of research.

[14] cf. Dora van Gelder in the *Spiritual Healing Seminar* reports. Those who engage in exorcism also often gain remarkable sensitivity. I Corinthians 12.10 includes among the gifts of the Spirit, "the ability to distinguish between spirits."

CHAPTER XIV

Gifts and Sacraments

Now there are varieties of gifts, but the same Spirit; and there are varieties of service, but the same Lord; and there are varieties of working, but it is the same God who inspires them all in every one.

I Corinthians 12.4–6

Healing Gifts

Some of the most intense focuses for healing power are to be found in the work of certain unusually gifted individuals. Such people are referred to by St. Paul in such passages as I Corinthians 12.4–11, as having been given, through the Spirit of God, "gifts of healing." The Greek word meaning "gifts" is *charismata*,[1] so we speak of such gifts (and their recipients) as charismatic. The Greek refers to a freely-given favor, an unmerited gift of grace, bestowed by the will of the Holy Spirit Himself.

Some Christian charismatics carry out their work in considerable independence of conventional church organizations. Others work within the traditional framework of the Church, though they certainly transcend established customs. Examples of the first type are Kathryn Kuhlman and Oral Roberts; the second would include Agnes Sanford and Gladys Falshaw.

The tendency is to consider the gifts of healing as something a few people have, for unknown reasons, and which the rest of us cannot share. If we were discussing natural talents

[1] χαρίδματα.

223

such as musical genius or a high I.Q., this might be so. But we are discussing instead supernatural gifts of the Holy Spirit. Such things are acquired, not inborn. The direction and intensity of expression of the gifts of the Spirit are indeed related to our natural endowments, but the Spirit acts with a freedom that can transcend numberless human limitations. St. Paul is not the least bit fatalistic about it. He says, "Earnestly desire the higher gifts." (I Corinthians 12.31) And actually *most* of those with outstanding healing gifts have not had them dropped in their laps, so to speak, but have received them as the result of their earnest desire in prayer. They asked and received, sought and found, knocked and saw the door move open.

If this is true of those with notable gifts, it is also true of those of us with more moderate gifts. Just because a man like Chopin is so rare is no reason to think that only a genius can play the piano. With enough ambition, discipline, and practice, innumerable people can enjoy piano playing. If this is so with natural talents, how much more ought multitudes of people to be encouraged to seek and find as much of the supernatural gifts of healing as possible. Indeed, *all* Christians are expected to share in the ministry of healing. The need is universal, and Christ's promise to answer prayer in His Name is universal. Some may be given grace to excel, but all are offered grace to participate.

It is especially distressing to hear clergymen refuse to develop a healing ministry by saying, "I don't have enough faith," or "I can't do it," or "I don't know how." If a man doesn't know how, he should set out to learn how from those who have done it. If he believes he can't do it, he is right: *God* does it. His job is to let God do it. If he lacks faith, he will never deepen his faith by wringing his hands. Let him *act* on what faith he has, and he will gain more. None of us were skilled preachers or pastors when we began. But we began. We had to begin. And through experience we learned. It is the same with the ministry of healing.

Jesus commanded the Apostles to heal the sick, and along with this He gave them the gifts of the Spirit that they needed to follow His command. The Church's Bishops are the successors of the Apostles in the pastoral ministry, and the Priests whom they ordain share the responsibility and the power of the Apostolic Ministry to the sick. In the same passage where St. Paul writes of the gifts of the Spirit and says "Earnestly desire the higher gifts," he also says that "God has appointed in the church first apostles." (I Corinthians 12.28) The Apostolic Ministry *includes* gifts of the Spirit; ordination itself conveys gifts, including the *charismata* of healing. *Every Priest is Charismatic, and is able to be a charismatic healer.*

On the other hand, a man's own personal endowments and his development as an individual affect the exercise of the gifts God provides at ordination. The gifts rest on the promise of God only, so they are always available. But the *practice* of the gifts is related in many ways to God's plan for each individual Priest and is influenced by the degree that Christian qualities are expressed in his thoughts, words, and actions.

Side-Effects

Charismatic healing is often accompanied by unusual effects on the body and the nervous system that suggest a tangible flow of power. Such phenomena are frequently reported by those who have engaged in spiritual healing, and I have experienced them many, many times. They may be vibrations or pulsations of the body; or a feeling like an electric shock; or a sensation of heat, usually deep in the body; or (more rarely) the feeling of something like a cool stream of air moving across the skin; or a distinct sense of a filling of the body with what can most closely be described as "peace"; or (once in a while) a sudden draining of energy almost to the point of collapse.[2] Some call this "the power of God." Such effects have been

[2] In unusual circumstances, fainting actually occurs.

in evidence in times of unusually strong spiritual resurgence. They are probably responsible for the names given to the *Quakers* and the *Shakers* in their early days, and were to be found in connection with the Wesleyan revival in the eighteenth century. Some such reaction may well have been involved in Jesus' healing of the woman with the hemorrhage: "she felt in her body that she was healed of her disease. And Jesus, perceiving in himself that power had gone forth from him, immediately turned about in the crowd, and said, 'Who touched my garments?'" (Mark 5.25–34) All sorts of interpretations of this passage have been given by Biblical scholars, but those who have been engaged in spiritual healing see in it a simple and direct parallel to their own sense of a flow of healing power through them into the sick.

Some will seek to explain all this in terms of hysteria and suggestion. Both of these factors are no doubt present in many cases, but as an all-embracing explanation such terms are too simple and too unrelated to what actually happens. Since these side-effects have never been studied scientifically in connection with spiritual healing, we have no genuine scientific explanation for them at the present time. We have some knowledge of similar things, but we do not know to what degree these healing phenomena parallel those similar things. We do not know whether there is a literal physical flow of power, or whether these effects are merely symbolic of healing power, or whether we are dealing with a sort of psychic energy which is not to be confused with physical energy, or whether we are sensing disruptions of normal functions due to pure and direct creative acts of God. We do not know to what degree these effects are physical—or purely neurological—or psychological. Their nature does suggest a close relationship to the nervous system, but their why and wherefore remain a mystery.

My experience is that the side-effects are often present when there is no visible or immediate evidence of healing, and healing—even instant healing—may occur with no noticeable side-effects. For this reason, and because spiritual healing itself is the main point, side-effects should not be overemphasized. But they do occur. They are often quite unpredictable, and may take place in a person who has never heard about them and is quite surprised by what he feels. After laying on hands, for instance, I have been told, "My, your hands are warm"; and when I immediately let the sick person touch my hands to see, there is no unusual warmth at all. Sometimes the person who receives the laying on of hands feels heat or tingling from head to toe—and this may happen when I do not sense much of anything.

These side-effects deserve careful scientific study.[3] It is possible that they may reveal highly significant processes which take place during spiritual therapy. And as our understanding increases, so will our effectiveness.

Sacramental Healing

The form of spiritual healing most easily adapted to a normal parish ministry is that which makes use of the grace offered by God in the Sacraments. It would seem that the exceptional healing activity within the Episcopal Church, compared with other major denominations, is due to two factors, one of which is its strong sacramental emphasis. (The other

[3] Such study, of course, is not easy. There is real danger, for instance, that thoughtless investigators may brashly trample in and by their own attitude destroy the atmosphere in which spiritual healing takes place. If we wanted to study the normal habits of rare birds, we could scarcely do it by noisily thrashing about in the jungle. Our birds, if we saw them at all, would always be in an abnormal state of fright. Even collectors of case histories of spiritual healings sometimes frustrate their own aims by manifesting their own skepticism in such a way that those who have been healed sense a desecration of the holy. Successful studies demand tact, understanding, sympathy, patience, and (so far as possible) unobtrusiveness, along with the scientific method. Observations of what happens *during* a healing can only succeed when the observer does not distract the participants. He must try to be like "the little man who wasn't there."

factor is its freedom and adaptability as contrasted with the Roman Church. Rome also stresses the Sacraments, but is hampered by medieval traditions which often tend to cancel out healing efficacy. The most striking example of this is their Extreme Unction, which began as anointing for healing but is now interpreted by Rome as mainly a preparation for death!) It is to be expected that the growth of healing within major Protestant groups will be accompanied by a wider appreciation of the spiritual power mediated by the Sacraments —including those outward and visible signs of inward and spiritual grace whose exact form has not been specified by Christ, but which are nonetheless means through which, by faith, we may receive the renewing energy of His risen life.

The peculiar effectiveness of sacramental healing comes from its direct dependence on the Word of God alone. When the appropriate outward and visible symbol is provided, whoever accepts the Sacrament is given God's assurance that through this symbol God provides His gifts. This works to free him from the personal shortcomings of the clergyman who administers the Sacrament, since here God's grace depends purely on His own promises, not on the worthiness or worthlessness of His ministers.

On the other hand, the effects of a Sacrament do depend on the attitude of the person who receives it. We might compare the Sacrament with a bank check. A check is a pledge to pay money, and depends on the honesty of its signer. Similarly, a Sacrament is God's pledge of gifts of the Spirit, and is absolutely dependable because of its trustworthy Giver. But a check cannot be used to buy anything unless the man who receives it is willing to do his part and cash it in to use the money at the store. Likewise, a Sacrament is not magic, and its benefits do not materialize in life unless the person who receives it is willing to meet the conditions to "cash in on it." These conditions are repentance, faith, and willingness to obey God. If you were to give me a check for a hundred dollars, and

I were to tear it up in front of you, I would indeed be ungrateful. In the same way, if I come to receive a Sacrament outwardly, but inwardly refuse God's gifts through the hardness of my heart, I ungratefully desecrate a holy thing. Woe to me if I do! My refusal does not change the fact that God offers His grace in the Sacrament. But since He does offer it, so much the greater is my condemnation if I reject it. Sacraments always do something; they are never empty symbols. But the one who receives the Sacrament is blessed or condemned according to the state of his own heart. However independent they may be of the personality of those who *minister* them, Sacraments do not magically lift personal responsibility from those who *receive* them.[4] They actually intensify that responsibility.

Now let us briefly review the Sacraments in relation to healing.

The fact that at present, Baptism is received mostly in infancy by members of Christian families tends to obscure its healing effects, though repentance from sin and redemption through faith in Christ are plainly at the heart of Baptism. Since spiritual healing in its full sense includes not only the body and the mind, but a restored relationship of love between men and God and between one another—and since this healing of the spirit is the matter of greatest importance, and, in fact, the test of effectiveness of spiritual healing, Baptism by its very nature, along with the other Sacraments, is a means of healing. This is seen particularly clearly in the Baptism of adult converts from paganism; in the early Church, Christ's healing power was stressed even further by the practice of immediately preceding Baptism by exorcism.

The Holy Communion offers us a share in the life of Christ:

---

[4] This is not to overlook the responsibility of the minister to help his people grow in that penitence, faith, and willingness to obey God which release the power of the Sacraments into our lives.

not only the body broken and the blood shed on the cross for our salvation, but His body, soul, and Spirit reunited and restored in His glorious resurrection and reigning in His ascension. The ancient Liturgy of St. James prays "that it may not be for condemnation to Thy people that the mystery of salvation has been administered by us, but for remission of sins, of renewal of souls and bodies," [5] and the Liturgy of St. Mark, probably also written before the third century, asks God regarding the reception of the elements of the Holy Communion, "That to all of us who partake thereof they may tend to healing . . . the renewal of soul, body, and spirit . . ." A similar emphasis upon the healing of both body and soul is seen in the Book of Common Prayer: [6] "Grant us therefore, gracious Lord, so to eat the flesh of thy dear Son Jesus Christ, and to drink his blood, that our sinful bodies may be made clean by his body, and our souls washed through his most precious blood, and that we may evermore dwell in him and he in us"; while during the administration of the Sacrament, the priest says, "the Body of our Lord Jesus Christ, which was given for thee, preserve thy body and soul unto everlasting life." Similar words accompany the delivery of the Cup. It is to be expected that the Real Presence of Jesus of Nazareth will be accompanied by the same power to heal that we see Him exercising as we read the Gospels.

Confirmation, which is the completion of Baptism, and a share in the Pentecostal gift of the Holy Spirit through the laying on of the Bishop's hands (or in some Christian communions by anointing), implies the promise of God to continue the spiritual gifts that characterized the Christians of the New Testament and the early Church.

This includes the gifts of healing. God has poured out the healing charisma in great power upon many whose tradition

[5] Frost, op. cit., p. 43.
[6] The American Book of Common Prayer of 1928, p. 82.

does not include Confirmation. How little faith, then, is shown by those who have received this Sacrament when they are reluctant to exercise the gifts of the Spirit!

Ordination, with its assurance of the pastoral authority and grace given to the Apostles, is incompatible with any notion that God intends to limit miracles to the days of the first century. Those of us who consider ourselves in the Apostolic Succession might do well to talk less about our venerable heritage and spend more of our time demonstrating it!

The harmonious knitting of family relationships that comes with a truly Christian marriage has probably become more and more evident as the problems of divorce and of juvenile delinquency have mounted. Holy Matrimony, with its enduring love and deep mutual responsibility before God, is a source of healing in its own way.

Absolution, the Sacrament of God's Forgiveness, is well known for its psychiatric benefits. But while the psychiatrist is primarily concerned with the emotional stresses caused by guilt feelings, the Gospel is the means of removing guilt itself. And while pastoral counseling is of great importance, it is no substitute for Absolution. The peculiar merit of private Confession and Absolution lies in these factors: (1) The explicit, crystallized recognition of sinful behavior and habits on the part of the penitent, making conscious much that he may have previously hidden from himself; (2) the honest confession of sin as sin, with no excuses; (3) the completely impersonal role of the priest; (4) the individual, authoritative assurance of the forgiveness of Christ to the faithful penitent; and (5) the opportunity for the penitent to make a concrete outward expression of repentance.

The usual dangers of auricular confession arise when it is considered to be compulsory, not voluntary. Points 1 and 2 can also be dealt with on a counseling basis; possibly 4 and 5 could be likewise, especially if 5 involved an act of restitution. On the other hand, valuable counseling can be given during a confession. In these ways counseling and auricular confession complement each other. But point 3 cannot really be duplicated in pastoral counseling, and its unique value is on shifting the emphasis from the pastor to God. For this reason, it is often very wise to conclude a counseling session with a formal Absolution, in the Church, with the priest in vestments to exalt his office and eliminate him as a particular personality.

An example of this use of Absolution was seen when Mrs. K. came to the Rev. L. M. in great distress because she had considered going out with someone other than her husband. Mr. K. was away for long periods because of his work, and a neighbor had asked Mrs. K. for a date. Out of loneliness (they had no children) she had impulsively agreed. When the time came, she did not keep the arrangement; but she had a tender conscience, and felt strongly that she had broken her marriage vow.

During counseling, the natural strain of living alone so much was pointed out, and so was the fact that she had not actually even gone out with the other man. Yet she had known these facts before, and still had not been able to escape a growing inner conflict. Possibilities for outside activities were discussed so that she might better avoid the temptation in the future, and she made some plans in that direction. But that still did not remove her sense of guilt for what she had already done. She could have been given Christ's promises of forgiveness, and prayer could have been offered that God would forgive and provide strength for the future. As a matter of fact, that was done. In some cases this might have been sufficient. Still, Mrs. K. had been a regular attendant at Church and had been hearing the promises of forgiveness, but somehow she had not been able to receive them and apply them to herself—that was why she had come to her pastor.

So it was suggested that she make a formal confession before leaving. She agreed, and after taking enough time to prepare herself, she made her confession at the altar rail and received Absolution. The next time she was in church, she told her minister that everything was all right again. She had been completely free of the problem ever since. Not only that, but she seems to have no emotional involvement with her minister other than a natural gratitude for his help; the personality entanglements that so often plague both the psychiatric and the counseling approaches were avoided.

We come finally to the one Sacrament specifically intended to be a channel of health: Anointing or Laying on of Hands for Healing. Anointing is considered more of a priestly function, since it is based partly on James 5.14–15, which enjoins calling for the "elders of the church" for prayer and unction. The Laying on of Hands is not only used in a sacramental sort of approximation to Anointing, but, as has been mentioned, is common in charismatic healing. It provides a simple link between the sacramental and the charismatic approach —though anointing is likewise associated with special spiritual gifts.

Healing Services in the Average Parish

The Laying on of Hands or Anointing, which we may call the Sacrament of Healing, opens up the possibility of regularly scheduled special services of spiritual healing in the average congregation. These services may incorporate some of the advantages of the prayer group and even of personal testimony, along with the advantages of emotional discipline and competent instruction. They fall into two main types, depending upon whether or not they are developed around a celebration of the Holy Communion.

An example of a rather nondenominational form of healing service using the Laying on of Hands is to be found on page 13 of *Religion and Health* by Alfred W. Price, D.D.[7] This is the sort of service that he has used with great effectiveness in a

[7] Rector of St. Stephen's Episcopal Church, Philadelphia, Pa.

downtown situation. Much of it can also be adapted to other types of services. It would be preceded by a sermon on healing, and consists of comforting Bible quotes; petitions, intercessions, and thanksgiving for healing; the Laying on of Hands at the altar rail, with prayer. It ends with a blessing.

Typical healing services using the liturgical forms of the Episcopal Church have been outlined by the Healing Commission of the Diocese of Pittsburgh. One type uses a shortened Evening Prayer Service (with the Psalm and Bible lesson relevant to healing) followed by an instruction, intercession for a list of the sick, thanksgiving for help received, and the Laying on of Hands, concluding with a blessing. The other type uses either a normal simple Communion service or else uses the Communion of the Sick (but in the Church), with an instruction on healing and with the Laying on of Hands and /or Anointing following the reception of Holy Communion.

Other types of healing services and prayers for healing are to be found in the *Manual of Christian Healing* of the Order of St. Luke, *The Order for the Ministration to the Sick*,[8] and Walter Dwyer's *Spiritual Healing in the United States and Great Britain.*

Some church leaders seem very reticent about public healing services. We have already mentioned dangers to the emotionally unstable in services of a hysterical sort. And the uninstructed and immature might run into pitfalls such as concentrating on physical healing without looking for a closer life with God. But the answer to these problems can be found by conducting healing services of the right *nature*; they need not be forbidden or abolished. They have their own very positive value. They stand as a public witness to Christ's healing work. The healing services in my own parish not only made it simple and natural for anyone to come there for healing for himself or for others, but also made crystal clear our Church's vital

---

[8] *Prayer Book Studies—III The Order for the Ministration to the Sick,* by the Standing Liturgical Commission.

concern with the healing ministry. As a result, many people came to me with their problems or asked for our prayers who otherwise might have hesitated to do so. My pastoral ministry and the people's prayer life were both immeasurably deepened through the strong focal point of the healing service.

If healing services are conducted in simplicity and dignity, in such a way as to witness to the peace and love of God, as well as His power, the emotional effect will be to integrate the personality, not to add new stresses. If balanced instruction, as well as inspirational material, is constantly used in meditations and sermons, healing will be kept in its true perspective, with a close spiritual relationship to God as of first importance. This is especially easy to accomplish when the healing ministry is conducted as part of the whole life of the parish, integrated with the fullness of Christian faith and living. Incidentally, some are over-fearful lest someone come for healing *before* he is properly instructed. But Jesus required neither courses nor diplomas before He healed. Once people knew God's love and power first-hand, and in that, knew Jesus as their Lord, there would be plenty of time for growth and instruction. We must *begin* where we *are*, and seek to grow to maturity. It is a life-time task. We found that our healing services promoted that maturity, and that the theoretical dangers supposed to attend them did not materialize.

The Pastoral Ministry

Whether or not a particular clergyman feels led to conduct public healing services, it is a rock-bottom necessity that he apply the principles of spiritual healing in his pastoral work with individuals. The pastoral ministry is already likely to be stressed in our Church life, both in counseling and in visitations, so we need not dwell on it here. What spiritual healing has to offer is an attitude and approach that adds enormous vitality and effectiveness to the work of a pastor. One of my clergy friends has told me how he spent many years without the victorious power of spiritual healing in his ministry; and now that he knows it, his entire ministry is changed. He spoke of a woman who was deathly ill. In the old days, he would have prepared her for dying, and she would have died. Instead, he prayed for healing and uplifted her faith. She lived. And the life he brings to his people, and the life he shares himself, is something far beyond physical and mental health. It is the joyous triumph of the life of the Spirit. It shines in him and in his work.

The Prayers of the People

A vital healing work needs the prayer-support of the people. There should be at least a nucleus of really concerned and dedicated Christians who seriously undertake to pray for the sick and for the whole ministry of the Church to the body, mind, and spirit.

Prayer groups can take various forms. Some meet at regular times; others pray together without meeting together. The members of some promise to pray daily. Some divide the hours of the day so that someone is praying for each sick person every hour, day and night. Some groups pray daily together only for the most seriously ill, and divide the other names among the group or through the days of the week, so that no one person prays for too many at once. Many individuals try to keep their own prayer list down to a dozen or so, in order to be able to picture each one clearly and lift that person effectively into the light of God. True prayer does not stop with easy words. It is hard work.

The intercessions themselves take many forms and patterns. Their effectiveness is tied to the deep inner attitude of the person who prays. A typical approach to God in prayer starts with time for relaxation, to let the cares and worries of the world drop away. Then there is the seeking after an awareness of the Presence of God. In the awareness of His perfection, we then realize our own littleness in faith and hope and love, and ask forgiveness and spiritual renewal through Jesus Christ, Who died for our sins and rose to bring us eternal life. All this is preparation. As we intercede for others we picture them as filled with the blessedness and the healing love of the Holy Spirit. We may even stretch out our hands, symbolically laying them upon the sick for whom we pray—anything that reinforces active faith and positive love is helpful. And we thank God for all His mercies, for His Son and for the new life He has given us. We thank Him especially that He is healing and renewing the one for whom we pray. In gratitude for Thine abundant gifts, O Lord, we give ourselves anew to Thee. Amen. So be it.

There is no *one* way to intercede for the sick. Each must look for God's leading, to find what is best for him and for his brothers in Christ who wish to pray with him.

Not long after we began our healing services, one of our most devoted young women heard about a critically ill Jewish man, whom we shall call David. He had a kidney infection, and the doctors did not know whether he would live. She began to pray for him, and put his name on the prayer list at our services. She also asked a number of her friends to pray for David. And she regularly inquired about his health. After several weeks, he recovered. When he was well on the road to health, she told David's wife that she had been praying for him, and that she had asked her Christian friends to do the same.

David's wife was exceedingly grateful. She told her sister about it. It so happened that her sister's son had married a Christian girl, and until that time the sister had not so much as allowed either of them to come into her home. But when she heard about the prayers of Christians for David, her heart warmed. She resolved to welcome her son once more, and his wife with him.

So it is that love can reach across every barrier to elicit love in return. We do not know exactly what part those prayers for David played in his own recovery. We believe they helped, though we do not know just how much or in precisely what way. But we thank God that He healed David. And we thank Him that through prayers for the strengthening of David's sick body, love was rekindled between Jew and Christian. It was rekindled through the compassion of one young woman who shared her concern with her Christian brothers and sisters in the Church. It was rekindled through the grateful responsiveness of David and his Jewish family. It was rekindled because both Christians and Jews had been vitally touched by the healing love of Jesus of Nazareth.

Who can stand unmoved by Thy love, Lord Jesus? Surely Thou hast borne our sicknesses and carried our pains. Thou wert wounded for our transgressions; Thou wert bruised for our iniquities. Upon Thee was the chastisement that made us whole, and with Thy stripes we are healed. Thou wert not given up to Death; the path of life is Thine. Show us Thy Way forever, that we may share with Thee the fullness of joy in the Presence of our Father. Thou art our healing. Thou art our life. Blessed by Thy Name, Lord Jesus.

On the Psychological Analysis of Jesus' Healing Ministry

A number of attempts have been made to analyze the psychological principles involved in the healing work of Jesus. We are unable to go into all the details here, but we can consider certain significant phases of such studies.

Three examples are: Dawson, *Healing: Pagan and Christian*, Chapter VIII; Weatherhead, *Psychology, Religion and Healing*, Section I, Chapter 1; and McCasland, *By the Finger of God*, which includes an introduction by David Cole Wilson, M.D.

These examples taken together lead to the following conclusions:

1. The only absolutely clear diagnosis in the cases healed by Jesus is the cutting off of the ear of the high priest's slave. (Luke 22.50–51) Dawson seems unsure what to say about this healing. Weatherhead doubts its historicity. It is not within the scope of McCasland's book.

2. The diagnoses next in clarity are:

a. The Gerasene demoniac (Mark 5.1–20), whose illness appears to be psychogenic and could be distinguished as manic. Weatherhead speculates on a cause, but does not provide convincing evidence that his guess is correct. Dr. Wilson agrees that the symptoms are manic, but says, "one would hesitate to make a final diagnosis." He also says, "It is quite safe to conclude that Christ cured a case of acute mania in this instance." Dawson does not deal with this case.

b. The epileptic boy (Mark 9.14–29, etc.): this general diagnosis is made by McCasland, and confirmed by Dr. Wilson. But its varieties are so great and its causes so many, both organic and psychological, that nothing is clear beyond the general diagnosis. There is no way to find out if it is true epilepsy. Weatherhead mentions scholars "that think that the illness may have been psychotic rather than merely epileptic, or a form of psychosis superimposed upon epilepsy" (p. 67). Dawson does not discuss this case.

3. The other cases are less certain in their diagnosis. All that can be said about the lepers is that they had some sort of skin disease of an unknown origin. We do not know why the blind were blind, though one was born that way. We cannot be sure why the "woman whom Satan had bound" (Luke 13.10–17) was bent over, though it seems more probable that her illness was psychogenic. We cannot be certain of the cause of the trouble with the woman who had a hemorrhage (Mark 5.25–34); Weatherhead says, "The disease is thought to have been menorrhagia or painful menstruation. Marr says, 'a uterine fibroid.' " The man with dropsy (Luke 14.1–6) may have had either an organic or a psychogenic illness. The same is true of the man with a withered hand (Mark 3.1–6). We do not know why Peter's mother-in-law had a fever (Mark 1.29–31). The possessed man at Capernaum (Mark 1.23–28) may have had hysteria or paranoidal schizophrenia, but Dr. Wilson is not certain. Nothing is known of the cause of his sickness. The dumb and blind demoniac (Matthew 9.32–33, 12.22) and the deaf stammerer (Mark 7.32–37) may have had psychogenic illnesses—but no proof is given that they did. The man by Bethesda's pool (John

5.1–18) may have been ill because he wanted to escape life's responsibilities, but we have no reason to be certain of this. Weatherhead suggests that the paralytic at Capernaum (Mark 2.1–12) was unable to walk because of psychological conflicts due to guilt—but the Gospel accounts do not necessarily mean that the paralysis was *caused* by unforgiven sin. They only say that the healing and the forgiveness of sins happened at the same time, and that the visible healing was evidence of the invisible forgiveness. We do not know the diagnoses of any of the other illnesses, though "demon-possession" would probably imply a psychosis.

4. McCasland mentions that both epilepsy and manic-depressive psychoses come in intermittent attacks and that both can return after a temporary cure. This means that in the two cases most clearly diagnosed, the Gerasene demoniac and the epileptic boy, we cannot demonstrate to the skeptical that the healings were permanent.

5. Though these analyses leave no reason to question the historicity of the diseases, they cannot supply enough details to know the actual causes in any instance other than that of the cutting off of the slave's ear.

6. Jesus' use of what we now call "suggestion" is plain enough in many of the healings. Certain other relevant psychological factors, such as an "atmosphere" of faith, can be distinguished. We also see instances of healing which is effective at a distance and healing without the active cooperation of those who are healed.

7. We lack the details that would describe the exact process of healing in any particular instance. We can distinguish certain factors, such as those just mentioned, but further psychological analysis is limited by the sketchiness of the evidence. When the diagnoses of the illnesses are so vague, the exact nature of the cures is bound to be even more uncertain.

8. The raising from the dead of the widow's son at Nain

(Luke 7.11–17) and Lazarus (John 11) are not treated in any of our three references. Weatherhead says, "The stories of raising from the dead are outside the scope of our present study, and are not dealt with here. They, of course, present still greater difficulties . . ." (p. 43).

9. On pp. 17–18 of McCasland, we read, "The field in which exorcism has been most successful has been that of illnesses which yield to suggestion. The principle of suggestion probably accounts for the cures which were achieved. In our own time, medicine is rediscovering the virtue of suggestion as an instrument of healing. Just how this principle operates in restoring deranged minds and ailing bodies appears still to be a mystery; but the fact of its healing power cannot be denied . . ." Dawson's first classification of Christ's cures (p. 115) is "(1) Those in which the psychological side is especially evident. They throw much light on psychological laws, and might almost be explained on the basis of what is known of mental and spiritual causation . . ." His word "spiritual" goes beyond psychology. But however much anyone might be inclined to explain any of Jesus' healing in terms *limited* to "suggestion" or known psychological laws, the Gospel records can give us no proof that such an explanation is correct. They never will provide such a proof, because no matter how much we may learn about psychology, we cannot fill in the details that are missing in the records.

10. Weatherhead rightly affirms that Jesus used what we now call psychological laws, and his classification of Christ's healings is "based on the psychological mechanisms which operated. This does not mean," he then goes on (p. 41), "that we can dismiss a miracle as merely an illustration of suggestion, for example. I have tried to make it clear already that in my opinion the healing works of Christ cannot be marshalled into psychological categories, as though the latter completely accounted for them." In his discussion of the Gerasene demoniac,

he says (p. 58), "I wish to make it very clear that the above description is not an attempt to explain away a miracle by using familiar psychological mechanisms. So far as I know, there is no parallel case in modern psychology. By no methods known to us can a patient as far advanced in psychosis as was the man from Khersa be brought back to sanity and to a desire to serve the Kingdom of God. The incident seems to me to illustrate the point already made, that the power of Christ broke through from that higher plane on which He habitually lived, and seems miraculous to us because we are unfamiliar with that plane and with what may happen on it."

This, of course, contradicts McCasland's explanation of exorcism in terms of suggestion. Weatherhead's conviction on these things is drawn from an over-all examination of the work of Jesus. McCasland's view comes from general psychological evidence, and assumes that the work of Jesus fits within typical psychological categories. This is a little strange, because the main argument of McCasland's book is that the New Testament exorcisms are historical and that they affirm Jesus' conception of Himself as the Messiah. We assume that McCasland has gone to this trouble because he, too, believes that Jesus is the Messiah. But if Jesus is the Christ, why is McCasland so sure that He always behaved within the usual limits of ordinary men? Did He have nothing new to reveal?

Dr. Weatherhead makes the point clear on p. 486: "It is futile, in my view, to equate the healing power of Jesus with the methods of modern psychotherapy. We may usefully note— as I tried to show—that Christ's healing powers made use of certain psychological mechanisms within men's personalities. But to compare the power released in personality by the slow and doubtful methods of psychotherapy with the power released immediately by Christ, is like comparing the power of rust to eat through an iron bar with the power of an oxyacetylene flame."

11. From all of this we may conclude that the psychological analysis of Jesus' healings leaves us with a very incomplete picture. It has certain values, but our progress in spiritual healing will be furthered the most by developing the *spiritual* principles of Jesus' healing, with psychology playing a subordinate role.

The Meaning of Greek Words Translated "Healed" in the Gospels

On pages 125 and 126 of his *Faith Healing and the Christian Faith*, Dr. Boggs claims that in certain passages concerning Jesus' healing, the Greek does not mean "healed." First he says:

There are two Greek words which are translated "healed" or "cured" in the English, "iaomai" and "therapeūo." Davis' 1939 revised edition of Liddell and Scott's Greek-English Lexicon says that the latter of these two verbs should be translated "treated" instead of "healed." [1]

A footnote directs us to "Liddell and Scott, *A Greek and English Lexicon*, p. 793. (Revised by Henry Stuart Jones in 1939.) Oxford: The Clarendon Press." This reference is a lexicon of *general* Greek usage, and on page 793 the seventh meaning which it gives for θεραπεύω (therapeuō) is "treat medically." None of the other translations that are given refer to healing. And the illustrations quoted as samples of the meaning "treat medically" include no New Testament passages.

[1] Dr. Boggs' transliteration of the Greek into "therapeūo" should be "therapeuō."

This is not surprising, however, since the Greek of the New Testament differs from classical Greek. Page ix of Liddell and Scott discusses their sources regarding New Testament Greek. One of them, it says, is "Moulton and Milligan's *Vocabulary of the Greek New Testament*, which (within its natural limits) may almost be regarded as a lexicon of the κοινή (that is, colloquial Greek) as a whole . . ."

Page xi of Moulton and Milligan says that the main feature of the Greek of the New Testament "was that it was the ordinary vernacular Greek of the period, not the language of contemporary literature, which was often influenced by an attempt to imitate the great authors of classical times, but the language of everyday life, as it was spoken and written by the ordinary men and women of the day . . ." This is what any student of New Testament Greek knows.

On page 289, we find a revealing comment on our word θεραπεύω: ". . . Ramsay (Luke, p. 16f.) has added the note that θεραπεύω, used as a medical term, means strictly 'treat medically' rather than 'heal'. . ." Now we are on the trail.

Luke the Physician, by W. M. Ramsay [2] discusses Acts 28.8–10, on pages 16 and following. He contrasts the healing of Publius through Paul's laying on of hands and prayer, with the statement that "the rest also which had diseases in the island came and were cured." The last word is our θεραπεύω, and Ramsay says that it would be more correctly translated "received medical treatment." He believes this was given by Luke. (We need not be concerned here with whether or not Ramsay is correct in this conclusion.) He goes on:

Here the Author recognizes a probable objection, but considers it has not any serious weight, viz., that Luke, like Paul, may have cured by prayer and not by medical treatment . . . Paul healed Publius (ἰάσατο), but Luke is not said to have healed the invalids who came afterwards. They received medical treatment (ἐθερα-

[2] (A. C. Armstrong and Son, N. Y., 1908.)

πεύοντο [a form of our *therapeuō*]). The latter verb is translated "cured" in the English version; and Professor Harnack agrees. Now in the strict sense ἐθεραπεύοντο, as a medical term, means "received medical treatment"; and in the present case the context and the whole situation demand this translation (though Luke uses the word elsewhere in the sense of "cure") . . .

We can now venture a reconstruction of how Liddell and Scott came by their translation of *therapeuō*. As a technical medical term it meant "treat medically," in much the same way as we use its derivative, "therapy." In the vernacular of the first century it meant "heal" or "cure." But Liddell and Scott may have been thrown off this track because one of their major New Testament sources, Moulton and Milligan, used the strict medical meaning. They in turn gave a wrong impression because they referred to Ramsay's argument about one particular New Testament passage where he felt that, because of the context, the medical term was correct. Yet Ramsay himself says, "Luke uses the word elsewhere in the sense of 'cure'."

We should note that these references do not translate as "treat," but as "treat medically." Ramsay's whole argument depends on contrasting Luke's medical treatment with Paul's healing through spiritual means. Jesus always used spiritual means, and even his occasional use of material aids was symbolic, not medical. The strict medical term could not apply to the work of Jesus.

That is why Thayer's *Greek-English Lexicon of the New Testament*,[3] along with the other lexicons *specializing in New Testament Greek*, is correct in translating θεραπεύω in the passages in question as "*to heal, cure, restore to health*." That is also why the English translations of the Gospels say "heal" or "cure." It is curious that the only authority chosen by Dr. Boggs was Liddell and Scott.

Dr. Boggs' second argument refers to ἰάομαι (*iaomai*), which, he says, "is ordinarily correctly translated 'healed,' but

[3] (American Book Co., N. Y.), p. 288.

not always. The imperfect tense of every Greek verb, according to the Greek scholar A. T. Robertson, always has a conative connotation, and should be translated, 'begin to (heal)' or 'try to (heal)'." [4]

The footnote refers to "Robertson, A. T., *A Grammar of the Greek New Testament in the Light of Historical Research,* p. 885. George H. Doran Company, 1915." What fascinating reading this volume brings!

Page 885 is in a section under the general heading, "The Imperfect for Past Time." Dr. Boggs' reference is to a particular subdivision called "The Inchoative or Conative Imperfect." But this section includes *ten* subdivisions on the meaning of the imperfect; and conative is only *one out of the ten.* Robertson certainly does *not* say—or so much as suggest— that "the imperfect tense of every Greek verb . . . always has a conative connotation." How could he say what a student of even elementary Greek knows is not true?

The scholars who translated the Revised Standard Version were right after all. The crowds came to Jesus, not because He "treated them" or "tried to heal them" but because He *was healing them.*

[4] The imperfect always refers to the past. Dr. Boggs should have said "'began to (heal)' or 'tried to (heal)'."

APPENDIX C

On the Creation and
Annihilation of Matter

In her fascinating chapter on "Some Healers To-day," [1] A. Graham Ikin also quotes Rebecca Beard's story of the healing of Alice Newton.[2] Miss Ikin makes the following observation:

But the striking feature of this case is the complete disappearance of thirty-eight pounds of matter in a night without leaving any trace of its passing—which is perhaps akin to the fact that when an electron moves from one orbit to another there is no trace of its existence in between the orbits, no trace of its passing. Some of these paranormal phenomena in healing may involve action on this level which is usually masked by the statistical averages of the large numbers of electrons in even the smallest organic molecules.

But the laws governing an individual electron in the tiny space inside an atom are radically different from the laws governing the transfer of thirty-eight pounds of matter over easily visible distances. And the evidence is that the matter did

[1] *New Concepts of Healing*, by A. Graham Ikin (Hodder & Stoughton, London, 1955), pp. 98–119.
[2] pp. 110–112. Quoted in our Chapter X.

not leave the body and go elsewhere. It left and did *not* go elsewhere. Nor was it transformed into an energy state—if it had been, it could have blown up the city! (It takes less mass than this turned into energy to make a nuclear bomb.) There are no physical laws to account for this sort of healing. From the point of view of physics, it is an absurdity.

Another hypothesis that has been applied to such healing is based on the random motion of molecules (or perhaps smaller particles). It is argued that there is a tiny statistical chance that the particles in one object might suddenly all move in one direction far enough to penetrate through the particles of another object. Aside from the problem raised by the lack of any "landing-place" for the thirty-eight pounds that disappeared, the "statistical chance" approach is fundamentally wrong. This is because it tries to explain in terms of pure chance something that is not chance or randomness at all.

Present-day scientific laws do not explain rare instances like this. The nature of the scientific method makes it doubtful that unrepeatable phenomena of such an exceptional nature can ever be incorporated into scientific description. The weight of today's scientific evidence would lead instead to the conclusion that some unknown error was made in observing this unique case, and that it really didn't happen that way!

However, those of us who have had experience with spiritual healing know that things really do happen that way. Not only do diseased tissues disappear, but healthy tissue sometimes appears out of nowhere. Alice Newton's healing is very striking, but it is not so unique as it seems. It is unlikely that it will be exactly duplicated, but it may be approximately reproduced. It cannot be produced on demand, however, and this is frustrating for experimental science. That is why we say it is "unrepeatable."

The simplest explanation of this healing comes by going beyond physical laws, in fact beyond the physical world itself, to the Creator of the world. Physics itself now lends some support to the theory of a point of creation of the whole universe. According to this scientific theory, everything started with a gigantic burst of energy at one particular moment, and nothing is known of anything before that moment. The Bible has often been misused as a text-book of science, but the Christian view that God has made His creation out of nothing, that creation is purely the expression of His own thought and action, is a theological necessity. It is necessary because we believe in *one* God, Who is the source of *all* being. "I bring to pass what comes to pass": this is God's Word. Christians cannot contemplate a physical world which has an independent principle of existence without God. The first article of our Creed is, "I believe in one God the Father Almighty, Maker of heaven and earth, And of all things visible and invisible . . ."

The explanation I would propose for the disappearance of Alice Newton's cancer is that it was a pure creative act of God. God simply cancelled that cancerous matter out of existence, and out of nothing He created healthy tissue. If the physical world derives directly from God's thought and action, He can think and act it out of existence or into existence as He wills.

God only does this sort of thing, however, in a personal and spiritual relationship of intense significance. Alice Newton's healing involved not only her spiritual need, but that of Rebecca Beard and of the many people whom they would touch. When Alice dreamed of Jesus looking sorrowfully at the sleeping disciples at Gethsemane and smiling at her, it was a symbol of her patient and untiring devotion to Christ, even beyond that of the Apostles. When she reached out to ease His suffering on the cross, her outgoing love became the channel through which He took away her suffering. The dream shows that her faith permeated her unconscious mind. It was the deepest kind of one-ness with God. The cancer could no longer exist in the face of it. Alice had passed from death to life.

Selected and Annotated

A very full bibliography can be derived by combining the following bibliographies:

1) *Manual of Christian Healing* of the Order of St. Luke, 7th Edition, 1956, pp. 49–58.
2) *Spiritual Healing in the United States and Great Britain,* by Walter W. Dwyer, 4th Edition, 1956, "Annotated Bibliography" at the end.
3) *Psychology, Religion and Healing,* by Leslie D. Weatherhead (Abingdon-Cokesbury, 1951), pp. 523–532.
4) *Faith Healing and the Christian Faith,* by Wade H. Boggs, Jr. (John Knox Press, 1956), pp. 187–194.
5) *The Healing Power of Faith,* by Will Oursler (Hawthorn Books, 1957), Appendix E, pp. 346–353.

A selected and annotated list of references (in alphabetical order) is as follows:

I. BOOKS

Beard, Rebecca—*Everyman's Search*, Merrybrook Press, Wells, Vt., 1950, 150 pp.

The fascinating story of a medical doctor who is led to practice spiritual healing. She has written sequels in *Everyman's Goal, Everyman's Mission* and *Everyman's Adventure.* Her thought shows the influence of Unity.

Boggs, Wade H., Jr.—*Faith Healing and the Christian Faith*, John Knox Press, Richmond, 1956, 216 pp.

A refutation of "faith healing," which he attributes to a widely inclusive group, from Aimee Semple McPherson to Agnes Sanford. Generalizes, with little discrimination between individual healers. No evidence of meaningful first-hand experience in spiritual healing. Wide range of reference material, large in quantity and inconsistent in quality. Considerable theological development, Calvinistically oriented. Weak in pastoral theology, essentially rationalizing the "status quo." His posing of the theological issues misses the main point.

Cranston, Ruth—*The Miracle of Lourdes*, McGraw-Hill, N. Y., 1955, 286 pp.

A full treatment of Lourdes in a popular style, but with the background of careful study. Miss Cranston is, however, a writer, not a scholar, and it is not easy to assess her qualifications for critical or scientific observation. Her father was a clergyman; she is very liberal in her own outlook. Her treatment of Lourdes is most sympathetic.

Dawson, George Gordon—*Healing: Pagan and Christian*, S. P. C. K., London, 1935, 332 pp.

A history of healing, physical, mental, and spiritual, from primitive times to the modern period. The book is written with fine scholarship and with deep faith.

Doniger, Simon (Editor)—*Healing: Human and Divine*, Association Press, N. Y., 1957, 254 pp.

A collection of articles by leading medical and theological authorities. Most of these were originally published in *Pastoral Psychology*. It is in four sections: I: Body, Mind, and Spirit; II: Religion and Psychiatry; III: Prayer; and IV: Spiritual Healing. A first-class reference.

Frost, Evelyn—*Christian Healing*, A. R. Mowbray, London, 1940 (2nd ed., 1949) or Morehouse, N. Y., 1940, 376 pp.

This is, as its title page says, "A consideration of the place of spiritual healing in the church of today in the light of the doctrine and practice of the ante-Nicene church." Unique in its study of patristics and perceptive in its analysis of the modern situation. Incarnational and sacramental, it is a piece of solid Anglican theology.

Hutchison, Harry—*The Church and Spiritual Healing*, Rider and Co., London, 1955, 164 pp.

An excellent book by a minister who has participated in the healing work in a large city church in the Church of Scotland. He covers the challenge of the healing ministry; the theological understanding of sickness; the scope, purpose and significance of spiritual healing; the conditions for healing; the methods of conducting the work; and the relationship of healing to personal religion.

Ikin, A. Graham—*New Concepts of Healing*, Hodder & Stoughton, London, 1955, 186 pp.

An imaginative exploration of the implications and relations of the various types of healing, both orthodox and unorthodox. Miss Ikin works to draw together medical, psychical, psychological, and spiritual healing. She includes everything from psychotherapy to parapsychology, from modern spiritual healing practices to the developments of the new physics. She paints with a broad stroke, but with valuable creativity. A Foreword by the the Bishop of Lincoln, Chairman of the Archbishops' Commission on Divine Healing, commends the book "most warmly, especially to doctors and particularly to the members of the Archbishops' Commission, as shedding light on many of the problems and questions with which we are grappling. It is a book too for the students in the theological colleges and medical schools, and for all who are seeking to understand the truths of Divine Healing." Its Appendices contain valuable reports of modern healing movements.

McCasland, S. Vernon—*By the Finger of God*, Macmillan, N. Y., 1951, 146 pp.

This is a "study of demon possession and exorcism in early Christianity in the light of modern views of mental illness." It is concerned to show the historical nature of the healings of the demon-possessed by Jesus. Its interpretation is that of liberal Protestant theology and contemporary psychotherapy. The supernatural element seems to be missing.

McGinley, Laurence J., S.J.—*Form-Criticism of the Synoptic Healing Narratives*, Woodstock College Press, Woodstock, Md., 1944, 173 pp.

"A study in the theories of Martin Dibelius and Rudolf Bultmann," from a Roman Catholic point of view. A thorough review of the principles, the results, and the shortcomings of form-criticism, with particular reference to the stories of healing in the first three Gospels.

Neal, Emily Gardiner—*A Reporter Finds God through Spiritual Healing*, Morehouse-Gorham, N. Y., 1956, 192 pp.

A popular story of a personal pilgrimage, unexcelled as an introduction to spiritual healing. A sparkling style, full of conviction. Considerable history, theology, and accounts of modern spiritual healing methods and results.

Oursler, Will—*The Healing Power of Faith*, Hawthorn Books, Inc., N. Y., 1957, 368 pp.

The most comprehensive review now available of the healing ministry in all churches in the modern period. Written by a distinguished author, novelist and reporter. It should be very popular, but should not be confused with a mere "popularization"; it is carefully done.

Richardson, Alan—*The Miracle-Stories of the Gospels,* SCM Press, London, 1941, 157 pp.

An outstanding Anglican theologian here considers carefully the meaning of Christ's miracles. He takes a positive and Christian approach to both their historical and religious value.

Roberts, David E.—*Psychotherapy and a Christian View of Man*, Charles Scribner's Sons, N. Y., 1950, 175 pp.

A valuable relating of theology with psychotherapy. No explicit reference to spiritual healing, but directly relevant. This is just a sample of many works in this field. His "Suggestions for Further Reading," pp. 155–6, include many such books.

Sanford, Agnes—*The Healing Light*, Macalester Park, St. Paul, Minn., 1947, 176 pp.

Probably the most widely used introductory book. Based on Mrs. Sanford's own experiences as a channel of healing. Theoretical analysis somewhat limited, and there is a tendency to overgeneralize from particular occurrences. A very positive approach, eliciting hope but often omitting difficulties. In actual practice, an unusually fruitful and popular book.

(Mrs. Sanford has written a number of other books which I will not include here. Curiously, one of the most helpful is written for children: *Let's Believe*, Harper & Brothers, N. Y., 1954, 121 pp. Her novels are based on actual experiences.)

Schaer, Hans—*Religion and the Cure of Souls in Jung's Psychology*, Bollingen Series XXI, Pantheon Books, N. Y., 1950, 221 pp.

A psychological treatment of religious experience with deep implications. Should be critically reviewed in the light of Biblical Christianity. The psychology of Jung is probably the most adaptable to the development of a Christian psychology, though a thorough reorientation of even his point of view is necessary.

Scherzer, Carl J.—*The Church and Healing*, Westminster Press, Philadelphia, 1950, 272 pp.

An unparalleled history of healing in the Christian Church. All types of healing are included, both medical and spiritual. The emphasis is on the mainstream of the Church's life, but all the most significant movements up to 1950 are covered.

Van Buskirk, James Dale—*Religion, Healing & Health*, Macmillan, N. Y., 1952, 167 pp.

Written by a man who is both a medical doctor and a Methodist minister. A general review of the relation of religious healing to mental, emotional, and bodily health.

Weatherhead, Leslie D.—*Psychology, Religion and Healing*, Abingdon-Cokesbury, N. Y., 1951, 543 pp.

"A critical study of all the non-physical methods of healing, with an examination of the principles underlying them and the techniques employed to express them, together with some conclusions regarding further investigation and action in this field." A classic, written by a man of great learning and experience. (Unduly negative, though, on public healing services: his criticisms do not really apply to services of the type usually held in our churches.)

Weiss, Edward and English, O. Spurgeon—*Psychosomatic Medicine*, W. B. Saunders, Philadelphia, 2nd ed., 1949, 803 pp.

A medical textbook. Dr. Weiss writes as Professor of Clinical Medicine at Temple University and Dr. English, as Professor of Psychiatry at the same institution. The book opens with a quote from Plato: "For this is the great error of our day . . . that physicians separate the soul from the body." The psychiatry appears much indebted to Freud, though not necessarily limited to him. As is to be expected, the book is oriented toward the problems of medical care, to help the physician in applying psychotherapy.

II. PERIODICALS

Good Health and Happiness, published quarterly by The Anglican Press. Editorial Address: Box 7245, Dallas 9, Texas. S. H. Lindsay, S.T.D., Editor.

Articles on health of body, mind, and spirit in a popular form.

Pastoral Psychology, particularly the special issue on "The Church and Spiritual Healing," May, 1954. (Vol. 5, No. 44).

This issue is completely devoted to spiritual healing and includes articles on various aspects of the field by theological and medical authorities. The writers include Otis Rice, Charles Braden, Cyril Richardson, Gotthard Booth, M.D., Wayne Oates, and Paul Tillich.

Religion in Life, Spring 1956 (Vol. XXV, No. 2), Symposium on "Spiritual Healing," pp. 163ff.

Articles reviewing spiritual healing in a favorable light. Authors: John Pitts, Cyril Richardson, Don Gross, Paul Johnson

The Healing Life, edited by the Rev. John Maillard, 8 Mountbatten Rd., Bournemouth W., Hants, England.

A monthly inspirational publication.

Sharing, monthly publication of the Order of St. Luke, edited by Ethel Tulloch Banks, 2243 Front St., San Diego 1, California.

This gives a running account of the work of the Order of St. Luke. It includes articles on healing, book reviews, letters, meditations, schedules of healing conferences, a directory of healing services, and a list of literature.

III. PAMPHLETS

Spiritual Healing in the United States and Great Britain, by Walter W. Dwyer (available from Samuel Weiser, Inc., 117 Fourth Ave., N. Y., 3, N. Y.), 4th ed., May, 1956, 37 pp.

A survey in four parts: 1) A Short History of Spiritual Healing; 2) Examples of Healing Procedure; 3) Appendix—Psychic Research Organizations; 4) Annotated Bibliography. Frequent revision keeps this booklet up to date. The next edition is to be titled *The Churches' Handbook for Spiritual Healing*.

Various tracts are available from the *Forward Movement*, 412 Sycamore St., Cincinnati 2, O., such as *Hope and Courage*, *What is Spiritual Healing?*, etc.

These are useful to give to the sick or to other interested laymen.

Various publications written by the Rev. Alfred W. Price, D.D., Rector of St. Stephen's Church, Philadelphia 7, Pa. The largest of these is *Religion and Health*, 63 pp.

The latter is a "Guide for the Practice of Spiritual Healing." It includes suggestions, meditations, prayers, articles, healing services, and testimonials.

IV. OTHER TYPES OF PUBLICATIONS

Divine Healing and Co-operation Between Doctors and Clergy, British Medical Association, London, 1956, 47 pp.

The "memorandum of evidence submitted by a special committee of the Council of the British Medical Association to the Archibishops' Commission on Divine Healing." Contains many helpful observations on cooperation between doctors and clergy. But the committee claims to have seen no evidence of any type of illness cured by spiritual healing alone which cannot be cured by medical methods.

Manual of Christian Healing of the Order of St. Luke, 8th Ed., 1958. Edited and arranged by John Gaynor Banks, Founder, OSL.

"A Handbook for the Order of St. Luke the Physician, and for Other Clergy and Laity Engaged in the Work of Spiritual Therapy." Includes healing services and missions, OSL information, healing agencies in various countries, books.

Healing Seminar reports from Wainright House, Rye, N. Y. Five Seminars have been held to date, with all proceedings published.

These involve discussions by many leaders in the field, including Leslie Weatherhead, Agnes Sanford, Alfred Price, Aldous Huxley, Cyril Richardson, Earl Loomis, etc. Spiritual healers, psychics, psychiatrists, physicians, theologians, pastors, and writers attended. Very useful for suggestions of future research.

Prayer Book Studies—III The Order for the Ministration to the Sick, by the Standing Liturgical Commission (The Church Pension Fund, N. Y., 1951).

An excellent proposed revision of the Episcopal Prayer Book with the theological, historical and liturgical reasons for the proposal.

Index